NUT**SHELLS**

Tort

NUT**SHELLS**

Tort

TENTH EDITION

by
VERA BERMINGHAM
Visiting Fellow,
Kingston Law School

JOHN HODGSON
Reader in Legal Education
Nottingham Law School

SUSAN WATSON
Senior Lecturer in Law
Kingston Law School

SWEET & MAXWELL   **THOMSON REUTERS**

First Edition – 1987
Second Edition – 1990
Third Edition – 1993
Fourth Edition – 1996
Fifth Edition – 1999
Reprinted 2000
Sixth Edition – 2002
Reprinted 2003
Seventh Edition – 2005
Eight Edition – 2008
Ninth Edition – 2011
Tenth Edition – 2014

Published in 2014 by Sweet & Maxwell, 100 Avenue Road, London NW3 3PF
Part of Thomson Reuters (Professional) UK Limited
(Registered in England & Wales, Company No 1679046.
Registered Office and address for service:
Aldgate House, 33 Aldgate High Street, London EC3N 1DL)

*For further information on our products and services, visit
www.sweetandmaxwell.co.uk

Typeset by YHT
Printed by Krips

*No natural forests were destroyed to make this product;
only farmed timber was used and re-planted*

A CIP catalogue record for this book is available from the British Library.

ISBN 978-0-414031913

Contents

Using this book

CHAPTER INTRODUCTIONS open every
chapter, providing an overview
of the topic to be discussed.

The Basis of Interv

INTRODUCTION

The process of judicial review involve
made by bodies exercising public l
᠂ legality of these decisions ᠁

᠁are in al᠁
᠁rendant is involved in a
to win.

CHECKPOINT

Approach adopted to incidents b
sporting events:
- In *Condon v Basi* (CA, 1985), a "᠁
  local amateur football match w
- In *Watson v British Boxing Boc*
  out that where the plaintiff cᵣ
  boxing ring he does not con
  safety arrangements by t'

CHECKPOINTS
highlight key concepts and define
complex terms, boxed for easy
identification and revision.

KEY CASES present the facts and
judgments in the most influential
case-law, boxed for easy
identification and revision.

᠁ comp᠁
᠁ secondly, since the ᵤ
plaintiff cannot be said to consᵤ
time (*Baker v T. E. Hopkins & Soᵣ*

KEY CASE

DANGER INVITES RESCUE; RESCUERS
RESCUE IS TO SAVE LIFE OR LIMB.
Chadwick v British Transport Com
assisted at the scene of a train cra
as a result of what he saw was hᵣ
was in no personal danger (for ᐧ
generally see Ch.2).

LEGISLATION HIGHLIGHTERS provide
extracts of the significant legislation,
boxed for easy identification and revision.

> **LEGISLATION HIGHLIGHTER**
>
> Section 149 of the Road Traffic Act (19
> the driver's liability to his passenger
> means that the *volenti* defence is now
> road traffic accidents.

4. Rescuers
If the defendant's negligence endang
rescue attempt is reasonably fores
~nes v Harwood (CA, 1935))
~d is actually the d

COLOUR CODING throughout to
help distinguish cases and legislation
from the narrative. At the first mention,
cases are highlighted in colour and
italicised and legislation is highlighted
in colour and emboldened.

..equent case law has decided ..
(a) Jews are an ethnic group (*Seide v*
(b) Gypsies are an ethnic group (*CRE v*
(c) Rastafarians are not an ethnic group
    ment [1993] I.R.L.R. 284)
(d) Jehovah's Witnesses are not an ethnic
    Norwich City College case 1502237/97)
(e) RRA covers the Welsh (*Gwynedd CC v*
(f) Both the Scots and the English are co
    "national origins" but not by "ethr
    Board v Power [1997], *Boyce v Brit*

should be noted that Sikh
~re also r

DIAGRAMS AND FLOWCHARTS condense and visually represent detailed information.

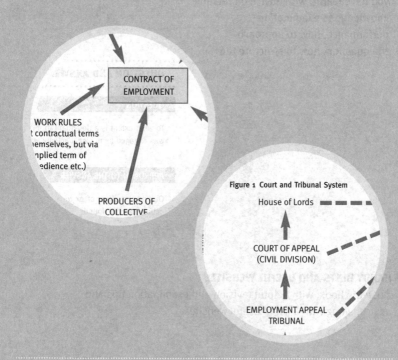

WORK RULES
t contractual terms
iemselves, but via
nplied term of
edience etc.)

CONTRACT OF
EMPLOYMENT

PRODUCERS OF
COLLECTIVE

Figure 1 Court and Tribunal System

House of Lords

COURT OF APPEAL
(CIVIL DIVISION)

EMPLOYMENT APPEAL
TRIBUNAL

**END OF CHAPTER REVISION
CHECKLISTS** identify the key take-aways from the chapter.

...was held th...
 liable because the pre₃
alleged negligence that, as the
criminal offence.

REVISION CHECKLIST

You should now understand:

☐ **The conditions within which the
and the overlap between the def**

☐ ***Volenti* is a complete defence ar
because it is more flexible;**

**END OF CHAPTER QUESTION AND
ANSWER SECTION** is a chance to practice what
you have learnt, with advice on relating
knowledge to examination
performance, how to approach
the question, how to structure the

•••••••••••••••••••••••••
QUESTION AND ANSWER
•••••••••••••••••••••••••

QUESTION

To what extent is a defendant in a
was engaged in an illegal activity at

APPROACH TO THE ANSWER

Outline the effect of *ex tur*
action can be founde

HANDY HINTS AND USEFUL WEBSITES
close the book, with helpful revision and examination tips and
advice, along with a list of useful websites.

HANDY HINTS

Examination questions in employme,
either essay questions or problem ques
format and in what is required of the ex
of question in turn.
      Students usually prefer one type
normally opting for the problem ques
examinations are usually set in a wa
least one of each style of question
      Very few, if any, questions
ows about a topic, and it
to make a p

USEFUL WEBSITES

Official Information
www.parliament.uk—very user-friendly.
www.direct.gov.uk—portal for governme
www.opsi.gov.uk—Office of Public Secto
      and statutory instruments available
www.dca.gov.uk—Department for Con
www.dca.gov.uk/peoples-rights/hum
      Unit at the Department for Con
www.homeoffice.gov.uk/police/
      the Police and Criminal

Table of Cases

Table of Statutes

Trespass to the Person

INTRODUCTION

Trespass to the person comprises a group of very long established torts. Essentially they impose liability for any intentional, direct and immediate interference with the person of the claimant. The act of the defendant must not be justifiable. Trespasses are actionable without proof of damage. This is because their real purpose is to vindicate the interest of the claimant in protecting his person against invasion, or his right to liberty. This is a critical distinction between trespass and negligence, where proof of damage is an essential ingredient of the tort.

As to the distinction between direct and indirect interference, the classic illustration is that given in *Reynolds v Clarke* (1725) of a man who throws a log into the highway. If the log hits someone when it is thrown, that, it was said, would be direct and a trespass, but if it merely lands in and obstructs the highway and someone later trips over it, that would be indirect and the claimant would have to sue in case (now the tort of negligence) and prove damage. However, today, it would be necessary in relation to trespass to show that the defendant threw the log at the claimant, because an action in trespass now requires intentional, not merely negligent harm. In *Fowler v Lanning* (HC, 1959) it was held that in an action of trespass to the person, it was not enough to allege the fact of direct harm (in this case gunshot wounds in the course of a shooting party). The claimant had the burden of at least proving negligence on the part of the defendant. This was taken further in *Letang v Cooper* (CA, 1965) where Lord Denning M.R. held that where the interference is negligent, as opposed to intentional, the proper cause of action is negligence and not trespass. This requirement of intention was confirmed in *A v Hoare* (HL, 2008).

There are three types of trespass to the person: assault, battery and false imprisonment. There are equivalent criminal offences, and in some respects the principles applicable are the same, so for some purposes criminal cases can be used as precedents in tort and vice versa. However there are some important differences. Firstly, in tort, there is a distinction between battery, which involves an actual application of force, and assault, which is the threat of a battery. In criminal law, assault is used to cover both, as in "assault occasioning actual bodily harm", or "assault by beating".

Secondly, in criminal law there are different levels of offence, of differing seriousness, in order to allow for differentiation in sentencing. Thirdly, in some areas criminal law will allow a defence if the defendant honestly believed something, e.g. that he needed to act in self-defence, while in tort the belief must be reasonable.

Figure 1: Trespass to the person: the present position

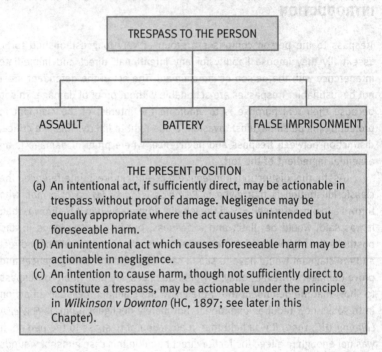

TRESPASS TO THE PERSON

ASSAULT   BATTERY   FALSE IMPRISONMENT

THE PRESENT POSITION
(a) An intentional act, if sufficiently direct, may be actionable in trespass without proof of damage. Negligence may be equally appropriate where the act causes unintended but foreseeable harm.
(b) An unintentional act which causes foreseeable harm may be actionable in negligence.
(c) An intention to cause harm, though not sufficiently direct to constitute a trespass, may be actionable under the principle in *Wilkinson v Downton* (HC, 1897; see later in this Chapter).

BATTERY

A battery may be defined as the direct and intentional application of physical force to the person of another without lawful justification. It is the act of making physical contact which must be intentional and there is certainly no requirement of an intention to cause injury. If A, intending to strike B, misses and hits C by mistake, it has long been a principle of the criminal law that A commits an offence. This is known as the doctrine of transferred intent, or transferred malice. The same principle applies to a civil action. In *Bici v Ministry of Defence* (HC, 2004), transferred intent applied in the case of a peace-keeping soldier in Kosovo who shot an unintended victim.

What constitutes "force" for the purposes of battery?
Any physical contact, however trivial, may constitute "force" for the purposes of the tort notwithstanding the absence of bodily harm. Apart from the more obvious examples of striking another with a fist or weapon, battery may take many forms. Thus, to spit in a person's face or to throw water over them, or to seize something from their hand, may be actionable wrongs. Since battery is sometimes used as a way of testing the legality of actions by the police or other officials, it could also be the force used in obtaining a fingerprint, or DNA sample, or in stopping someone moving away while being questioned, as in *Collins v Wilcock* (HC, 1984).

The defendant's act must be a positive one, voluntarily done; merely to obstruct the claimant's passage by standing still is not sufficient: *Innes v Wylie* (1844). In *Fagan v Metropolitan Police Commissioner* (HC, 1969) the defendant was held liable for criminal assault in respect of what appeared, on the face of it, to be a mere omission to act. The accused in that case accidentally drove his car on to the foot of a police officer and then deliberately delayed in removing the vehicle once the officer drew his attention to the situation. One judge dissented on the ground that at the time of driving onto the officer's foot the defendant had no mens rea, and that after forming an intention to allow the car to remain there he did no positive act. The reasoning of the majority was that, where the defendant's act is a continuing one, the mens rea need not be present at the inception of that act but could, at some later time, be superimposed upon it. In civil law terms, we can substitute "intention" for mens rea.

Although the application of force must be direct, this is not strictly interpreted. Battery can be committed with a missile such as a stone or bullet, and there are cases indicating other extensions. It is battery to strike the horse on which the claimant is riding (in the case this caused the horse to rear and throw the rider): *Dodwell v Burford* (1669), or to touch the claimant's clothing: *Piggly Wiggly Alabama Corp v Rickles* (1925) (USA). In *Haystead v Chief Constable of Derbyshire* (HC, 2000) the defendant punched a woman, causing her to drop the child she was holding. This amounted to the criminal offence of "assaulting by beating" the child, which requires a battery.

There has been much debate over how to deal with the ordinary and sometimes inevitable physical contacts of everyday existence (e.g. jostling in a crowded place (although this is not necessarily intentional contact) or touching a person for the purpose of engaging his attention). There is no doubt that these are not actionable. This qualification has been explained on the ground either that that they are justified because the claimant impliedly consents to such contact or, according to *Collins v Wilcock* (HC, 1984), that cases of this nature are to be treated as "falling within a general exception embracing all physical contact which is generally regarded as acceptable in the ordinary conduct of daily life".

KEY CASE

COLLINS V WILCOCK (1984)

A woman police officer tried to question a woman whom she suspected of soliciting contrary to the Street Offences Act 1959. When she took hold of the woman's arm in order to detain her and administer a caution, the officer was not exercising a power of arrest.

Held: (HC) Battery is the actual infliction of unlawful force on another person. Any physical contact, no matter how trivial, is sufficient "force". The officer had gone beyond the scope of her duty in detaining the woman in circumstances short of arresting her and had therefore committed a battery.

Historically, there was also a requirement that the act must be "hostile", applying the dictum in *Cole v Turner* (1704) that the least touching of another "in anger" is a battery, but, although confirmed as a requirement in *Wilson v Pringle* (CA, 1986) no clear indication was given as to the meaning of "hostile", save to say that it was not necessarily to be equated with ill-will or malevolence, the existence or otherwise of which was a question of fact.

In *F v West Berkshire Health Authority* (HL, 1989) Lord Goff doubted whether hostility was a requirement in battery and said that to hold otherwise would be difficult to reconcile with the principle that any touching of another's body is, in the absence of lawful excuse, a battery. Thus, he said, a prank which misfires, an over-friendly slap on the back, or surgical treatment in the mistaken belief that the claimant has consented, are prima facie actionable. However, he pointed out that physical conduct (such as jostling in a crowded street) which is generally accepted in the ordinary conduct of everyday life would not constitute a battery.

On balance, having regard to the current state of the case law it is preferable to treat incidental contact as justified by implied consent, and to consign the label "hostile" to the history books.

ASSAULT

An assault may be defined as an act which directly and intentionally causes the claimant reasonably to apprehend a battery is about to be inflicted by the defendant. Although the term "assault" is popularly (and in criminal law) used to include a battery, a person may be liable for an assault even though no battery is committed, for all that is required is the reasonable apprehension by the claimant of immediate violence. For example, to shake one's fist in another's face, or to aim a blow which is intercepted, is an assault, but the claimant must reasonably believe that the defendant has the means of carrying the threat into effect, so that there is no assault where the claimant is in such a position as to be inaccessible to physical force.

CHECKPOINT

Apprehension of an "immediate" battery
The defendant's apprehension of an immediate battery must be reasonable. In *Thomas v National Union of Mineworkers* (HC, 1985) there was no assault when picketing miners made violent gestures to working colleagues who were being transported across the picket line under police escort. The claimants had no reasonable belief that the defendant had the intention or the ability to carry out the threat immediately.

Just as there may be an assault without a battery, so there may be a battery without assault, as where the claimant is struck from behind, or whilst asleep, by an unseen aggressor. Even if the defendant is for some reason unable to carry out the threat or equally has no intention of so doing, there seems to be no logical reason why he should not be guilty of an assault, provided that his act induces in the claimant a reasonable apprehension that force is about to be inflicted upon him. A commonly cited illustration of this problem is that of pointing an unloaded gun at the claimant. In the civil case of *Blake v Barnard* (1840) it appears to have been held that this would not constitute an assault, although the decision has been explained on the procedural ground that the claimant, having claimed in his pleadings that a loaded gun was pointed at him, then sought a verdict on the basis that it was unloaded, so the court never addressed the substantive point. In the criminal case of *R v St George* (1840) the court was clearly of the view that it would be a common law assault to point an unloaded gun at the claimant (unless he knows it to be unloaded), and this would seem to be correct in principle.

As with battery there must be a positive act by the defendant, so that passive obstruction unaccompanied by any threatening move or gesture cannot amount to an assault (*Innes v Wylie* (1844)). For many years it was erroneously thought that words alone could not amount to an assault. However, as Lord Steyn said in *R v Ireland* (HL, 1997), "A thing said is also a thing done." Now the question is whether the words, in the precise context, create the necessary apprehension. So if they are said in a transatlantic telephone call, they will not, but if the call is from someone who may be close at hand, they may do. Words which accompany a threatening act may negate what would otherwise be an assault where they clearly indicate no intention to carry out the threat: *Tuberville v Savage* (1669). A conditional threat accompanied by gestures may constitute an assault, at least where the defendant has no authority to require compliance with the condition: *Read v Coker* (1853).

KEY CASE

TUBERVILLE V SAVAGE (1669)
The defendant placed his hand on his sword and said: "If it were not Assize time, I would not take such language from you."

Held: By his own words the defendant had negated the possibility of a battery so no assault was committed. This principle was applied in *Thomas v National Union of Mineworkers* (above) because there was no danger of an immediate battery.

FALSE IMPRISONMENT

This may be defined as an act which directly and intentionally places a total restraint upon the claimant's freedom of movement without lawful justification. The term "false" means wrongful and "imprisonment" signifies that the claimant has been deprived of their right to go where they will. It does not require cells and warders. Thus, a person may be imprisoned in their own home, in a motor car, or even in a public street, as long as their movements have been totally constrained by the defendant's will. Such constraint may be evidenced by the use of actual physical force amounting to an assault and battery, or simply by the reasonable apprehension of such force. However, whilst the wrong of false imprisonment is often that of assault or battery also, it is not necessarily so. For example, to unjustifiably lock a person in a room into which she or he has freely and voluntarily entered is a false imprisonment but clearly not assault, although it is not clear whether a mere negligent lack of awareness of the claimant's presence in the room would suffice for the purposes of the tort.

The act of imprisonment

It has been seen that there need be no imprisonment in the ordinary sense of the word. An unlawful arrest is in itself a false imprisonment, as is the continued detention of someone who, though originally in lawful custody, has acquired the right to be discharged. On the other hand, an arrest which is initially unlawful on the ground that no reason was given for the arrest may subsequently become lawful as from the time a reason is given: *Lewis v Chief Constable of South Wales* (CA, 1991).

The restraint must be total

The deprivation of the claimant's liberty must, however, be complete, and a mere partial interference with their freedom of movement is not an imprisonment.

KEY CASE

BIRD V JONES (1845)

The defendants wrongfully closed off part of a public footpath over Hammersmith Bridge in order to erect a grandstand as part of the arrangements for a boat race. The claimant (Bird) tried to enter and pass through the closed off area but was refused permission to proceed and was told that he might make a detour by crossing to the other side of the bridge.

Held: There was another route which Bird could take to proceed so there was no false imprisonment. Provided the restraint is total, how large the area of confinement can be must depend on the circumstances of the case.

An imprisonment usually involves some positive act, and there is generally no duty to assist another to obtain their liberty. In *Herd v Weardale Steel, Coke & Coal Co* (HL, 1915) the claimant miner refused to do certain work in the mine which he believed to be dangerous and demanded that the defendants take him to the surface. The defendants refused for some 20 minutes to do so and, in an action for false imprisonment, it was held that the defendants' omission to accede to the claimant's demands did not amount to an imprisonment. The claimant had voluntarily accepted a restriction upon his liberty by initially going into the mine for the period of his shift of duty, and it was he who was in breach of contract by refusing to complete the shift.

It may be that the defendants could have been liable had they been in breach of their own contractual duty. To similar effect is *Robinson v Balmain New Ferry Co Ltd* (PC, 1910) where the claimant, having paid a penny to enter the defendants' wharf to catch a ferry, discovered that he had just missed one and wished to leave. He was directed to the exit turnstile where he refused to pay a further penny which, as was clearly stated on a notice-board, was chargeable upon leaving. [Note—there were no turnstiles on the far bank—all fares were collected at this terminal of the service.] It was held that there was no false imprisonment because the claimant had entered the wharf upon the terms of a definite contract by which the parties contemplated that he would take the ferry, and, since there was no agreement as to the terms on which he might go back, the defendants were not obliged to make the exit from their premises gratuitous but were entitled to impose a reasonable condition for the privilege.

There are numerous instances in which a person may voluntarily accept a degree of restraint upon their freedom of movement, but the above cases do not necessarily support the proposition that that person cannot thereafter revoke their consent and demand that the restraint be terminated, even though that would put them in breach of contract. Whether the defendant is obliged to comply with the demand will presumably depend, in particular, upon the degree of inconvenience caused in so doing.

KEY CASE

IQBAL V PRISON OFFICERS ASSOCIATION (2010)
The claimants sued in false imprisonment because a sudden unannounced strike in breach of contract by prison officers meant that prisoners spent an extra six hours of their day locked in their cell.

Held: (CA) The claimant did not succeed in false imprisonment because a mere failure of the prison officers to work at the prison involved no positive action on their part. Following *Herd* the Court of Appeal held that since the strike was a mere failure to act there was no liability and, as a general principle, a defendant was not to be held liable in tort for the result of his inaction unless there was a specific duty to act, arising out of the particular relationship between the claimant and defendant.

A prisoner does not retain a degree of residual liberty such as to enable an action in false imprisonment to be maintained against the prison governor if he or she is further unlawfully restrained (e.g. by segregation from other prisoners in breach of the Prison Rules). This was decided in *Hague v Deputy Governor of Parkhurst Prison and Weldon v Home Office* (HL, 1991). However, there may be a public law claim in respect of a failure to apply the Prison Rules or other regulations properly. Similarly, a remand prisoner detained after expiry of the statutorily prescribed time limit cannot sue the prison governor for false imprisonment, since only an order of the court can terminate the period of custody: *Olotu v Home Office* (CA, 1997). Furthermore, no action for false imprisonment lies where the detention is carried out under an order of the court. In *Quinland v Governor of HMP Belmarsh* (CA, 2002) the judge made an arithmetical error in calculating the claimant's sentence but his appeal against his sentence was not heard until after his release. The governor was not liable for false imprisonment because until the court order was set aside it justified the claimant's detention. Nevertheless, if the governor has authority to release the prisoner without an order of the court to terminate the period of custody, there may be liability.

Intention to restrict movement is required but it is not necessary for the defendant to have intended to act unlawfully.

KEY CASE

R. v Governor of Brockhill Prison, Ex p. Evans (2000)

The claimant, Evans, was kept in prison for 59 days longer than she should have been because of the miscalculation of the date for her release. The governor calculated the date for release correctly according to the principles earlier laid down by the Court of Appeal. Evans herself successfully raised the issue of the incorrect calculation.

Held: (HL) The prison governor was liable in false imprisonment. Although the excessive imprisonment arose because of a judicial reinterpretation of the law in the case itself and the governor had not been at fault, because it is a tort of strict liability, the prisoner was entitled to compensation for false imprisonment.

The claimant's knowledge

In *Meering v Grahame-White Aviation Co Ltd* (CA, 1919) it was held to be immaterial that the claimant was unaware of the fact of his detention, though this conflicted with the earlier decision in *Herring v Boyle* (1834). In *Murray v Ministry of Defence* (HL, 1988) the House of Lords approved *Meering*, but expressed the view that a claimant who did not know of the detention would normally receive only nominal damages.

Means of escape

If a reasonable means of escape is available to the claimant there will be no imprisonment. An escape route will be unreasonable if it exposes the claimant to a risk of injury. If the claimant is unaware that such a route exists, the question is probably whether a reasonable man would have realised that there was an available means of escape.

INTENTIONAL PHYSICAL HARM

We have seen above that some contact or physical force is required for an action in trespass; emotional distress is not enough to establish liability for intentionally inflicted bodily harm. Nevertheless, if severe emotional distress causes bodily harm and the defendant either intended this or was reckless as to the consequences, there may be liability. This represents a common law extension of liability outside the boundaries of trespass, but it is considered here because it is closely linked to the trespass torts.

KEY CASE

WILKINSON V DOWNTON (1897)

The defendant, as a practical joke, told the claimant that her husband had been seriously injured in an accident. As a result the claimant suffered a severe nervous disorder but the specific requirements of assault and battery, the application, or threat, of force, were not present.

Held: (HC) Conduct amounting to a battery was extended to include situations where no contact or physical force is used. Where an act wilfully calculated to cause physical damage does actually cause such harm there will be liability in trespass. Note that at the time of this case there was no liability in negligence for nervous shock.

To amount to acts "calculated to cause harm" under the principle in *Wilkinson v Downton* there must be both actual harm and an intent to cause damage. In *Wong v Parkside Health NHS Trust* (CA, 2001) a campaign of rudeness and unfriendliness by colleagues was not regarded as the intentional infliction of harm. Although this decision restricts the principle in *Wilkinson v Downton*, the Protection from Harassment Act 1997 might now apply in circumstances such as the "course of conduct" to which the claimant in *Wong* was subjected (see *Majrowski v Guy's and St Thomas's NHS Trust* (HL, 2006) below).

In *Wainwright v Home Office* (HL, 2003) a mother and son had been subjected to a strip search carried out in a manner which breached the Prison Service Rules. Their claim for breach of privacy and the intentional infliction of harm was dismissed on the ground that emotional distress is not enough to establish liability for intentionally inflicted bodily harm. The House of Lords also rejected a general right to of privacy in English common law and said that the coming into force of the Human Rights Act 1998 weakens the argument for saying that a general tort of invasion of privacy is needed. In this case no contact or physical force is used and even if there was an intention to cause harm, *Wilkinson v Downton* was not authority for the proposition that damages for distress falling short of psychiatric injury were recoverable.

Wilkinson v Downton was approved in *Janvier v Sweeney* (CA, 1919) which also concerned a false statement causing shock, and both cases were relied upon in *Khorasandjian v Bush* (CA, 1993) as authority for the grant of an injunction where the defendant's campaign of harassment by means, inter alia, of threatening telephone calls was likely to injure the claimant's health, even though at the time of the action no damage had in fact been caused. In *Hunter v Canary Wharf Ltd* (1997) the House of Lords was prepared to preserve the rule in *Wilkinson v Downton* as a general cause of action but it anticipated that claimants in these cases ought to rely on new statutory provisions contained in the **Protection from Harassment Act 1997** rather than the common law. It also rejected an extension of private nuisance in this type of case.

LEGISLATION HIGHLIGHTER

Protection from Harassment Act 1987

Section 3(1) of the Act creates a statutory tort of harassment and provides remedies by way of damages and injunction. Damages may be awarded for consequential anxiety and financial loss (s.3(2)). There must be an actual or apprehended course of conduct by the defendant which amounts, or would if pursued amount, to harassment of the claimant and which the defendant knows or ought to know amounts to harassment (s.1(1)).

The legislation is very widely drawn and may potentially impact upon numerous spheres of everyday life, including the conduct of the press, conduct in employment (in *Majrowski v Guy's and St Thomas's NHS Trust* (HL, 2006) it was held that an employer could be vicariously liable under the Act for harassment committed by one of its employees in the course of employment), disputes between neighbours and family members, and the activities of protesters. In *Huntingdon Life Sciences Ltd v Curtin* (HC, 1997) Eadie J. said that the Act was clearly not intended by Parliament to be used to clamp down on the discussion of matters of public interest or upon the rights of political protest and public demonstration and that the Act should be interpreted accordingly. It would now clearly have to be applied so as to respect the right to freedom of expression under art.10 of the European Convention on Human Rights.

DEFENCES

The following justifications are available in an action of intentional trespass to the person:

Consent

If the claimant expressly or impliedly consents to an act which would, but for that consent, amount to the commission of a tort, the defendant is not liable. Thus, the claimant may give their consent to physical contact within the rules of a lawful sport or to the performance of a surgical operation. This is also the better way of dealing with intentional but incidental contact in everyday life.

Although consent is not a defence to a criminal assault occasioning actual harm, Lord Denning M.R. in *Murphy v Culhane* (CA, 1977) suggested that a person could, in an appropriate case, either be taken to have "assumed the risk" or be defeated by ex turpi causa (see Ch.5). This might be so where, for example, the claimant was the aggressor and "got more than he bargained for". This view is further supported by *Barnes v Nayer* (CA, 1986), but it cannot apply where the defendant's response to the provocation is a "savage blow out of all proportion to the occasion": *Lane v Holloway* (CA, 1968).

In the context of medical treatment the principles applicable to the defence continue to evolve. Treatment without consent is prima facie a battery, and an adult of full mental capacity has an absolute right to choose whether or not to consent to treatment (see *Airedale NHS Trust v Bland* (HL, 1993); *Re MB (Medical Treatment)* (CA, 1997)). A consent need only be in general terms; once there is such a consent, the case will not be one of trespass: *Chatterton v Gerson* (HC, 1981), although an issue as to whether proper information was given in accordance with General Medical Council guidelines may raise issues of informed consent in an action for medical negligence (see *Chester v Afshar* (HL, 2004)).

KEY CASE

CHATTERTON V GERSON (1981)

The claimant was suffering from severe pain caused by a trapped nerve for which the defendant, a specialist in the treatment of chronic intractable pain, gave her spinal injections. This helped the pain for a while but it rendered her right leg numb. She claimed in trespass on the ground that her consent to the injection was invalid as she had not been warned of the risk or informed of the potential consequences.

Held: (HC) The defendant was not liable in trespass. Although medical treatment involving the direct application of force administered without the patient's consent, or giving treatment different from that for which consent has been given, constitutes a battery, where a patient is informed in broad terms of the nature of the procedure and consent is obtained, failure to disclose the associated risks does not invalidate the consent.

Comment

An action in respect of failure to disclose sufficiently the risks inherent in medical treatment must be based in negligence (see *Sidaway v Bethlem Royal Hospital Governors* (HL, 1985)). In *Chester v Afshar* a neurosurgeon who failed to warn a patient of a small inherent risk of injury was liable in damages for injuries resulting when a serious side-effect occurred, even though there was no negligence in the actual performance of the surgery. The majority of the court held that, unless the full award was made, the duty to warn would be a hollow one.

If there is no consent, an action will lie: *St Georges NHS Trust v S* (CA, 1999) This right to personal autonomy or self-determination was also in issue in *Secretary of State for the Home Department v Robb* (HC, 1995) where, following *Airedale NHS Trust v Bland*, a declaration was granted that prison officials and nursing staff responsible for the care of a prisoner of sound mind who went on hunger strike could lawfully abide by his refusal to receive nutrition, for so long as he retained the mental capacity to do so. In reaching this decision the court declined to follow *Leigh v Gladstone* (HC, 1909), which had held the forcible feeding of an imprisoned suffragette on hunger strike to be justified on the ground of necessity.

Where an adult patient is not in a fit state to give or withhold consent, a practitioner may nevertheless administer treatment in an emergency, in which case the practitioner may rely on the defence of necessity (see below). Otherwise, if the practitioner reasonably considers it to be in the best interests of the patient to administer treatment, the guidance of the court in the form of a declaration that the proposed treatment would not be unlawful should be sought.

A minor of 16 or 17 may consent to treatment without parental approval (Family Law Reform Act 1969, s.8) as may a minor below that age, provided that he or she has sufficient intelligence and understanding to know precisely what is involved: *Gillick v West Norfolk & Wisbech Area Health Authority* (HL, 1986). It seems, however, that no minor of whatever age can refuse medical treatment to which a parent has validly consented, and that the court can, in all cases involving minors, override the wishes of the patient in the exercise of its inherent wardship jurisdiction: *Re W* (CA, 1992).

Consent must be freely given and will therefore be vitiated if obtained by duress. It may also be invalid if obtained by fraud or misrepresentation, but only if the claimant is thereby mistaken as to the essential nature of the act (but see *Appleton v Garrett* (HC, 1996)). As noted earlier, a mistake merely as to the consequences of the act does not affect consent, so that a patient need only be informed in broad terms of the nature of any proposed treatment (see *Chatterton v Gerson* (HC, 1981)). Failure to disclose known risks associated with the treatment cannot therefore give rise to a battery but may be actionable in negligence (see again *Sidaway v Governors of the Bethlem Royal Hospital* (HL, 1985) and *Chester v Afshar* (HL, 2004)).

Necessity

The basis of this defence is that the defendant was obliged to act as they did in order to prevent greater harm either to the claimant or a third party. The giving of emergency treatment to one who is unable to consent, for example, may be justified on this ground: *F v West Berkshire Health Authority* (HL, 1989). The defence is not available where the occasion of necessity is brought about by the defendant's negligence, and once this matter is raised it is for the defendant to show that he or she was not negligent: *Rigby v Chief Constable of Northamptonshire* (HC, 1985).

Self-defence

An individual may use such reasonable force as is necessary to protect their person or their property, and to prevent the entry of, or to eject, a trespasser upon their land. The use of reasonable force to prevent crime is statutorily sanctioned (Criminal Law Act 1967, s.3(1)), so a defence is available to one who goes to assist another under attack. However, the test in tort is whether the use of force of the kind actually employed was reasonable in all the circumstances: *Ashley v CC of Sussex* (HL, 2008).

KEY CASE

ASHLEY V CHIEF CONSTABLE OF SUSSEX POLICE (2008)
Ashley was shot by the police during an armed drugs raid at his home the early hours of the morning. The police admitted negligence but disputed liability for battery on the basis that the officer in question had acted in self-defence.

Held: (HL) A defendant who had mistakenly but honestly thought it was necessary to defend himself against an imminent risk could not rely on self-defence if his mistaken belief, although honestly held, had not been a reasonable one.

Lawful authority

We have already looked at some of the cases. *Quinland v Governor of HMP Belmarsh* (CA, 2002) confirms that a lawful warrant of commitment from a court is a complete justification for detention, providing that detention does not extend beyond the time in fact authorised (see *R. v Governor of Brockhill Prison, Ex p. Evans* (HL, 2000)). At common law any person may take reasonable steps to stop or prevent an actual or reasonably apprehended breach of the peace, and such steps may include the detention of a man against his will: *Albert v Lavin* (HL, 1982).

Arrest raises many issues. Statute, in the form of the general powers in s. 24 of the Police and Criminal Evidence Act 1984 (and many specific powers in other statutes) and the common law, gives powers of arrest to constables. Action taken to exercise such a power of arrest is a justification, both for the detention, and for the use of reasonable force. However, the defendant must be able to satisfy all the conditions in relation to the use of the power, and, where he cannot, absence of malice is irrelevant. Note that under art.5 of the European Convention on Human Rights the state must provide for compensation for improper deprivation of liberty, but this will not apply to cases where the arrest and detention were objectively justified. In other cases damages for false imprisonment represent that compensation.

CHECKPOINT

For the arrest by a constable to be lawful, he or she must have a reasonable suspicion that an offence has been, is being or is about to be committed, as the case may be, and also that the person arrested is guilty. This is an objective test, and it is not enough for the claimant to show that he was in fact not a wrong-doer, e.g. *Al Fayed v Metropolitan Police Commissioner* (CA, 2004).

We also need to consider how the rules apply to citizen's arrests, which are regulated by s.24A of the **Police and Criminal Evidence Act**. These powers are significantly narrower than those of constables. They now apply to a person committing or reasonably suspected of committing an indictable offence while he is in the act of committing the offence, and, where an indictable offence has been committed, to a person guilty or reasonably suspected of having committed it. Reasonable suspicion that an offence has been committed does not count: *Walters v W H Smith* (CA, 1914). However there is also a requirement that it must not be practicable for the police to effect the arrest, and the arrest must be necessary to prevent injury, damage to property or the suspect making off before the police can "assume responsibility" for him. There is no doubt that the intention is to discourage citizen's arrests except when the suspect is "caught in the act", and to encourage reporting to the police for them to take over the investigation.

In *Davidson v Chief Constable of North Wales* (CA, 1994) the claimant and her friend were arrested by the police after a store detective wrongly suspected they had stolen a cassette. The action against the police failed because of their reasonable suspicion based on the initial statement of the store detective. Could the store detective, however, be said to have "instigated, promoted and actively incited" the arrest, thus rendering herself and her employer liable for false imprisonment? No, according to the Court of Appeal. The police had exercised their own judgment, even though the detective said in evidence that she was accustomed to the police acting on her information, and clearly expected them to.

In *Lumba v Secretary of State for the Home Department* (SC, 2011) the Supreme Court ruled that breach of a public law duty authorising detention is capable of making a detention unlawful in the context of immigration detention.

KEY CASE

LUMBA V SECRETARY OF STATE FOR THE HOME DEPARTMENT (2011)
A group of foreign nationals detained pending deportation under the Immigration Act 1971 claimed in false imprisonment. Although official policy was that a foreign prisoner who had been released from prison would not normally be detained pending deportation, the Home Office introduced a secret ban on release pending deportation.

Held: (SC) The breach of a public law duty authorizing detention was capable of making that detention unlawful and the claimants had therefore been falsely imprisoned. The fact that the appellants would have lawfully been detained in any event did not affect liability in false imprisonment. However, since false imprisonment is actionable per se the question of damages arose. In these circumstances a majority ruled that no more than nominal damages should be awarded.

Restraint of movement by "kettling"

KEY CASE

AUSTIN V METROPOLITAN POLICE COMMISSIONER (2009)
The police, acting on the basis of intelligence that the anticipated violent protests on May Day 2001 would create one of the most serious threats to public order ever seen in the city, adopted kettling as a strategy to prevent violence. This involved placing an absolute cordon

to contain protestors and restrict movement around areas at particular risk of personal injury and damage to property. The appellants, not themselves protestors, were caught within this police cordon and prevented from leaving the "kettle" for up to seven hours. They claimed that this amounted to false imprisonment and deprivation of liberty within the meaning of art.5 (1) of the European Convention on Human Rights.

Held: (HL) The level of restraint did not in fact amount to imprisonment at common law. On the basis of the specific and exceptional facts of this case, kettling also did not amount to a deprivation of liberty so art.5 was inapplicable. However, the court went on to say: "Had it not remained necessary for the police to impose and maintain the cordon in order to prevent serious injury or damage, the "type" of the measure would have been different, and its coercive and restrictive nature might have been sufficient to bring it within article 5."

Damages in trespass

All forms of trespass are actionable per se without proof of damage but:

- nominal damages only may be awarded where no actual loss is suffered;
- aggravated damages may be awarded where, for example, an assault or battery takes place in humiliating or undignified circumstances;
- in an appropriate case, exemplary or punitive damages may be awarded.

A significant punitive award of exemplary damage was awarded in *Muuse v Secretary of State for the Home Department* (CA, 2010) because of the malicious and oppressive conduct of the officials during his unlawful imprisonment.

KEY CASE

MUUSE V SECRETARY OF STATE FOR THE HOME DEPARTMENT (2010)
Muuse had been unlawfully detained pending deportation to Somalia even though there was no right to deport him. Verification of his claims to establish this could have been carried out quite simply but nothing was done and letters from his solicitors to the relevant officials went unanswered. During his detention Muuse was treated by officials in a malicious and oppressive manner and was terrified that he would be deported. On the basis of this treatment by the officials in question, the judge awarded a significant punitive award of exemplary damages. The Home Secretary did not dispute the award of compensatory or aggravated damages for unlawful imprisonment but made an appeal against the award of exemplary damages.

Held: (CA) The Home Office appeal was dismissed. Sir Scott Baker observed: " . . . it is to be hoped that the worrying issues raised by this case have been or will be addressed. Nothing less is acceptable in a true democracy." In reaching its decision, the court relied on *Rookes v Barnard* (1964) where Lord Devlin said an award of exemplary damages is made where its effect will serve "a valuable purpose in restraining the arbitrary and outrageous use of executive power".

REVISION CHECKLIST

You should now understand:

- ☐ Trespass requires a *direct* and *intentional* interference, for example, unwanted touching or hitting a person. The tort of negligence covers *un*intentional or negligent conduct and *in*direct interference.

- ☐ An assault is the reasonable apprehension of an *immediate* battery; a battery can take place without an assault and even the slightest force may amount to a battery, for example, an unwanted kiss.

- ☐ An imprisonment usually involves some positive act and if a reasonable means of escape is available to the claimant there may be no false imprisonment.

- ☐ The principle of *Wilkinson v Downton* applies to cases of deliberate, but indirect infliction of harm, including psychiatric harm, but not mere distress.

- ☐ The **Protection from Harassment Act 1997** protects against repeated harassment and situations involving a "course of conduct" causing physical or emotional harm.

QUESTION AND ANSWER

QUESTION

1. Dan threw a stone at Ana which hit her in the eye. He also carelessly left his garden hose on the pavement outside his house causing Sylvia to fall over it. Which forms of action in tort are open to Ana and Sylvia?

2. Niamh quietly crept up behind Forbod and hit him on the back of

the head with a stone. Has she committed an assault? Has she committed a battery?

3. A large crowd was jostling at the bus stop and as Josh went to board the bus he bumped into Zak causing him to fall to the ground. Can Zak sue Josh in battery?

4. Millie lives alone and her beloved cat, Mog, is her greatest companion. As Nick walked past Millie's house he noticed Mog sleeping in the warm sunshine on top of Millie's greenhouse. As a practical joke, he knocked on Millie's door and told her that Mog had been killed by a passing car.

   What action (if any) is available to Millie in trespass to person?

APPROACH TO THE ANSWER

1. Trespass requires a *direct* and *intentional* interference (*Reynolds v Clarke* (1725)) so the question is whether Dan's conduct in throwing the stone amounted to a direct and intentional interference? The tort of negligence covers *un*intentional or negligent conduct and *in*direct interference (*Letang v Cooper* (1965)). Did Dan's conduct in leaving his garden hose on the pavement outside his house amount to unintentional or negligent conduct and an indirect interference?

2. When Niamh crept up behind Forbod did he apprehend an immediate battery? Did the stone hitting Forbod on the back of the head amount to a battery? (*Thomas v National Union of Mineworkers* (1985))

3. Would jostling at a bus stop amount to conduct generally accepted in the ordinary conduct of everyday life? (*Collins v Wilcock* (1984)) If yes, then Josh's conduct would not constitute a battery.

4. Millie would need to be advised that the tort of trespass to the person has three elements: assault, battery, and false imprisonment. A battery requires the direct and intentional application of physical force to the person of another without lawful justification. There must be physical contact, however trivial, to constitute "force" for the purposes of the tort. (*Collins v Wilcock* (1984)). The facts state that Nick called to Millie's house and "told" her the falsehood so the requirement of physical contact is missing and she will be unable to claim battery.

   An assault does not require physical contact, it is defined as an act which directly and intentionally causes the claimant to apprehend that a battery is about to be inflicted by the defendant. The apprehension of an immediate battery must be reasonable (*Tuberville v Savage* (1669)). For example, in *Thomas v National Union of Mineworkers* (1985) there was no assault when picketing miners made violent gestures to working miners being transported across the picket line under police escort because there was no danger of an immediate battery. Although Millie suffered harm when Nick called to tell her that Mog had been killed, this would not amount to an assault as she did not apprehend that a battery was about to be inflicted by Nick.

Although there is no basis for an action in assault or battery, the circumstances in which Nick wilfully made a statement calcu-lated to cause, and actually did cause, physical harm to Millie may be come within the tort of *Wilkinson v Downton* (1897). This case extended the conduct which could amount to a battery to include situations where *no* contact or physical force is used. Liability can arise where words calculated to cause physical injury (including psychiatric harm) are spoken. In *Wilkinson v Downton* the defen-dant was held liable for falsely telling the claimant, by way of a perverted practical joke, that her husband had met with a serious accident, in consequence of which she suffered physical illness through nervous shock. At the time this case was decided, how-ever, there was no recovery in negligence for psychiatric harm and the specific requirements for assault and battery—the application, or threat, of force—were not present. However, on the particular facts of the case, the court distinguished *Wilkinson v Downton* from trespass to the person and found the defendant liable for wrongful interference. The conduct was not merely negligent but was intended to cause harm. On this basis Nick may be liable under the principle established in *Wilkinson v Downton* because his act was wilfully calculated to cause physical harm to Millie and it did actually cause such harm.

Negligence: Duty of Care

INTRODUCTION

Negligence as a tort may be defined as the breach of a duty of care, owed by the defendant to the claimant, which results in damage to the claimant. The tort of "negligence" uses the word "negligence" in a special sense. Negligence is commonly used as a synonym for carelessness. In the present context it is shorthand for "the tort which is the action for breach of duty". The breach is usually negligent in the ordinary sense; it arises from a careless lapse. However, it could arise from a deliberate act. E.g. in the case of *Condon v Basi* (CA, 1985) a claim was brought in negligence arising out of an incident in a football match. The defendant was alleged to have committed a deliberate foul. When playing contact sports such as football there is a duty on the part of the players to act in accordance with the "spirit of the game". The fact that this was said to be a deliberate act did not affect the fact that it was also a breach of the duty in question.

What we now refer to as the tort of negligence emerged during the 17th and 18th centuries as an extension of the torts of trespass. As we have seen in Ch. 1 these torts require intention and direct infliction of harm. Originally this action was known as the action of "trespass *in consimilitudini casu*". This is Latin for "trespass in a similar case". It was then shortened to the phrase "action on the case" or sometimes simply "case". If you read old cases you will sometimes see these expressions. As you should be aware the common law normally developed by a process of analogy. The ratio decidendi of a case would be extended to a case in which the material facts were seen as so similar that the same principle of law could be applied. This is how the action on the case developed. It dealt with specific situations where there was a relationship between claimant and defendant which justified the imposition of a duty on the defendant to take care to protect the claimant against certain types of harm. Usually this was limited to protection against physical injury or physical damage to property. The main differences between trespass and case were that in case it was sufficient to prove negligence as opposed to intention, and the harm could be caused indirectly. However, it was an essential ingredient of the action on the case that harm be caused. For a considerable period of time each of the duty situations was treated separately. There was a group of cases concerning the liability of physicians and surgeons to their patients when the patient was not paying for their service under contract. There was a group of cases involving the liability of those using the highway to other highway users. These categories were extended by analogy. Once it had been established that a surgeon owed a duty to a patient, this could be extended to physicians, dentists and pharmacists. In highway cases, once it had been established that horsemen and wagon drivers owed a duty of care, when the bicycle was invented, and then the traction engine and motor vehicles the duty could be extended to these modes of transport. However, little thought was given to the question of whether these various duty situations arose from a single underlying principle until the end of the 19th century. As we will see shortly the question of whether there is an effective unifying principle has been a major concern of the courts and academic tort lawyers since then.

CHECKPOINT

It is however important to recognise that the vast majority of claims in negligence arise out of well-established duty situations. In addition to the liability of clinicians and road users referred to above, other major categories include employer and employee, occupier of property and visitor and teacher and pupil. In such cases it is unnecessary to ask whether a duty of care is owed because the point has already been established.

There will however always be a small number of novel cases where it is alleged that a duty arises in circumstances which are not covered by the existing categories. Although small in number these cases raise important issues of principle. The courts have to establish whether a duty ought to exist. In order to do this they need to have some mechanism for distinguishing between cases where it is appropriate to find the duty exists and those where it is inappropriate. You must also remember that, even where it is appropriate to hold that a duty exists, it is necessary to establish the limits of that duty.

Liability in the tort of negligence requires that each of the essential elements, namely duty, breach and damage must be established. The concept of duty of care serves to define the interests protected by the tort of negligence by determining whether the type of loss suffered by the claimant in the particular way in which it occurred is actionable. That is, in a novel situation, does it arise in a context where the defendant "ought" to be responsible for seeing that harm does not befall the claimant, causing her loss, thus establishing a new type of "duty situation"? The loss in question may arise through misfeasance (doing something wrong) or nonfeasance (failing to act when action was required), and may consist of personal injury, physical damage to property, financial loss consequent on personal injury or physical damage (for example loss of earnings as a result of injury, or loss of profit where property is used for business purposes) or what is categorised as pure economic loss, which is financial loss not associated with personal injury or physical damage. Personal injury can also be subdivided. Until recently there was great reluctance to award compensation in respect of psychiatric harm. This was particularly the case where psychiatric harm occurred without physical injury. A duty of care in respect of psychiatric harm alone can now exist, but it is subject to special rules. In this chapter the development of the *duty of care* and the tests for establishing if a duty exists will be discussed, Ch.3 will examine what amounts to *breach of that duty*, and *damage* (causation and remoteness) will be the subject of Ch.4. However, it might be useful at this point to note that the elements of negligence frequently overlap and sometimes fail to provide a clear answer as to whether a claim should be allowed. It should also be noted that the claimant must establish all the elements, while the defendant will succeed if any one of them is not proved, so will focus on the areas of weakness in the particular case.

In *Lamb v Camden LBC* (CA, 1981), Lord Denning M.R. said: "it is not every consequence of a wrongful act which is the subject of compensation". He added that the lines have to be drawn somewhere:

> "Sometimes it is done by limiting the range of persons to whom a duty is owed. Sometimes it is done by saying that there is a break in the chain of causation. At other times it is done by saying that the consequence is too remote to be a head of damage. All these devices are useful in their way. Ultimately, it is a question of policy for judges to decide".

Figure 3: Elements of Negligence

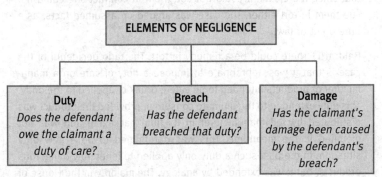

Note: the elements of negligence frequently overlap.

APPROACHES TO DUTY OF CARE

As the law developed to allow actions on the case we have seen that it came to be recognised that certain relationships gave rise to a legal duty, such that carelessness by one of the parties in that relationship which caused damage to the other would entitle that other to bring an action for damages. In this way a number of specific "duty situations" were created, and the claimant had either to prove that their case fell within one of these existing categories of relationship or to persuade the court to recognise a new duty situation.

Some judges and academics then tried to identify an underlying principle linking these duty situations, which would allow novel situations to be assessed against general criteria. The first successful attempt was that of Lord Atkin in *Donoghue v Stevenson* (HL, 1932). Lord Atkin, in attempting to trace a common thread through existing authority, formulated a general principle (the "neighbour principle") for determining whether, in any given case, a duty of care should exist.

KEY CASE

DONOGHUE V STEVENSON (1932)

The claimant went to a café with a friend who ordered some drinks. When the drinks arrived the claimant drank some of the contents and alleged that when her friend poured the remainder of the drink into her glass it contained the remnants of a decomposed snail. As a result she became seriously ill. She could not sue the retailer with whom she had no contract nor could she plausibly claim that he was negligent because the bottle was opaque and the snail could not be seen. Instead she sued the manufacturers of the drink in negligence. The manufacturers raised the defence of privity of contract and claimed that since the claimant could not sue them in contract she could not sue them in tort either. The case was argued on assumed facts, as a pure point of law.

Held: (HL) There could be a remedy in tort. The ratio decidendi of the case is that it was appropriate to impose a duty of care on a manufacturer of products intended to be eaten, drunk or applied to the body. This duty extended to the ultimate consumer, provided the product was distributed by the manufacturer in its final packaging and was not modified in the meantime. This was determined to be a new duty situation. In the past such a duty only applied to inherently dangerous products, but it was extended by analogy. The majority in the House of Lords recognised that such a duty had become appropriate in an era of mass production where any industrial manufacturer, rather than a local artisan who dealt directly with the consumer, was responsible for the product, and products could harm not only the purchaser, who had a contractual remedy against the seller, but also others such as family members or, as in the case, friends.

Comment

(1) Liability for negligent conduct had previously been recognised only in certain specifically defined circumstances. The court allowed actions for damages in cases where the special circumstances gave rise to a duty of care such as, for example, doctor-patient, innkeeper-guest, or where fire damage resulted from negligence. The case added manufacturer and consumer to the list of these.

(2) Lord Atkin, obiter, sought to unify these disparate duties of care in a single general theory and stated that the courts had previously been "engaged upon an elaborate classification of duties as they existed in various fact situations." He regarded this as unnecessary, adding "And yet the duty which is common to all the cases where liability is established must logically be based upon some element common to the cases where it is found to exist."

(3) This "neighbour principle" was founded on two elements. The first was that there must be foresight and reasonable contemplation of harm. The second was the need for a relationship of proximity between the parties, but this does not necessarily mean that the claimant must be in a close physical or spatial relationship to the defendant. Proximity is used to describe the nature of the relationship between the parties giving rise to a duty of care.

CHECKPOINT

The neighbour principle
Lord Atkin:

> "You must take reasonable care to avoid acts or omissions which you can reasonably foresee would be likely to injure your neighbour."

"Neighbour", in the legal sense, he defined as

> "persons who are so closely and directly affected by my act that I ought reasonably to have them in contemplation as being so affected when I am directing my mind to the acts or omissions which are called in question."

The significance of the *Donoghue v Stevenson* principle was that it potentially established negligence as an independent tort (rather than a "bundle" of torts each focussed on a duty situation) and provided a basis for its expansion to cover situations not already governed by precedent where a relationship between the parties existed such as doctor-patient or innkeeper-guest. This is not to say, however, that cases in which no duty had been held to exist prior to 1932 would thereafter be decided differently simply on the basis that the damage in question was reasonably foreseeable, since it is clear from the neighbour principle itself, as emphasised in a number of subsequent decisions, that there must also be a sufficient *relationship of proximity* between the parties.

The term "proximity" means legal, rather than geographical, proximity and, according to Lord Keith in *Yuen Kun Yeu v Att Gen of Hong Kong* (PC, 1987), is referable to

" ... such close and direct relations that the act complained of directly affects a person whom the person alleged to be bound to take care would know would be directly affected by his careless act."

The unforeseeable claimant

Even where the courts are prepared to find that the circumstances are such as to be capable of giving rise to a duty, the claimant will still fail if she was an unforeseeable victim of the defendant's negligence. In imposing a duty it is not sufficient to establish that the circumstances give rise to a duty—the court must also be satisfied that the particular defendant owed a duty to the particular claimant. Thus, simply to say that a motorist owes a duty of care to other road users does not answer the question whether, in any given case, harm of the type suffered by the particular claimant was in the circumstances foreseeable.

In *Bourhill v Young* (HL, 1943), the claimant heard, but did not see, a crash caused by the defendant motorcyclist's negligence. The claimant later saw part of the aftermath of the accident and suffered nervous shock. She failed to establish the existence of a duty of care to prevent nervous shock—she was an "unforeseeable" claimant and harm to her of that type was not foreseeable.

The development of the *duty of care*

In *Hedley Byrne v Heller* (HL, 1963), the House of Lords extended the neighbour principle to cover cases of pure economic loss not resulting from physical damage in circumstances where a "special relationship" arises between the parties.

HEDLEY BYRNE V HELLER (1963)

The appellants, advertising agents, became doubtful about the financial status of one of their clients, Easipower Ltd. They made enquiries of the defendant bankers with whom Easipower had an account. The defendants replied, first orally and then in writing, that Easipower was financially sound. The appellants relied on this advice and suffered financial loss when Easipower went into liquidation.

Held: (HL) A duty of care would arise in relation to statements where there is a "special relationship" between the giver and the recipient of the advice.

Comment

(1) The nature of a "special relationship" was not fully defined by the court but the requirements for its existence appeared to be:

  (i)   the existence of a relationship based on professional or other skill or expertise;

  (ii) a reliance by the claimant on the defendant's special skill and judgment;

  (iii) knowledge, or reasonable expectation of knowledge on the part of the defendant, that the claimant was relying on the statement;

  (iv) it was reasonable in the circumstances for the claimant to rely on the defendant;

  (v)   in some cases that the relationship was close to being contractual (since liability in contract for negligent advice is well-established).

(2) The concept of "a voluntary assumption of responsibility" has subsequently been used to establish proximity in determining the existence of a duty of care. This arises from an undertaking either expressed or implied that the defendant will exercise care in giving information or advice. However doubt has been expressed as to whether this criterion was necessary or useful. In *Smith v Bush* (HL, 1990) Lord Griffiths suggested that it is not a helpful or realistic test for liability, but in *Henderson v Merrett Syndicates Ltd* (HL, 1995) Lord Goff said that the criticism of the concept of a voluntary assumption of responsibility in *Smith v Bush* is misplaced. It seems to be regarded as the most useful way of identifying whether a special relationship exists by most judges today. However some also look at the issue in terms of reasonable reliance. Really these are the two sides of the same coin. A crucial factor in assessing whether reliance by the claimant was

reasonable will be whether the claimant could reasonably conclude that the defendant was assuming responsibility.

(3) The duty of care under *Hedley Byrne* has been restated in more restricted terms by the House of Lords in *Caparo Industries v Dickman* (HL, 1990). A distinction must be drawn between advice specifically given in defined circumstances to a particular individual (even if the identity of the individual is unknown as in *Smith v Bush*) and advice which is published more generally. In the latter class of case, responsibility will normally be assumed only in respect of the specific purpose for which the advice was published. In *Caparo* the auditors of a company produced the statutory annual audit report which was intended to enable the shareholders, as owners of the company, to decide whether they were satisfied with the management of the company by the board of directors on the basis of the company's past performance. It was not intended as a basis for a decision to invest in the shares of the company. Advice on this would be based on different criteria. There was no voluntary assumption of responsibility towards potential investors, nor would it be reasonable for such an investor to rely on this report for that purpose.

Later, in *Home Office v Dorset Yacht Co Ltd* (HL, 1970) some borstal trainees escaped from custody during the night when, it was alleged, the three officers in charge of them were asleep. The escapees caused damage to the claimant's yacht. It was argued by the Home Office that it would be contrary to public policy to hold it (or its officers) liable to a member of the public for the acts of others (the borstal trainees) by failing to restrain them. The majority of the House of Lords concluded that a duty of care was owed on the grounds that a "special relationship" existed. In extending Lord Atkin's neighbour principle, Lord Reid suggested that a duty of care based on reasonable foreseeability and proximity ought to apply in all cases unless there was some justification or valid explanation for its exclusion. This approach was affirmed by the House of Lords in *Anns v Merton LBC* (HL, 1978). At this point it is clear that the judicial opinion was firmly behind the principled approach, and the old approach of extension by analogy in relation to separate duty situations had been abandoned. Lord Wilberforce stated that the enquiry into the existence of a duty of care is to be approached in two stages.

First one has to ask whether, as between the alleged wrongdoer and the person who has suffered damage there is a sufficient relationship of proximity or neighbourhood such that, in the reasonable contemplation of the former, carelessness on his part may be likely to cause damage to the latter—in which case a prima facie duty of care arises. Secondly, if the first question is answered affirmatively, it is necessary to consider whether there are any considerations which ought to negative, or to reduce or limit the scope of the duty or the class of person to whom it is owed or the damages to which a breach of it may give rise.

In one sense Lord Wilberforce's formulation is merely a paraphrase of the neighbour principle originally stated by Lord Atkin, followed by a recognition that there would inevitably be some cases where policy considerations would arise. Unfortunately the new formulation was interpreted as changing the significance of the two elements of foreseeability and proximity. This interpretation was that if the claimant established foreseeability of harm, this alone raised the presumption of the existence of a duty of care. It was almost as though proximity had been written out. This meant that, at the second stage of the test (the policy stage) the courts were left to restrict the scope of negligence liability by reference to policy considerations. The extent to which policy considerations will carry weight with judges will vary. In *McLoughlin v O'Brian* (HL, 1983) (below) the policy arguments, which were said to justify the restrictions on liability, were criticised. Lord Bridge, dismissing the floodgates argument, said:

> "I believe that the floodgates argument ... is, as it always has been, greatly exaggerated".

This period of expansion of negligence liability reached its high-water mark in *Junior Books v Veitchi Co Ltd* (HL, 1983). This was a case where the flooring in a factory which had been installed by a nominated specialist subcontractor proved to be defective. Normally the building owner would claim against the main contractor in contract. In this case that option was not available. A claim was brought against the subcontractor. The decision could be justified on its facts because this particular subcontractor had been in very close contact with the building owner and had made a number of claims about the quality of its product. The House of Lords held that this gave rise to a special relationship which justified overturning the normal rule that claims arising under construction contract should be pursued in contract. This would enable the main contractor to pass on the claim to the subcontractor where appropriate (for application of the normal principle see *Simaan v Pilkington* (CA, 1988).

During the 1980s the courts became increasingly concerned that the Wilberforce version of the two-stage test was leading to a large number of actions which were unjustified. In *Governors of the Peabody Donation Fund v Sir Lindsay Parkinson & Co Ltd* (HL, 1985) the House of Lords warned against the more liberal approach of the Wilberforce test, and in subsequent decisions the courts have sought to reassert limits on the scope of liability that had traditionally been recognised in the case law.

Carriage of goods by sea involves a large number of contracts between those who own the goods and those responsible for transporting them. In essence the goods can be carried at the owner's risk, or at the carrier's risk, and all these contracts should be set up to reflect this. This will mean that the party at risk will ensure the goods but the party at risk will not. If something goes wrong with the insurance arrangements, and the goods are damaged, the contracts will ensure that those who would not supposed to bear the risk will not have it imposed on them. If the person who has sustained the uninsured loss can ignore this contractual framework and sue the person allegedly responsible for the damage in tort, this destabilises the entire basis of the transaction. However such claims were brought on the basis that this was a case where harm was foreseeable, as was the claimant. The claims were rejected (see *The Aliakmon* (HL, 1986) but were taking up judicial time and wasting resources. There were similar concerns where claims were brought, not against the person who had caused the loss, but against a regulator who had failed to prevent the real tortfeasor from doing so, in circumstances where the loss was foreseeable. These claims were also rejected (see *Yuen Kun Yeu* (PC, 1987)) but there was the same concern. Lord Keith said "In view of the direction in which the law has since been developing, their Lordships consider that for the future it should be recognised that the two-stage test in Anns is not to be regarded as in all circumstances a suitable guide to the existence of a duty of care." *Anns* was eventually overruled by the House of Lords in *Murphy v Brentwood District Council* (HL, 1990).

The question then arose as to what approach should henceforth be taken to identifying whether or not a duty of care should be acknowledged in a novel situation. In *Caparo v Dickman* (HL, 1990), the House of Lords rejected not only the broad approach taken by Lord Wilberforce in *Anns* but any overarching principle. Lord Roskill observed that: "it has now to be accepted that there is no simple formula or touchstone" in the formulation of the test for existence of a duty of care:

"Phrases such as 'foreseeability', 'proximity', 'neighbourhood', 'just and reasonable' 'fairness', 'voluntary acceptance of risk' or 'voluntary assumption of responsibility' will be found used from time to time in the different cases. But ... such phrases are not precise definitions. At best they are but labels or phrases descriptive of the very different factual situations which can exist in particular cases and which must be carefully examined in each case before it can be pragmatically determined whether a duty of care exists and, if so, what is the scope of that duty."

Their Lordships all approved a dictum in the Australian case of *Sutherland Shire Council v Heyman* (1985) where Brennan J said that the law should develop "incrementally by analogy with established categories." As Lord Bridge put it after discussing the neighbour principle in its original Atkinian form, and also in the Wilberforce modified version:

> "The concepts of proximity and fairness embodied in these additional ingredients are not susceptible of any such precise definition as would be necessary to give them utility as practical tests, but amount in effect to little more than convenient labels to attach to the features of different specific situations which, on a detailed examination of all the circumstances, the law recognises pragmatically as giving rise to a duty of care of a given scope. Whilst recognising, of course, the importance of the underlying general principles common to the whole field of negligence, I think the law has now moved in the direction of attaching greater significance to the more traditional categorisation of distinct and recognisable situations as guides to the existence, the scope and the limits of the varied duties of care which the law imposes."

KEY CASE

CAPARO INDUSTRIES PLC V DICKMAN (1990)

The claimants owned shares in a public company whose accounts were audited by the defendants for the purposes of the annual statutory audit. The claimants purchased further shares and made a successful takeover bid for the company. They subsequently suffered a substantial loss and brought an action against the auditors. It was alleged that the shares had been purchased in reliance on the audit which was negligently prepared and gave a misleading impression of the company's financial position.

Held: (HL) The claimant's claim failed. The auditors owed no duty of care in respect of the accuracy of the accounts to either members of the public or existing shareholders if they sought to rely on such an audit report to invest in the company; there was not sufficient proximity between the claimants and the defendants. Also, the audit was prepared for the purpose of enabling the shareholders as a body to exercise control over the company; it was not prepared for the purpose of providing information for investors.

Comment

(1) In this case the statement was placed into general circulation as

opposed to the "one to one" advice situations in *Hedley Byrne* and *Smith v Bush*. Lord Bridge said that an essential ingredient of the required proximity in situations where a statement is put into more or less general circulation is to prove that: "the defendant knew that his statement would be communicated to the claimant, either as an individual or as a member of an identifiable class, specifically in connection with a particular transaction or transactions of a particular kind, . . . and that the claimant would be very likely to rely on it.".

(2) This approach to liability was applied in *Al-Nakib Investments (Jersey) Ltd v Longcroft* (HC, 1990) where directors issued a prospectus inviting shareholders to subscribe for additional shares in the company. The purpose of the prospectus was specifically to invite existing shareholders to apply and a claim brought by purchasers in the market was struck out.

The speeches in *Caparo* make it very clear that the Law Lords are firmly rejecting any overarching principle, and therefore any test of general application based on that principle. As we have seen they did identify a number of factors which are likely to be significant. Nevertheless on the rare occasions when it is necessary to undertake this exercise though they are firmly indicating that there must be a specific enquiry considering the precise facts and context, with each of the various factors being given appropriate weight. This will result in a specific ruling which can of course subsequently be applied by analogy to similar situations. The House of Lords has subsequently confirmed this approach in *Commissioners of Customs & Excise v Barclays Bank* (HL, 2006). However, judges, legal representatives and even law students often like to have a test or checklist to deal with complicated issues such as the existence of a duty of care. As a result some cases have interpreted *Caparo* as identifying a set of criteria which can be articulated into a three stage checklist. This has become known as the *Caparo* test, although it was not laid down as such in that case in any meaningful sense.

CHECKPOINT

The *Caparo* criteria—the three stage test used to establish a duty of care

Under this test, for a duty of care to arise:

(i)   the loss must be reasonably foreseeable;

(ii) there must be a relationship of proximity between the parties; and

(iii) it must be fair, just and reasonable that the law should impose a duty—this enables the court to take account of any underlying policy concerns.

Cases differ infinitely in their circumstances. In most cases involving personal injury or physical damage it will be proximity and foreseeability which are most important considerations. In *Barrett v Ministry of Defence* (CA, 1995), there had been a pattern of excessive drinking amongst naval airmen at a remote Navy base. A rating collapsed after a bout of heavy drinking and the duty officer arranged for him to be taken to his room where he was left unsupervised. The rating later died due to choking on vomit. The Navy was not liable for preventing the deceased from excessive drinking or for anything that happened prior to his collapse but when he collapsed the Navy assumed responsibility and was liable in negligence. There was sufficient proximity. Its supervision of the deceased following his collapse was inadequate and the measures taken fell short of the standard reasonably to be expected.

In some cases of physical damage, the third criterion may be relevant. The case of *Marc Rich & Co v Bishop Rock Marine Co Ltd* (HL, 1996) arose following the sinking of a cargo ship. Some of the cargo was inadequately insured. The cargo owners were therefore looking to make a claim in relation to their uninsured loss. They could not claim against the shipowner because the goods were being carried at the cargo owners' risk. Prior to sailing, the ship had been inspected by a surveyor acting for a marine classification society. These are responsible for classifying ships in terms of their seaworthiness. It was alleged that the survey was negligent. If the correct classification had been issued the ship would not have been allowed to sail until repairs had been carried out. The classification society were of course aware that the ship would be carrying cargo. Their relationship with the cargo owners arguably satisfied the requirements of proximity, and the loss was entirely foreseeable. The House of Lords stated that notwithstanding proximity and foreseeability were present, the claim failed because, on the grounds of policy, it would not be fair, just and reasonable to impose a duty in this type of case. The law of international trade, underpinned by a network of contracts and supported by insurance cover, already covered the events which occurred. To allow this to be evaded to the claimant's advantage by imposing liability on the marine classification society could undermine the whole system of international trade in the future. At the very least it would mean that the classification society would have to take out insurance to cover any possible claims. This would be extremely expensive and the cost would be passed on through their fees and in turn increase the cost of shipping goods. In most cases this would be entirely unnecessary double insurance. This is why it was not in the public interest and therefore failed to satisfy the "fair just and reasonable" test. In *Perrett v Collins* (HC, 1998) a passenger injured in an aircraft accident, allegedly caused by the non-airworthy condition of the aircraft, claimed in negligence against the inspector who had certified that the aircraft was fit to fly. The defendant sought to rely on the reasoning in *Marc Rich* but the Court of Appeal held that *Marc Rich* was based upon broad policy considerations relating to the organisation of maritime trade which were peculiar to that situation. In *Perrett* the inspector had an independent and critical role because the aircraft could not lawfully fly unless such a certificate had been issued. He therefore owed a duty to potential passengers to use reasonable care in inspecting the aircraft and issuing the certificate.

KEY CASE

MARC RICH & CO V BISHOP ROCK MARINE CO LTD (1995)
A vessel, "The Nicholas H", developed a crack while carrying a cargo from South America to Italy. A surveyor employed by a marine classi-fication society pronounced that, with temporary welding work, the vessel was fit to complete the voyage. A few days later the ship sank with a total loss of the cargo.

Held: (HL) The classification society owed no duty of care to the cargo owners. Although the damage was physical harm (damage to property) rather than pure economic loss resulting from the surveyor's negligent statement that the vessel was seaworthy, this was insufficient to give rise to a duty of care. Whatever the nature of the harm suffered by the claimant, all three elements of the tripartite test, foreseeability, proximity and questions of justice and reasonableness, must be applied. As noted above, a number of policy factors pointed against a decision in favour of the owners. Classification societies were inde-pendent non-profit making entities, operating for the sole purpose of promoting the collective welfare, namely, the safety of ships and lives at sea. A finding of liability might lead to classification societies adopting a more "defensive position". If a duty of care was to be recognised it would enable cargo owners, or their insurers, to upset the balance of the international conventions governing shipowners' liabi-lity to cargo owners. In addition, another layer of insurance cover would be wastefully introduced into the structure.

Comment
In *Watson v British Boxing Board of Control* (CA, 2001) a boxer who suffered brain damage following a boxing match alleged that the Board which regulates boxing had been negligent in not providing a better level of ringside medical care. Lord Phillips in the Court of Appeal described the case as a unique one because here, rather than pre-venting it, the causing of physical harm was the object of the activity. Taking account of the boxer's reliance on the Board to reduce the

effects of injuries once they occurred the court concluded that in all the circumstances of the case it was fair, just and reasonable to impose a duty of care. It should be noted that the fact that the Board was a non-profit making organisation (like the defendant in *Marc Rich*) was not enough to deny the justice of finding liability.

However, inextricably interconnected as these requirements are, the relationship of one with the other is far from clear. In *Davis v Radcliffe* (PC, 1990), for example, Lord Goff said that proximity referred to such a relation between the parties as rendered it just and reasonable that a duty should be imposed, and Lord Oliver in *Caparo Industries Plc v Dickman* (HL, 1990) suggested that lack of proximity could in some cases be attributed to a failure of the just and reasonable requirement. It could indeed be said, which appears to be what Lord Oliver is suggesting, that proximity is not an independent criterion, but an aspect of what is just and reasonable. Further, the relative significance to be attached to each requirement will depend upon a variety of factors including, inter alia, the status of the parties and their relationship with one another, the nature of the harm suffered, and the particular way in which that harm arises.

The language used by judges in dealing with the duty issue has tended to mask the fact that the decision whether or not a duty exists as a matter of law is ultimately based upon policy, a fact which has now come to be more openly acknowledged. As Lord Pearce observed in *Hedley Byrne & Co v Heller & Partners Ltd* (HL, 1964):

> "How wide the sphere of the duty of care in negligence is to be laid depends ultimately on the courts' assessment of the demands of society for protection from the carelessness of others."

In other words, the concepts of proximity and what is just and reasonable, flexible and elusive as they are (and quite incapable of definition), merely serve as convenient tools which the courts can manipulate in order to achieve the result which they perceive the merits of the case to justify.

Figure 4: Questions relevant to establishing the elements of a duty of care

> **What is the relationship between the parties and the nature of the harm suffered?**
> The relative significance to be attached to each requirement will depend upon a variety of factors including, *inter alia*, the status of the parties and their relationship with one another, the nature of the harm suffered, and the particular way in which that harm arises

> **Was the claimant's physical harm the result of a positive act on the part of the defendant?**
> Where positive conduct by the defendant causes direct physical injury to the claimant or the claimant's property, reasonable foresight of such harm will generally be sufficient to satisfy the other criteria for the existence of a duty (see, e.g. Lord Oliver in *Murphy v Brentwood District Council* (HL, 1990)).

> **Does the claim involve pure economic loss or an omission to act?**
> Where the claimant's claim is in respect of *pure economic loss*, or where the defendant has failed to prevent damage by *omitting* to act, mere foreseeability of the harm is never sufficient to establish a duty; in cases of this type, questions of proximity and whether it would be just and reasonable to impose a duty assume much greater significance and must be weighed more carefully in the balance.

The rest of this chapter deals with some of the more well-defined circumstances in which no duty, or a duty of limited scope only, has been held to exist.

PURE ECONOMIC LOSS

Financial loss consequent upon negligently inflicted injury to the person or to property is ordinarily recoverable. This covers such heads of damage as loss of earnings where an injury makes the claimant unable to work, the cost of private medical treatment or other care as a result of disability, and losses caused where damage to property used for business purposes results in loss of profits. Using the ordinary principles of causation which we consider in Ch. 4, these are seen as simply part and parcel of the harm caused to the individual or the property concerned. There are however situations where financial loss is caused without there being any injury or damage. One obvious example is negligent advice on investment. The only result is loss of money. This type of harm is referred to as pure economic loss. Such loss can arise from a negligent act or from the provision of negligent information or advice. The law has developed very differently in relation to the two areas.

Negligent acts

There has never been liability for pure economic loss caused by negligent acts. This was first established in *Cattle v Stockton Waterworks Co* (HL, 1875)), although economic loss consequent upon damage to the claimant's property has always been recoverable. This principle was challenged in *Spartan Steel & Alloys Ltd v Martin & Co (Contractors) Ltd* (CA, 1973), but the majority of the Court of Appeal reaffirmed that as a matter of policy such a loss should not be recoverable. As a result the claimants succeeded in the first part of their claim (resulting from damage to their property consequent upon a power cut) but failed to recover in respect of the profit which they would have made but for the power cut (pure economic loss).

KEY CASE

SPARTAN STEEL & ALLOYS LTD V MARTIN & CO (CONTRACTORS) LTD (1973)
This case illustrates the distinction between "pure economic loss" and economic loss which is consequent upon physical damage to person or property. Economic loss which results from physical damage is recoverable. Here, the defendant contractor, in the course of digging the road, negligently cut a power cable causing the claimant's smelting works to be shut down. At the time of the power cut there was a "melt" in progress and to stop the steel solidifying it had to be drawn out of the furnace. This reduced its value by £368. The claimants claimed for the reduced value of the melt and for the profit which would have been made had it been completed. They also claimed for the loss of profit from four further melts which would have been processed but for the 14-hour power cut.

Held: (CA) The claimants recovered the reduction in the value of the solidified melt, which was property damage, and the profits they would have made from its sale. However, they obtained nothing for the loss of profits on the four further melts which could have been processed before the electricity was restored; that was pure economic loss independent of the physical damage.

Comment

(1) Lord Denning made clear the public policy justifications for this decision. He stated:

" ... the risk of economic loss should be suffered by the whole community who suffer the losses, usually many but comparatively small losses, rather than on the one pair of shoulders ... ".

(2) In *Weller & Co Ltd v Foot and Mouth Disease Research Institute* (1966) livestock auctioneers were unable to continue their business because the defendants had negligently released a virus which caused an outbreak of foot and mouth disease. Their indirect loss of business was denied because it was purely economic

(3) Essentially in relation to negligent acts the issue of pure economic loss is an issue of remoteness of damage. The policy is to disallow such claims, not for want of factual causation, but because it is not in the public interest.

(4) Under the influence of *Anns v Merton* (HL, 1978) liability in negligence for the cost of repair of defective property was allowed. This is treated as pure economic loss since no damage has been done to the property, it is merely less valuable because of the need for further expenditure. This line of cases was overruled in *Murphy v Brentwood DC* (HL, 1990). There is no justification at common law for departing from the normal rules. However, in certain circumstances there is a statutory right to compensation under the Defective Premises Act 1972.

(5) Exceptionally, where there is a particularly close relationship between a building owner and a subcontractor who is responsible for defective work, there will be a special relationship analogous to that in negligent statement cases (discussed in the next section) which justifies recovery for pure economic loss: *Junior Books Ltd v Veitchi Co Ltd* (HL, 1983).

Negligent statements

In this area there are two distinct issues. The first is whether there is a duty of care in relation to the statement itself. The second is whether damages are recoverable pure economic loss if in the particular case there is a duty and it is broken. These issues need to be addressed separately.

Liability for negligent statements

Prior to 1964 liability for misstatements only existed in contract, in the tort of deceit (*Derry v Peek* (HL, 1889)), or for breach of a fiduciary duty (*Nocton v Lord Ashburton* (HL, 1914)). In *Hedley Byrne & Co Ltd v Heller & Partners Ltd* (HL, 1964) where the claimants suffered financial loss when they relied on the information provided by the defendant bank it was held that in the particular case no duty arose because of a disclaimer attached to the information, but that, in appropriate circumstances, a duty could arise in relation to negligent provision of information or advice.

Tests imposed as the basis of liability for negligent statements

(1) In *Hedley Byrne* their Lordships accepted that reasonable foresight of the harm was not in itself sufficient because of the potentially far-reaching effect of the spoken (or written) word, and spoke of the need for a "special relationship". It appeared that such a relationship would exist where, to the defendant's knowledge (actual or constructive), the claimant relied upon the defendant's skill and judgement or his ability to make careful enquiry, and it was reasonable in the circumstances for the claimant to do so. The essence of *Hedley Byrne* could thus be equated with the concept of "reasonable reliance".

(2) In *Caparo Industries Plc v Dickman* (1990) Lord Bridge said that, in order for a duty to arise, it was necessary to show that the defendant knew that his statement would be communicated to the claimant, either as an individual or as a member of an identifiable class, specifically in connection with a particular transaction or transactions of a particular kind, and that the claimant would be very likely to rely on it in deciding whether or not to enter into the transaction.

There has also been a tendency to explain the existence of a duty as resting upon a voluntary assumption of responsibility by the defendant. Thus, in *Henderson v Merrett Syndicates Ltd* (HL, 1994), it was held that where a person assumed responsibility to perform professional or quasi-professional services for another who relied on those services, the relationship between the parties was in itself sufficient to give rise to a duty on the part of the person providing those services. This broad statement of principle cuts across the traditional distinction between negligent statements and negligent acts in the context of liability for professional negligence. Although in many instances the relationship between the parties will be contractual, it was held in *Henderson* that this did not preclude the simultaneous existence of a tortious duty.

Most of the cases have involved professional advisers, and the view of the majority in *Mutual Life and Citizens' Assurance Co Ltd v Evatt* (PC, 1971) was that the duty was limited to such persons, or to those holding themselves out as possessing a comparable skill and competence. The minority view, on the other hand, was that the duty would arise whenever a businessman in the course of his business gave information to a person who let it be known that he was seeking considered advice upon which he intended to act. This more liberal approach found favour in *Esso Petroleum Co Ltd v Mardon* (CA, 1976), although the fact that the adviser is not in the business of giving advice of the type sought may be relevant in determining whether the claimant was reasonably entitled to rely on it for the particular purpose in question or whether, for example, he might reasonably have been expected to undertake further enquiries or obtain independent advice. For a more detailed breakdown of the factors which may be relevant to the existence of a duty, see Neill L.J. in *James McNaughton Papers Group Ltd v Hicks Anderson & Co* (CA, 1991).

Figure 5

Negligent statements: relevance of the defendant's knowledge (actual or constructive) of the purpose for which the information is required	
Auditors	**Surveyors**
The scope of the duty in the context of auditors does not extend to the use for a different purpose of a standard report (*Caparo*). It will apply in situations where the defendant is specifically requested to prepare a report for the purpose of showing it to an actual or prospective bidder in a proposed take-over. (The dissenting judgement of Denning L.J. in *Candler v Crane Christmas* (CA, 1949) was expressly approved in *Hedley Byrne*.)	In contrast to the position of auditors, surveyors appointed to value a house for mortgage purposes may owe a duty to the purchaser even though the primary purpose of the valuation is to enable the lender to decide whether to advance a loan (*Yianni v Edwin Evans & Sons* (HC, 1982), approved in *Smith v Eric S. Bush* (HL, 1989) and *Harris v Wyre Forest DC* (HL, 1989)).
Reason for this distinction	
This distinction has been justified on the basis that valuers are paid for their services at the mortgagor's expense and must know that, in the case of a typical house purchase, the majority of buyers in fact rely upon their report and cannot afford an independent valuation. A warning note was sounded in *Smith v Bush* that the duty would not necessarily apply to commercial property or to houses at the more expensive end of the market, where the purchaser might be expected to obtain their own independent survey.	

Hedley Byrne does not apply to information or advice tendered "off the cuff" or on a purely social occasion, nor is there any general duty to volunteer information. However, the duty has been held to apply to pre-contractual negotiations (*Esso Petroleum Co Ltd v Mardon* (CA, 1976)), though where the claimant is induced to contract as a result of a negligent misstatement he may, apart from a possible action in tort, sue under s.2(1) of the Misrepresentation Act 1967. The advantage of the statutory action is that the defendant has the burden of proving that he or she had reasonable grounds to believe, and did believe up to the time the contract was entered into, that the facts represented were true (see *Howard Marine & Dredging Co Ltd v A. Ogden & Sons Ltd* (CA, 1978)). This case also provides a useful indication of what type of advice or information will be treated as sufficiently formal and professional to attract liability, and what will be seen as too informal. The case concerned an agreement to hire barges to transport excess soil from a building site to be dumped at sea. The hirers were concerned to ensure that the barges had a suitable carrying capacity in terms of both weight and volume. Early in the negotiations, during a telephone call, a representative of the owner was asked about this. He gave an immediate response based on his general recollection. It was held that that did not amount to a formal statement on which reliance could be placed. Later the question was repeated, and on this occasion the owner's representative took time to consult his files relating to the barges and then gave an answer. This was held to be a formal answer for which the owners had assumed responsibility, and which it was reasonable for the hirers to rely on.

The application of Hedley Byrne
Provided that the defendant is aware of the existence of the claimant either as an individual or as a member of an ascertainable class, there is clearly no need for the defendant to know the identity of the claimant. A crucial ingredient of the duty is the defendant's knowledge (actual or constructive) of the purpose for which the information is required. In *Caparo Industries Plc v Dickman* (HL, 1990), it was held that, in preparing the statutory audit of the accounts of a public company, the defendants owed no duty to the claimants either as potential investors or as existing shareholders. The purpose of the audit was to report to the shareholders to enable them to exercise their rights in the management of the company, not to provide information which might assist them in making investment decisions. It follows from this that auditors owe no duty to existing or potential creditors of the company (*Al Saudi Banque v Clark Pixley* (HC, 1989), approved in Caparo). Similarly, it was held in *Al-Nakib Investments (Jersey) Ltd v Longcroft* (HC, 1990) that information in a prospectus inviting shareholders to subscribe for additional shares by way of a rights issue can be used only for that specific purpose, and not for the purpose of deciding to buy additional shares in the stock market (see also *James McNaughton Papers Group Ltd v Hicks Anderson & Co* (CA, 1991)).

Reliance by a third party
There are situations in which a duty of care will be imposed upon A who makes a statement to B, as a result of which B acts upon it to C's financial detriment. Although it is well established that, in performing a service for their client, a solicitor generally owes no duty of care to third parties (see, e.g.

Clarke v Bruce Lance & Co (CA, 1988)), it was held in *Ross v Caunters* (HC, 1980) that a solicitor who failed to inform his client, the testator, that the spouse of a beneficiary should not witness the will was liable to an intended beneficiary for the loss of her bequest. In *White v Jones* (HL, 1995) a majority of the House of Lords held the defendant solicitors liable for failing to carry out their client's instructions regarding his will, with the result that the claimants (the intended beneficiaries) lost their legacy. One of the principal arguments in support of the imposition of a duty in these cases was that to hold otherwise would lead to the unjust result that the solicitor would escape liability for the consequences of his or her negligence, because the deceased testator and his estate had suffered no loss and would therefore have no claims (other than for nominal damages for breach of contract). A solicitor also owes a duty to an intended beneficiary under a will notwithstanding the fact that the estate may also have a claim against the negligent solicitor. In *Carr-Glynn v Frearsons* (CA, 1998) a first instance decision that no duty was owed where the effect of the solicitor's negligence is to cause a loss to the estate, since it is unacceptable that the defendant should be at risk of two separate claims for identical loss, was overruled by the Court of Appeal.

Figure 6

The duty under *White v Jones* is not confined to cases relating to wills	
Pensions and Life Insurance	**Employment References**
In *Gorham v British Telecommunications Plc* (CA, 2000), Mrs Gorham sued Standard Life for breach of a duty of care owed to her and her children. Her deceased husband had been incorrectly advised that the BT pension scheme was preferable to a personal pension. However, on his death she and the children received considerably less because of the negligent advice given to her husband. The Court of Appeal held that if an insurance company owed a duty of care to the customer, this duty was also owed to the customer's dependant wife and family where he had intended to create a benefit for them on his death.	In *Spring v Guardian Assurance Plc* (HL, 1994) an employer supplying a reference about an employee to a prospective employer was held to owe a duty to the employee to avoid negligently making untrue statements. There was clear proximity of relationship as between employer and employee, so that it was fair, just and reasonable that the law should impose a duty on the employer. In *McKie v Swindon College* (HC, 2013) an unsolicited email (not a reference) containing largely erroneous and untrue statements sent by the former employer of a lecturer led to his dismissal from a new job. Although the email was not a reference, the defendant was nevertheless liable for the negligent statement.

In the opinion of the majority in *Spring* economic loss in the form of failure to obtain employment was clearly foreseeable if a careless reference was given and there was clear proximity of relationship as between employer and employee, so that it was fair, just and reasonable that the law should impose a duty on the employer. By analogy with *Spring* it has been held that, in carrying out a pre-employment medical assessment on behalf of a company, a doctor could owe a duty to the would-be employee (*Baker v Kaye* (HC, 1997)).

Statements on websites

In *Patchett v Swimming Pool & Allied Trades Association Ltd (SPATA)* (2009), the Court of Appeal considered liability for statements on a website which the claimant alleged were inaccurate and misleading. Here, financial loss was suffered when the installer of a swimming pool became insolvent before the pool was completed and the question was whether the defendant, SPATA, owed a duty of care to internet users for statements on its website. The Court of Appeal found there was no assumption of responsibility, because the degree of reliance by its customers which SPATA intended, or should reasonably have expected, was limited by its advice in a statement to customers to obtain an information pack for further details. It was held that the state-ments on the website had to be taken as a whole and it was reasonable to expect potential customers to have regard to all the information available on the website. In these circumstances, it would not be fair, just and reasonable to hold that SPATA owed the claimants a duty of care and that to find such a duty would be an unwarranted extension of existing case law.

To summarise the effect of all these decisions, we can say that a duty of care may arise in relation to negligent advice or information. The question of whether it does is dealt with using the various criteria referred to in the so-called *Caparo* test. However when considering whether there is sufficient proximity the courts look for a much closer relationship in the shape of the "special relationship", although exactly how that is characterised depends on the context and to some extent on the particular approach to the problem of the individual judge. As Lord Bingham pointed out in *Commissioners of Customs & Excise v Barclays Bank* (HL, 2006), the same result seemed to be reached whatever formulation was adopted.

What loss is recoverable

Where negligent words cause physical harm the claimant usually needs only to prove that the harm was foreseeable, as was the case with the workman in *Clayton v Woodman & Son (Builders)* (CA, 1962) who was injured when an architect negligently instructed a bricklayer to remove the keystone of an archway. It is obvious in this case that there was proximity and no conceivable policy reason to deny recovery.

Where negligent words cause pure economic loss the courts take a much more restrictive approach which was justified by Lord Pearce in *Hedley Byrne* v *Heller* (HL, 1964) on the basis that: "words are more volatile than deeds, they travel fast and far afield, they are used without being expended." Liability for pure economic loss without injury to person or property mainly arises with negligent misstatements. However, once a statement is put into circulation it may be broadcast and relied on in different ways by many different people so the criterion of reasonable foreseeability of the loss was rejected as giving rise to potentially too wide a liability. However, once it was accepted that there could be liability in negligence for negligent statements, since pure economic loss is the typical consequence of such statements, clearly pure economic loss has to be recoverable albeit subject to specific restrictions.

CHECKPOINT

Restriction of liability for negligent words
The courts have always been wary in cases of financial loss resulting from negligent statements of burdening the defendant with liability "in an indeterminate amount for an indeterminate time to an indeterminate class" (per Cardozo CJ in in the American case of *Ultramares Corp* v *Touche* (1931)). Liability for harm caused by negligent *behaviour* is normally recoverable but where harm is caused by negligent *words* the courts are now inclined to approach the issue on a case-by-case basis, identifying discrete categories of liability. Cases of financial loss may arise as a result either of negligent information or advice, or of negligent conduct, although the distinction between word and action is not always clear. For example, if you ask a stockbroker for advice about investing in a particular security, this would be potentially liability for words, but if you are instructing him to manage your portfolio and he decides to invest part of it in that security, this would be liability for action. However, the loss is the same and its root cause is the same, i.e. negligent misjudgement of the investment opportunity.

Although *Hedley Byrne*, which made a major inroad upon the principle that economic loss was generally not recoverable in tort, was originally confined to misstatements, there followed a trend towards the formulation of a broader principle, applying to both statements and acts, which would permit recovery where there was no prospect of indeterminate liability (see, e.g. *Ross* v *Caunters* (HC, 1980)). This development blurred the distinction between statements and acts, and reached its highwater mark in *Junior Books Ltd v Veitchi Co Ltd* (HL, 1983). While it is the case that the *Hedley Byrne* duty can arise in the context of the provision of professional services (*Henderson v Merrett Syndicates Ltd* (HL, 1994)), the search for a generalised principle covering all cases of economic loss has largely been abandoned.

CHECKPOINT

In the development of the duty of care, the above cases show current judicial thinking is that the law should develop incrementally by ana-logy with established categories of duty, with the result that economic loss caused by negligent acts is normally irrecoverable unless the case can, exceptionally, be brought within the parameters of *Hedley Byrne*.

PSYCHIATRIC ILLNESS

In this section we are only considering psychiatric illness arising from a traumatic event. Psychiatric illness may result in other situations. Workplace stress is one example. However these cases are dealt with as cases of employer's liability in the usual way.

Those who are involved in traumatic situations may suffer psychiatric illness in one of three distinct situations. The first is where they suffer phy-sical injury and this leads to psychiatric harm. The second is where they are in an area where they are at risk of physical injury but managed to avoid this but suffer psychiatric injury. The third is where they are not themselves at risk, but suffer psychiatric harm as a result of what they have seen and heard.

The first situation has not caused any particular difficulty. The psy-chiatric harm is simply treated as part and parcel of the overall personal injury claim. The second situation involves what we call primary victims. In general they will be allowed to recover. The third situation involves what we call secondary victims, it is in relation to them that significant difficulties have arisen. A secondary victim may be actively involved in the event as a rescuer, may be emotionally involved because friends and relatives are or may be among the victims, or may simply be a passive bystander. The sec-ondary victim may be physically present, but at sufficient distance to be safe, may arrive at the scene of the accident in time to witness its aftermath, may witness it on television, or may be informed of it by some other means. This means that there is potentially an enormous number of claimants and the extent of liability needs to be managed as a matter of policy.

Figure 7: Shock victims

Adopting Lord Oliver's classification in Alcock, shock victims may fall into one of two broad groups:	
1 those who are unwilling participants in the events causing shock (primary victims)	2 those who are merely passive and unwilling witnesses (secondary victims)

The law also limits the types of psychiatric or psychological harm for which there can be recovery. Mere distress or grief are seen as ordinary emotions, not harm for which recovery is possible. There must be a recognisable psychiatric illness: *Hinz v Berry* (CA, 1970). There are various medical listings of these, and there must be medical evidence demonstrating that the claimant is suffering from at least one of them. Furthermore there is still generally a requirement that this results from "shock." According to Lord Ackner in *Alcock v Chief Constable of South Yorkshire* (HL, 1992), shock "involves the sudden appreciation by sight or sound of a horrifying event, which violently agitates the mind". It must then manifest itself in some recognisable psychiatric or physical illness. Lord Ackner also made it clear that, as the law presently stands, there can be no recovery for psychiatric illness "caused by the accumulation over a period of time of more gradual assaults on the nervous system". However, later cases appear to have relaxed this requirement to some extent.

Primary victims

With regard to this group, if the defendant's negligent conduct foreseeably puts the claimant at risk of injury it follows that there will be a sufficiently proximate relationship between them, so if personal injury of some kind to the claimant is reasonably foreseeable as the result of an accident, the defendant is liable for psychiatric injury (even though no physical injury occurs), and the claimant need not prove that psychiatric injury as such was foreseeable because the defendant must take his victim as he finds him. This principle was established many years ago in *Dulieu v White* (HC, 1901). The modern formulation of the rule is to be found in *Page v Smith* (HL, 1995).

PAGE V SMITH (1995)

This case illustrates that a "primary victim" is a person directly involved as a participant in the traumatic event and, if personal injury of some kind is foreseeable, it is not necessary to show that injury by shock was foreseeable. However, where the claimant is a "secondary victim" (such as a witness to the accident) the defendant will not be liable unless psychiatric injury is foreseeable in a person of reasonable fortitude. Here the claimant was driving with due care when a car driven by the defendant turned into his path. This caused an accident of moderate severity and although there was damage to the cars, the claimant was physically unharmed in the collision. However, he had suffered from myalgic encephalomyelitis (ME) for 20 years which at the time of the accident was in remission. He claimed that the accident resulted in the reactivation of this condition.

Held: (HL) Provided personal injury of some kind is foreseeable the defendant is liable for the psychiatric injury, irrespective of whether psychiatric injury was foreseeable.

Comment

It is by no means clear that ME is actually psychiatric in origin. What the case effectively says is that a primary victim is one who is at risk of *some* personal injury whatever its kind. A rescuer who is in the danger area will qualify as a primary victim. It is foreseeable that rescuers will intervene and a duty is owed to them.

In *Dooley v Cammell Laird* (HC, 1951) a crane driver whose load slipped and caused injury to his colleagues was held entitled to recover on the basis that he was an involuntary participant in the event. Lord Oliver in *Alcock v Chief Constable of South Yorkshire* (HL, 1992) treated such claimants as an anomalous kind of primary victim. Subsequently, in the Scottish case of *Salter v UB Frozen & Chilled Foods Ltd* (2003) a forklift truck operator, not himself in danger, who suffered psychiatric injuries because he believed that he was the involuntary cause of a colleague's death, was held to fall within the class of victims identified in *Alcock*. The defendant *in Salter* argued that in nervous shock cases caused by witnessing the death of another, damages were only recoverable if the claimant was at risk of physical injury or reasonably believed he was, or if the secondary victim control mechanisms in *Alcock* were fulfilled. Although not in any danger himself, the claimant was a primary victim because he was actively involved in the accident which led to the death.

Injury by shock—three types of primary victim

Persons in these categories will recover if shock to them was reasonably foreseeable or if personal injury of some kind was foreseeable (in which case it need not be proved that psychiatric injury was foreseeable (*Page v Smith*, above)):

1. Those who are put in reasonable fear for their own safety (as in *Dulieu v White & Sons* (HC, 1901)).
2. Rescuers who are in reasonable fear for their own safety (see e.g. *Chadwick v British Transport Commission* (CA, 1967)).
3. Those who reasonably believe that they are about to be, or have been, the involuntary cause of another's death or injury (see e.g. *Dooley v Cammell Laird & Co Ltd* (HC, 1951)).

Secondary victims

Secondary victims are subject to a series of criteria which they must satisfy in order to be regarded as foreseeable victims to whom a duty of care is owed. This is because of the potentially very large number of claims which need to be regulated. A duty to secondary victims was first acknowledged in *Hambrook v Stokes Brothers* (CA, 1925). The criteria to be satisfied were set out in the leading case of *Alcock v Chief Constable of South Yorkshire* (HL, 1992). This case arose from the Hillsborough football disaster. Sixteen relatives of those killed or injured brought claims alleging they had suffered psychiatric harm as a result. Fifteen of the claims were ultimately rejected. These claimants failed to satisfy one or more of the criteria.

ALCOCK V CHIEF CONSTABLE OF SOUTH YORKSHIRE (1992)

In this case the claimants based their claim on the argument that the sole test for a duty in nervous shock was reasonable foreseeability. However, the courts have traditionally adopted a cautious and restrictive approach to the imposition of liability. In *Victorian Railway Commissioners v Coultas* (PC, 1888) it was held that harm through nervous shock was not compensatable at all. The reason for the restrictive approach is that physical damage caused by negligence will be limited to those within the range of the harmful event, but psychiatric harm may affect a wide range of persons beyond the direct victim of negligent conduct. These actions for psychiatric harm were brought against the police arising from the Hillsborough football stadium disaster. As the result of overcrowding, 95 people were crushed to death and hundreds more were injured. The tragedy was witnessed by thousands of fans at the match and others witnessed the horrific events on live television broadcasts. Claims were brought by relatives and friends of the victims who suffered psychiatric illness as a result of their experiences. A number of them had been in other parts of the stadium from where they had witnessed the events and others had seen the disaster live on television. Some of the claimants had identified bodies at the mortuary and others suffered solely from being told the news.

Held: (HL) The claimants' actions were dismissed. The House of Lords applied a set of criteria which must be met by secondary victims. As in all cases of psychiatric harm and there must be a medically recognised psychiatric disease or condition. The criteria are:

(1) The secondary victim must have a close tie of love and affection with a primary victim. That close tie is presumed to exist between spouses and between parent and child. It is not presumed to exist in the case of other relationships, or between friends. However evidence may be led to demonstrate that such a tie does in fact exist.

(2) The secondary victim must be able to demonstrate physical proximity in time and space to the accident. This means present at the scene or witnessing the immediate aftermath in accordance with the conditions set out by Lord Wilberforce in *McLoughlin v O'Brian* (HL, 1983).

(3) The secondary victim must have perceived the accident or aftermath with his own unaided senses. In general terms being informed by a third party or witnessing the television coverage would not count.

These criteria are intentionally restrictive. It should be noted that they constitute a set of legal constraints which do not relate to current medical opinion. For example psychiatrists acknowledge that pathological reactions to the death of a loved one may as easily occur when the death occurs on the other side of the world as when it is witnessed. This is at odds with the second *Alcock* criterion.

The first criterion applies in all cases. This means that a rescuer who is not a primary victim is highly unlikely to recover because he will not satisfy this criterion. This was established in *White v Chief Constable of South Yorkshire* (HL, 1998). This case was brought by a number of police officers who claimed to have suffered psychiatric harm while on duty on the occasion of the Hillsborough disaster. One group of officers who were actually in the crowd where the fatalities and injuries occurred were able to recover as primary victims. Other officers whose duties did not put them at personal risk did not qualify as primary victims, and failed to meet this criterion. In earlier cases such as *Chadwick v BRB* (HC, 1967) it was held that a duty of care was owed to a rescuer as such. The claimant in *Chadwick* would have qualified as a primary victim, but *White* made it clear that there was no separate category of liability for rescuers, or indeed on the basis that the officers were employed by the defendant. Generally speaking, the relationship between workmates is not seen as close enough to meet this criterion. See the Scottish case of *Robertson v Forth Road Bridge* (1995).

KEY CASE

WHITE V CHIEF CONSTABLE OF SOUTH YORKSHIRE POLICE (1998)

In determining liability for psychiatric damage this case shows that an employee is in no special position just because the incident was due to the negligence of the employer. Unless the employees were exposed to the risk of physical harm they remain "secondary victims" and therefore subject to the control mechanisms in *Alcock*. Here, four police officers who were actively helping to deal with the human consequences of the Hillsborough tragedy claimed for the post-traumatic stress disorder they suffered as the result of their experiences. They argued that there was no justification for regarding physical and psychiatric injury as different kinds of damage. It was also contended the employer was under the conventional employer's liability principles to protect employees from harm through work. In addition, three of the officers claimed as rescuers and argued that as such they were not subject to the control mechanisms in *Alcock*.

Held: (HL)
(1) Nowadays courts accepted that there was no rigid distinction between body and mind and in that sense there was no qualitative difference between physical and psychiatric harm. However, it would be an altogether different proposition to say that no distinction was made or ought to be made between principles governing the recovery of damages in tort for physical injury and psychiatric harm. Policy considerations had undoubtedly played a part in shaping the law in this area. To allow the claims of the police officers would substantially expand the existing categories in which compensation could be recovered for pure psychiatric harm. Moreover, the awarding of damages to them sat uneasily with the denial of the claims to bereaved relatives by the decision in *Alcock*.
(2) The rules to be applied to an action against an employer for harm

suffered in the workplace were governed by the ordinary rules of the law of tort, which contained restrictions on the recovery of compensation for psychiatric harm. The rules governing such recovery do not at present include police officers who sustained such injuries while on duty. If such a category were to be created by a judicial decision, the new principle would be available in many different situations, for example, doctors and hospital workers who were exposed to grievous injuries and suffering. In addition, police officers who were traumatised by something in their work had the benefit of statutory schemes which permitted them to retire on pension. In that sense they were better off than the bereaved relatives in *Alcock*.

(3) None of the four police officers were at any time exposed to personal danger and none thought he was so exposed. In order to contain the concept of rescue in reasonable bounds the claimant must at least satisfy the threshold requirement that he objectively exposed himself to danger or reasonably believed that he was doing so.

Comment

Although the majority held that in order to claim for psychiatric injury, rescuers must have been exposed to physical danger or would need to satisfy the *Alcock* criteria, *Chadwick* (above) was distinguished on its facts. By entering the wrecked train carriages Chadwick had been objectively exposed to physical danger and he had therefore been within the range of foreseeable personal injury.

A mere bystander will also not be able to recover. This has been the law since *Bourhill v Young* (HL, 1943). Such a claimant was always outside the scope of the duty of care because it was not foreseeable that a mere bystander would be so affected as to suffer psychiatric harm, but she would now be excluded specifically by this criterion. In *Alcock* the House of Lords left open the possibility that there might be a disaster of such magnitude that liability would extend to mere bystanders, but in *McFarlane v EE Caledonia* (CA, 1993) a witness to the Piper Alpha oil rig disaster which killed many workers, some of whom were his colleagues, was held not entitled to claim as he was not close enough to the event to be at actual risk. His genuine belief that he was at risk did not assist as it was not a reasonable one.

The second criterion has evolved somewhat. Originally a secondary victim had to be present at the actual incident. Even being a matter of yards away was enough to defeat some claims. In *McLoughlin v O'Brian* (HL, 1983) the claimant's family were involved in a serious road accident. She was notified of this and went to the hospital to which they had been taken. She saw various members of her family still in much the same state as when the accident occurred. She also learned that one child had died. Clearly she had not been present at the incident itself, but the House of Lords considered that what she had seen was sufficiently traumatic to be treated as equivalent to presence at the scene. She had witnessed enough of the aftermath to be within the duty of care. Subsequent cases have consistently accepted the concept of the aftermath, but what constitutes relevant aftermath depends on all the circumstances of the case, and there is some inconsistency between decisions. In *Galli-Atkinson v Seghal* (CA, 2003) a mother went to the scene of what proved to be her daughter's fatal accident, but after the body had been removed, and then went to the mortuary. This was held, perhaps controversially, to constitute participation in the aftermath. Generally if all that the secondary victim participates in is viewing a corpse decently presented in a mortuary, or an injured patient in a hospital bed, this will not be accepted as aftermath, see *Taylorson v Shieldness* (CA, 1994). In *Palmer v Tees Health Authority* (CA, 1999), the Court of Appeal held that no duty of care was owed to a mother in respect of psychiatric injury following the abduction, sexual assault and murder of her four-year-old daughter by a psychiatric outpatient. Although she was involved in the search for her daughter and was in the vicinity at the time the body was discovered, she had not witnessed any part of the central events herself and did not therefore satisfy this criterion. (The claim also failed for "lack of proximity" based on the decision in *Hill v Chief Constable of West Yorkshire* (HL, 1988) (below) where it was held that the police do not owe a duty of care in negligence to the victims of crime.)

This is also connected to the requirement that there be a single sudden shocking event. If the primary victim deteriorates over a lengthy period, this requirement is normally not satisfied: *Sion v Hampstead HA* (CA, 1994). In *Crystal Taylor v A Novo (UK) Ltd* (CA, 2013) the question of proximity or alternatively, the timing of the "immediate aftermath" were considered by the Court of Appeal. A daughter who was not present at the scene of a workplace accident in which her mother was injured, claimed for the psychiatric injury she suffered when her mother suddenly died of complications at home, three weeks later. The Court of Appeal reaffirmed the reasons for the strict controls and the centrality of legal policy in this area and held that to permit recovery from an event three weeks after the accident would be to extend the law impermissibly. However, in *North Glamorgan NHS Trust v Walters* (CA, 2002) the events witnessed by a mother over the 48 hours during which her child deteriorated and died due to the negligence of those treating him was treated as a single prolonged shocking event.

The third criterion excludes those cases where the secondary victim's only source of knowledge and information is from a third party. Normal television coverage is not treated as the equivalent of direct perception. This is because it is subject to editing, even when it is a live broadcast, and the broadcasting authorities are subject to codes of practice which should ensure that particularly harrowing images are not shown. The question of whether liability could attach where images are broadcast unedited remains open. There has been an example of this. The Challenger space shuttle disintegrated shortly after takeoff. This was shown live and unedited, and one of the astronauts was a primary school teacher participating in the citizen astronaut programme. No claims arising from this have been reported. Given the litigation culture in the United States this might be seen as surprising.

However, if the information from the third party leads to the secondary victim actually participating in the event or its aftermath, the contribution of the initial information appears to be overlooked. This was the case in *McLoughlin v O'Brian*. The single successful claimant in *Alcock* was the father

Figure 8: Alcock criteria applied

Application of the above *Alcock* criteria	
Requirement (a)	**Requirements (b) and (c)**
With regard to requirement (a) the claimant must generally show that he had a relationship of "love and affection" with the primary victim, though this might be presumed in the case of parents and spouses (and, per Lord Keith, fiancés) unless there is evidence to the contrary. Less close relations such as brothers and brothers-in-law do not have the benefit of the presumption and must therefore adduce evidence of the closeness of the emotional tie. Despite this general requirement three of their Lordships expressed the view that a bystander might succeed if he or she witnessed at close hand a particularly horrific catastrophe, provided that a person of reasonable fortitude would be likely to suffer shock but such a possibility was rejected by the Court of Appeal in *McFarlane v E.E. Caledonia Ltd* (CA, 1994).	Requirements (b) and (c) rule out the possibility of a claim by one who is informed of the event by a third party and who does not come upon the scene of the accident or its immediate aftermath. A point directly in issue in Alcock was whether a person who witnessed the events of a disaster on television (or radio) could be regarded as sufficiently proximate in time and space. Their Lordships held that, on the facts, such a person could not, because broadcasting guidelines forbade the suffering of identifiable individuals to be televised, and any perception of the actual consequences of the disaster to his relatives came later. In principle, however, Lords Ackner and Oliver thought that there could be circumstances where the simultaneous broadcast of a disaster would be equivalent to direct sight or hearing.

of a victim who had travelled to the match without a ticket, and was sitting in a coach parked near the stadium watching the match on television when he realised that the tragedy was unfolding. He then went to the stadium, got in, and witnessed the scenes involving large numbers of panicking, injured, dying and dead supporters. He clearly satisfied the first criterion as a parent, and in the circumstances met both the others.

Miscellaneous psychiatric harm cases

In *AB v Thameside & Glossop Health Authority* (CA, 1997) the defendant health authority wrote to inform a number of patients of the slight risk that they might have been exposed to the HIV infection. Some recipients of the letters alleged that they suffered psychiatric illness as a result of the communication of bad news by letter rather than face-to-face. The authority admitted that it was under a duty to transmit this information in a sensitive way.

In *Attia v British Gas* (CA, 1988) the claimant returned to her home to find it on fire as a result of the negligence of workmen employed by the defendant. Her claim for psychiatric harm succeeded. She could of course have a claim in respect of property damage. The court merely treated her psychiatric harm as being in principle a part of the overall claim which was entirely foreseeable.

OMISSIONS

As a general rule the defendant does not owe a duty to take positive action to prevent harm to others. Thus, the rescuer who goes to the assistance of others in peril is certainly under no legal obligation to do so. So, too, the failure of a public authority to exercise a statutory power will not normally give rise to a common law duty (*Stovin v Wise* (HL, 1996)). The House of Lords further held that the mere existence of statutory powers and duties did not create a parallel common law duty and a highway authority's failure to paint a marking or to erect a road sign warning of a dangerous stretch of road did not give rise to a duty of care to the claimant (*Gorringe v Calderdale* (HL, 2004)).

CHECKPOINT

The term "omission" in this context is taken to mean passive inaction, since tortious negligence can invariably be characterised as a failure to take reasonable precautions.

EXCEPTIONS TO THE RULE

Most of the cases involving liability for nonfeasance are concerned, directly or indirectly, with the extent to which a defendant is under a duty to prevent harm to the claimant caused by the independent act of a third party. It may be the nature of the relationship between the parties which gives rise to the duty, such as employer and employee (*Hudson v Ridge Manufacturing Co Ltd* (HC, 1957), though the duty does not extend to protecting the employee from economic loss; *Reid v Rush & Tomkins Group Plc* (CA, 1989)), or occupier and visitor (see Ch.6). Alternatively, there may be a special relationship between the defendant and third party such that there is a positive obligation to control the third party. Examples of such a relationship include gaoler and prisoner (*Home Office v Dorset Yacht Co Ltd* (HL, 1970)), parent and child (*Carmarthenshire CC v Lewis* (HL, 1955)) and employer and employee (*Hudson v Ridge Manufacturing Co Ltd* (HC, 1957) where the claim related to horseplay by a fellow employee; the employer was found liable because he was aware of the employee's propensity to horseplay). Liability might also arise where the defendant negligently causes or permits to be created a source of danger, and it is reasonably foreseeable that third parties may interfere with it and thereby cause damage (as in *Haynes v Harwood* (CA, 1935)); or where the defendant fails to abate a known risk created by third parties upon his or her property (*Sedleigh-Denfield v O'Callaghan* (HL, 1940); see Ch.11).

Where the wilful wrongdoing of a third party causes damage then, in the absence of any of the exceptional cases referred to above, it is very unlikely that the defendant will be liable. Thus, in *P. Perl (Exporters) Ltd v Camden London BC* (CA, 1983) the defendants were held not to owe a duty to make their premises secure in order to prevent thieves from breaking in thereby gaining access to neighbouring properties and stealing from their occupiers.

No liability for pure omissions

Liability for acts of third parties was further considered by the House of Lords in *Smith v Littlewoods Organisation Ltd* (HL, 1987) where the defendants bought a disused cinema with the intention of demolishing it to make way for a supermarket. While the premises were empty, vandals gained access and attempts were made to start a fire, though neither the defendants nor the police knew of this. A fire was eventually started which spread and caused damage to adjacent property belonging to the claimants. Lord Goff said that there was no general duty of care to prevent a third party from causing damage to the claimant by deliberate wrongdoing, however foreseeable such harm might be, because the common law does not normally impose liability for pure omissions. His Lordship concluded that none of the exceptional circumstances which might give rise to a duty applied and, since the defendants were unaware of the presence of the vandals, the risk was therefore not foreseeable. Lords Brandon and Griffiths said that the duty owed by the defendants was to take reasonable care to ensure that the cinema was not, and did not become, a source of danger to neighbouring occupiers, but since there was nothing inherently dangerous on the premises, and because the defendants did not know of the vandals' activities, the risk was unforeseeable. Lord Mackay, too, adopted the test of reasonable foresight, but indicated that there might be circumstances where the risk would have to be "highly likely" before it could be regarded as reasonably foreseeable; in this case, he said, whilst it was probable that persons might attempt to enter the vacant premises, it was by no means a probable consequence of the vacation of those premises that they would be set on fire.

In *Mitchell v Glasgow City Council* (HL, 2009), the House of Lords applied *Smith* and held that liability for the criminal act of a third party would arise only where the person who was said to be under that duty had by his words or conduct assumed responsibility for the safety of the person who was at risk. Here the question was whether the local authority had assumed a responsibility to protect one of its social housing tenants who, following a long campaign of abuse and threats, was murdered by a fellow tenant. Although the local authority had been aware that the victim's neighbour might resort to violence after being informed that he risked being evicted, the required element of a relationship of responsibility was absent, as it would not be "fair, just and reasonable" to impose this duty on a public authority coping with an onerous burden of anti-social behaviour amongst tenants.

SPECIFIC IMMUNITIES

The police and other emergency services

In performing the function of investigating and preventing crime the police owe no duty of care to an individual member of the public. In such circumstances even where harm was reasonably foreseeable, there is insufficient proximity between the police and the victim: *Hill v Chief Constable of West Yorkshire* (HL, 1988). The claim was brought by the mother of the last victim of Peter Sutcliffe, the so-called Yorkshire Ripper. It was at least arguable that the police had failed to investigate the case effectively. If they had done so, they might well have caught Sutcliffe before his last offence. However Sutcliffe's offences were fairly random. Any woman was at risk. There was no special relationship between the police and this particular victim. This case also shows that public policy is capable of constituting a separate and independent ground for holding that liability in negligence should not be imposed. Imposing a general duty of care to protect all members of the public from the consequences of crime would be impracticable and, on grounds of public policy, deeply damaging to police operations. The police would be put under pressure to deploy their resources in ways that might minimise claims, but would not be the best use of their resources in overall terms of crime prevention, protection of public order etc.

KEY CASE

HILL V CHIEF CONSTABLE OF WEST YORKSHIRE POLICE (1988)

The claimant was the mother of the last victim of the mass murderer Peter Sutcliffe, the "Yorkshire Ripper". She claimed damages on the basis that the police had negligently failed to apprehend the murderer before her daughter was killed.

Held: Notwithstanding that harm was reasonably foreseeable, there was insufficient proximity between the police and the victim. The requirement of foreseeability was fulfilled in the sense that the harm to victims such as Miss Hill was reasonably foreseeable if Sutcliffe were not apprehended. However, under the *Anns* test (which was then applicable) more was needed to establish a duty of care: either a relationship of control between the police and the killer (similar to that between the prison guards and the boys in *Dorset Yacht*) or a proximity of the police to the victim. As Sutcliffe could not be said to have been under their control and there was nothing to set Miss Hill apart as being more at risk than the rest of the female population, then this element of the *Anns* equation was not fulfilled and there been no duty of care. This would certainly be the case today applying the *Caparo* criteria. It would not be fair just and reasonable to impose liability.

Comment

In *Brooks v Commissioner of Police for the Metropolis* (HL, 2005) a friend of Stephen Lawrence who witnessed Stephen's murder, suffered post-traumatic stress as the result of the way he was treated by the police following the murder, first as a suspect and later as a witness but not as the victim of crime. In rejecting a claim in negligence against the police the approach in *Hill* was applied. According to Lord Steyn:

"[T]he core principle of *Hill* has remained unchallenged in our domestic jurisprudence and in European jurisprudence for many years. If a case such as the Yorkshire Ripper case, which was before the House in *Hill*, arose for decision today I have no doubt that it would be decided in the same way. It is, of course, desirable that police officers should treat victims and witnesses

> properly and with respect: ... But to convert that ethical value into general legal duties of care on the police towards victims and witnesses would be going too far."

The public policy immunity granted in *Hill* was extended beyond the failure of police to apprehend criminals to include police failure to act on warnings in *Osman v Ferguson* (CA, 1993). The police failed to act on warnings that a teacher was a known threat to his victims. The claimant and his father were subsequently shot by the teacher and although the Court of Appeal was prepared to accept that in the circumstances of this case a sufficient relationship of proximity existed between the claimant's family and the police, the *Hill* immunity was applied and the case failed on grounds of public policy.

However, following this denial of liability, the Osman family brought a case against the United Kingdom alleging a violation of their rights under the European Convention of Human Rights. Subsequently, in *Osman v UK* (1998) the European Court of Human Rights held that a rule forbidding action against the police regardless of the circumstances and effectively granting a "blanket immunity" in negligence was in breach of Art.6 of the European Convention (the right to a fair trial). The Convention does not prevent courts taking into account public policy issues and although a public interest in protecting police from civil claims could be asserted, this must be balanced with other competing public interests. Under the Human Rights Act 1998 (incorporating the European Convention on Human Rights into UK law) courts are required to balance whether granting such immunity to a defendant is proportionate to the interference with the claimant's human rights.

The police do not, however, have total immunity; in *Swinney v Chief Constable of Northumbria Police* (CA, 1996) it was held that the immunity could be displaced by other, more compelling, policy considerations. In that case the claimant supplied confidential information to the police about a serious crime, naming a person who, to the knowledge of the police, was of a violent disposition. As a result of police negligence, that information came into the hands of the person named, and the claimant suffered psychiatric injury in consequence of the threats made against him. It was held that the police could owe a duty in these circumstances, since it was in the public interest that informants should be encouraged in their activities without fear that their identity might become known to the suspect. Although the court refused to strike out the claim, the claimant failed when the case proceeded to trial on the ground that there had been no breach of duty. The police, in leaving the information in a locked briefcase in a locked car, had not been negligent: *Swinney v Chief Constable of Northumbria Police (No 2)* (1999). However, it should be noted that in *Smith* (below), the Court of Appeal remarked that in cases involving the police the very proximity of the parties can not only create a duty of care, but can overcome the public policy considerations which would otherwise bar the claim (as in *Swinney*) and said that whether under art.2 or at common law, it cannot be a valid ground of distinction that an informer is entitled to protection while a witness is not.

Where the police owe no duty under the common law, a positive obligation to protect life under the Human Rights Act 1998 (Convention art.2 right to life and the art.8 right to private and family life) may be relied on.

Rescue services

The Court of Appeal has ruled that there is no proximity of relationship between the fire brigade and a building owner: fire brigades are not under a common law duty of care to answer an emergency call nor under a duty to take reasonable care to do so. Unless the fire service negligently increased the damage or caused additional damage, liability in negligence in tackling a fire will not arise (*Capital and Counties Plc v Hampshire CC* (CA, 1997)). Similar reasoning was applied in *Harris v Evans* (CA, 1998) where the claimant sued for the economic losses he had suffered when the advice of the specialist inspector from the Health and Safety Executive had been inconsistent with the Executive's policy. The Court of Appeal held that it was not fair, just and reasonable to impose a duty on the Health and Safety Executive: the imposition of a duty of care would probably have a detrimental effect by producing an unduly cautious and defensive approach by inspectors.

By contrast in *Kent v Griffiths* (CA, 2000) the Court of Appeal held that in certain circumstances an ambulance service could be liable in negligence. Although no duty is owed to the public at large to respond to a call for help, once a 999 call in a serious emergency has been accepted, the ambulance service assumes responsibility and has an obligation to provide the service for a named individual at a specified address.

For a discussion of police liability see figure 9 overleaf.

Public bodies generally

In *X (Minors) v Bedfordshire CC* (HL, 1995), the House of Lords ruled that there is no common law duty of care on local authorities when they are carrying out their discretionary statutory functions. The question is whether it is fair, just and reasonable to impose a duty of care in negligence upon a body exercising a public function. The impact of litigation on a local authority exercising its public function could lead to that function being performed in a detrimentally defensive manner and contrary to the public interest.

Figure 9: Justification for the Hill immunity

The justification for the *Hill* immunity against police liability was considered by the House of Lords in *Van Colle v Chief Constable of Hertfordshire* and *Smith v Chief Constable of Sussex* (HL, 2008) where the question was whether the Court of Appeal had been correct to find that the police were not immune from negligence liability in the two cases.

In *Van Colle* a prosecution witness was shot dead shortly before he was due to give evidence at trial. The Court of Appeal found that the police were, or should have been aware, of the real and immediate threat to the witness and that they had failed to take preventive measures to protect his life. This case was not brought under common law negligence; it was based upon human rights and litigated under art.2 of the ECHR and compensation was therefore payable for breach of art.2. The chief constable appealed against this finding.	In *Smith* the claimant, who had repeatedly informed the police that his former partner had threatened to kill him, brought an action under the common law. He claimed that the police had ample evidence of these threats and had no excuse for not preventing his partner from carrying out the threatened hammer attack which caused him serious injuries. This was a claim in common law negligence.

Both appeals were allowed:

- in *Van Colle* the *Osman* test, that the police knew or ought to have known "at the time" of the shooting of "a real and immediate risk to the life" of an identified individual from the criminal acts of a third party, was not met;
- in *Smith* the balance of advantage in this difficult area lay in preserving the principle set out in *Hill* that imposition of liability would result in defensive policing and, in the absence of special circumstances, the police owed no common law duty of care to protect individuals against harm caused by criminals;
- in the context of the future of the *Hill* immunity it is important that the dissenting views in these cases are noted;
- in *Sarjantson v Chief Constable of Humberside Police* (CA, 2013) the Court of Appeal held that the duty to avert a real and immediate risk to life or injury under articles 2 and 3 of the Convention of Human Rights was not limited to identified persons, as long as there was a clear and specific threat arising from a particular incident.

X (Minors) v Bedfordshire County Council (1995)

Actions were taken by children against a number of local authorities for alleged breaches of the Children Act 1989. The cases against Bedfordshire and Newham concerned abuse: in one case the local authorities had negligently failed to take abused children into care, and in the other, had identified the wrong person as the abuser and wrongly taken the child into care. In the cases involving Dorset, Bromley and Hampshire, it was alleged that the authorities had failed to properly identify and provide for the special educational needs of the claimants.

Held: (HL) It would not be fair, just and reasonable to subject the authorities to a common law duty to take care in carrying out their discretionary statutory functions.

Comment

(1) In addition to their case in common law negligence, the children brought an action for breach of statutory duty, claiming that their injury resulted from breaches of the Children Act 1989 by their local authority. Their Lordships held that in the light of the other range of remedies under the Act (e.g. the statutory appeals procedure in the education cases) it was inconceivable that Parliament intended an additional right of action for breach of statutory duty. A tortious duty of care was incompatible with these remedies and would also cut across a complex statutory framework (e.g. educational bodies, doctors, police, etc.) established by Parliament for the protection of children at risk.

(2) The imposition of a duty on a local authority in exercising its public function could lead to social services departments performing their duties in an "unduly defensive frame of mind". The resources directed towards the investigation and defence of spurious claims, together with awards of damages and costs, would diminish the limited funds available for other child protection activities.

(3) A distinction is made between a statutory "duty" on a local authority which places it under a duty to provide a service, and a statutory "power" where a local authority has a power (but not a duty) to act (see *Stovin v Wise* (HL, 1996)).

In *Barrett v Enfield London BC* (HL, 1999), concerning a claim for the various psychiatric problems the claimant suffered as a result of the authority's negligence during his time in their care, the House of Lords reversed the Court of Appeal's decision to strike out the claim. In the light of *Osman* (above) the claimant is entitled to have his or her case tried and the facts found before excluding a duty simply because the actions of the local authority involved the exercise of discretion. The decision in *X (Minors) v Bedfordshire CC* involved the exercise of statutory discretion as to whether or not to take the claimant into local authority care.

In *Z v United Kingdom* (ECtHR, 2001), which is the same case as *X v Bedfordshire*, the European Court of Human Rights held that failure to provide children with appropriate protection against serious long-term neglect and abuse amounted to the infliction of inhuman and degrading treatment in breach of art.3 of the European Convention of Human Rights. The court further held that the applicants had not been afforded an effective remedy in breach of art.13 of the Convention concerning the right to an effective remedy before a national authority. What these cases collectively show is that in procedural terms the merits of the case must be investigated, rather than granting blanket immunity.

CHECKPOINT

The distinction between *Barrett* and *X* is that in *Barrett* the alleged negligence took place after the child had been taken into the local authority's care. Having taken the child into care it was at least arguable that the local authority could be liable for negligence in its decisions concerning his foster placements and supervision. This is not a matter of the exercise of discretion, but of carrying out the statutory functions of the authority. There have been numerous cases where individual officials have been found to be in breach of a duty of care, for example in relation to educational psychological support, and the employing authority has been found vicariously liable. Again these cases relate to the performance of the function, rather than any discretionary element.

In *Phelps v Hillingdon London BC* (HL, 2000) it was held that an educational psychologist, employed by the local authority, could be under a duty of care to the claimant for failing to diagnose her dyslexia. In reversing the Court of Appeal decision, the House of Lords further held that Hillingdon could be vicariously liable for the educational psychologist's breaches of duty. *Phelps* was applied in the case of *A v Essex CC* (CA, 2003) where, although it was not fair, just and reasonable on professionals involved in compiling reports for adoption agencies to impose a broad duty of care to the adopting parents, the adoption agency was found vicariously liable for the failure of its social workers to communicate information to the adopting parents which the agency had decided they should have.

> **Public bodies—the same action may give rise to a duty to one of the parties involved in a case but not to another.**

In *JD v East Berkshire Community Health Trust* (HL, 2005), a boy's allergic reaction was interpreted wrongly by the social service department as indicating mistreatment by his mother and the child was put on the at-risk register for some months until the mistake was discovered. The mother contended that the health care professionals' duty to exercise due skill and care in the investigation of suspected abuse extended to the child's parents as primary carers as well as to the child. The mothers claim was dismissed on grounds of public policy. Health professionals, acting in good faith in what they believed were the best interests of the child, should not be subject to potentially conflicting duties when deciding whether a child might have been abused. It was not fair, just and reasonable to impose such a duty, *Caparo Industries Plc v Dickman* (HL, 1990) applied.

JD was distinguished in *Merthyr Tydfil CBC v C* (HC, 2010), where the children in question had been sexually abused by a neighbour's child. The mother of the children claimed that she had suffered psychiatric harm caused by the local authority's negligence in failing to properly deal with her reports of abuse. The local authority claimed that owing a duty of care to a parent would potentially conflict with the duty of care that it owed to the children and sought to rely on the decision in JD. The Court said that the decision in JD did not lay down any general principle that, where an authority owed a duty of care to a child, it could not as a matter of law at the same time owe a duty of care to parents of that child; a duty of care may be owed to parents as well as children, provided the parents are not suspected of abuse.

Affirmative duty to prevent harm

In *Watson v British Boxing Board of Control* (CA, 2001), a non-profit making organisation controlling the rules of boxing and the licensing of boxers was held to owe a duty of care to inform itself adequately about the risks inherent in a blow to the head and to ensure the provision of adequate resuscitation facilities at the ringside. In *Vowles v Evans* (CA, 2003), a referee of a rugby match, acting in an amateur capacity, owed a duty of care to players when carrying out his refereeing duties. In applying the rules of the game, it was fair, just and reasonable that the players should be entitled to rely on the referee for their safety. It was further noted that it was possible for the referee or Welsh Rugby Union, the body who appointed him, to take out insurance cover against third party liability.

REVISION CHECKLIST

You should now understand:

☐ **The function of duty of care as the first of the three main elements of a claim in negligence.**

☐ **How the duty concept is determined by proximity and foreseeability.**

☐ **The just and reasonable requirement.**

☐ **The role of policy, special duty situations and specific immunities in limiting liability.**

QUESTION AND ANSWER

QUESTION

Explain and discuss the public policy reasons for denial of negligence claims against public bodies

ANSWER

In the context of the liability of public bodies, the concept of a duty of care is a key limiting device. The main policy arguments against imposing negligence liability on public bodies are that liability is met by the tax payer and that public bodies which carry out particular functions on behalf of society need to be as efficient and effective as possible, and this will not be achieved if they are constantly acting defensively for fear of an action. Also, bodies such as social services and education authorities are given discretionary powers by Acts of Parliament and many of the decisions they make involve public policy, so they must look at the "bigger picture", rather than on the basis of a duty to "look after" individuals.

One important case discussing and illustrating these arguments is *X v Bedfordshire CC* (1995) which considered the local authority's liability for children's welfare. In the *Bedfordshire* case five children had been supervised by the local authority and the authority had failed to take them into care in spite of the neglect and mistreatment they suffered at the hands of their parents. When the children, who were now adults, sued the local authority it was held by Lord Browne-Wilkinson that although the decision about whether or not to take the children into care was justiciable (i.e. it involved weighing up factors which the court could evaluate judicially), it was not fair just or reasonable for a number of policy reasons, to impose a duty of care on the local authority in carrying out their discretionary statutory functions. The impact of litigation could lead to that function being performed in a detrimentally defensive manner and contrary to the public interest. The underlying policy reason for not imposing a duty on a local authority in exercising its public function was that it could lead to social services departments performing their duties in an "unduly defensive frame of mind". The resources directed towards the investigation and defence of spurious claims, together with awards of damages and costs, would diminish the limited funds available for other child protection activities.

However in *Barrett v Enfield* (2001) a duty was owed where the local authority had taken a child into care and then failed to act in the child's best interests; in this case the authority had assumed responsibility and was under a duty to act responsibly. The case was not concerned with whether they ought to assume responsibility. Later in *JD v East Berkshire Community Health Trust* (2005) an action was taken by the parents of children who had been wrongly diagnosed as suffering from child abuse. It was held that no duty should be owed to the parents for a range of policy reasons and in addition to those already mentioned, here there was an additional reason. If a parent was owed a duty of care there would be a conflict of interest if a child was owed a duty of care at the same time. Lord Rodger said:

> "Acting on, or persisting in, a suspicion of abuse might well be reasonable when only the child's interests were engaged, but unreasonable if the interests of parents had to be taken into account. Of its very nature, therefore, this kind of duty of care to the parents would cut across the duty of care to the children."

The Court of Appeal in *JD v East Berkshire* had concluded that the decision *in X v Bedfordshire* that a local authority owes no duty at all in respect of the decision whether or not to take a child into care could not survive the Human Rights Act. The court held that that the obligation to respect a child's Convention Rights meant that recognition of a duty of care would not adversely impact the way in which the authorities performed their duties: "In the context of suspected child abuse, breach of duty of care in negligence will frequently amount to a violation of article 3 and article 8." The next question would be whether it were fair, just and reasonable to impose a duty of care.

In the context of the police, public policy is capable of constituting a separate and independent ground for holding that liability in negligence should not be imposed. In *Hill v Chief Constable of West Yorkshire Police* (1988) notwithstanding that harm was reasonably foreseeable, the House of Lords held there was insufficient proximity between the police and the murder victim. The court further stated that a general duty of care to protect all members of the public from the consequences of crime would be impracticable and, on grounds of public policy, deeply damaging to police operations.

In *Brooks v Commissioner of Police for the Metropolis* (2005) the policy reasons outlined in *Hill* were preserved by the House of Lords and a claim in negligence against the police by a witness was rejected. The court held that a duty of care in negligence would detrimentally affect the work of the police by causing them to act defensively in order to avoid negligence claims and divert police resources away from their primary function of investigating and suppressing crime. The justification for the *Hill* immunity against police liability was reiterated by the House of Lords in *Van Colle v Chief Constable of Hertfordshire* and *Smith v Chief Constable of Sussex* (2008).

The public policy immunity granted in *Hill* was extended beyond the failure of police to apprehend criminals to include police failure to act on warnings that a teacher was a known threat to his victims in *Osman v Ferguson* (1993). Following the rejection of their claim, the applicants brought a case against the United Kingdom alleging a violation of their rights under the European Convention of Human Rights. Subsequently, in *Osman v UK* (1998) the European Court of Human Rights held that a rule forbidding action against the police regardless of the circumstances and effectively granting a "blanket immunity" in negligence was in breach of art.6 of the European Convention (the right to a fair trial). The Convention does not prevent courts taking into account public policy issues and although a public interest in protecting police from civil claims could be asserted, this must be balanced with other competing public interests. In *Sarjantson v Chief Constable of Humberside Police* (CA, 2013) the Court of Appeal held that the duty to avert a real and immediate risk to life or injury under articles 2 and 3 of the European Convention on Human Rights was not limited to identified persons, so long as it applied to a defined situation.

Negligence: Breach of Duty

INTRODUCTION

The first step in establishing a claim in negligence is to show that the defendant owed a duty of care to the claimant. Once the existence of a duty is established, the second step for the claimant is to show that the defendant has breached this duty and failed to reach the standard of care required in the particular circumstances. The key elements in showing a breach of duty are to determine:

(a) The *standard of care* the defendant was required to meet in the particular circumstances.

(b) Whether the defendant met the standard of care: this question requires an assessment of the facts to see if the defendant acted *reasonably in all the circumstances* of the case.

The reasonable man

Once it is established that the defendant owed a duty of care to the particular claimant, it must then be proved that the defendant was in breach of duty. Negligence was defined in *Blyth v Birmingham Waterworks Co* (Ex., 1856) as:

> "the omission to do something which a reasonable man, guided upon those considerations which ordinarily regulate the conduct of human affairs, would do, or doing something which a prudent and reasonable man would not do".

As a matter of law, therefore, the standard of care required of the defendant is that of the hypothetical, reasonable man and, whilst no man is expected to attain perfection, that standard is objective in the sense that it generally takes no account of the idiosyncrasies of the person whose conduct is in question: *Glasgow Corp v Muir* (HL, 1943). However, whether the defendant has reached the required standard in any given case is a question of fact, so that previous decisions should not be relied upon as precedents for what constitutes negligence. The House of Lords made this clear in *Qualcast v Haynes* (HL, 1959), stressing that such decisions might throw light on the factors which are relevant, but should not be cited as precedents.

The standard of reasonable care is therefore invariable in the sense that the law does not recognise differing degrees of negligence, but it is an infinitely flexible concept enabling the court in any given situation to impose standards ranging from very low to very high. Employers, for example, are often held to a high standard. The standard expected in the context of sporting activities is often low, since competitors are entitled to compete vigourously: *Wooldridge v Sumner* (CA, 1963). The cases below illustrate recent judicial concern that setting too high a standard of care in negligence could lead to inhibiting desirable activities from taking place. The **Compensation Act 2006** also aims to address the deterrent effect of potential liability in setting too high a standard of care in negligence by providing that in considering the standard of care required of the defendant, the court should have regard to whether it might prevent a desirable activity from being undertaken at all or discourage persons from undertaking functions in connection with a desirable activity.

KEY CASE

COLE V DAVIS-GILBERT (2007)

The claimant brought an action against the organisers of a May Day fête. As part of the fête, a maypole was placed into a hole on the green that had been dug for that purpose. At the end of the fête the hole was filled with soil and stones and subsequently with a bung. Two years later, the hole had become exposed and while walking across the green the claimant had stepped into it and suffered injury to her leg. The judge held that the organiser had breached its duty of care to the claimant as it had not taken adequate steps to ensure that the hole had been filled in properly.

Held: (CA) The defendants succeeded on the ground that it was not possible to establish that the accident was caused by any negligence on the part of the organiser. The court observed that accidents sometimes happen for which the victim cannot recover damages because fault cannot be established. It was also noted that if the law courts were to set a higher standard of care than what is reasonable, the consequences would quickly be felt.

Comment

(1) In *Hopps v Mott MacDonald Ltd* (HC, 2009) s.1 of the Compensation Act was applied on the ground that a finding of liability on the employer would prevent the desirable activity of reconstructing the infrastructure of Iraq being undertaken.

(2) The Court of Appeal specifically referred to s 1 of the Compensation Act in *Sutton v Syston Rugby Club* (CA, 2011). The claimant was injured

when he fell on part of a cricket boundary marker which had been left on the pitch. It was not easy to spot. The Court of Appeal held that a reasonable walk over of the pitch to inspect it for dangers was sufficient to discharge the club's duty of care. The court noted that games of rugby are desirable activities within the meaning of the Act.

Perry v Harris (CA, 2008) was another case where the Court of Appeal considered that the judge had imposed too high a standard, in saying that a mother supervising children on a bouncy castle should supervise "continuously"; again in the view of the court what happened was a freak accident not involving breach of duty.

CHECKPOINT

What is reasonable care?
The standard expected will depend on all the circumstances of the case. The standard required of a participant in a competitive sport vis-à-vis spectators and fellow players may be described as low (see, e.g. *Wooldridge v Sumner* (CA, 1963)). This is because it is reasonable for the competitor to focus on performing to the best of his ability. Other competitors accept the "normal risks of the game", and so should others who choose to put themselves "in harm's way".

High standards are imposed on motorists and the Court of Appeal in *Nettleship v Weston* (CA, 1971) held that the learner driver must exercise the skill of a reasonably competent, experienced driver. This also applies to a driver who loses control of the vehicle being driven on account of some disabling condition of which he or she knew or ought to have known. Such a driver will be liable, but there will be no liability if the driver is wholly unaware of the disability (*Mansfield v Weetabix Ltd* (CA, 1997)). The imposition of such high standards may be justified where the defendant is engaged in a high-risk activity, and there can be little doubt that, in some instances, compulsory liability insurance has influenced the court in fixing the level of care.

THE CONCEPT OF RISK

What is reasonable conduct varies with the particular circumstances, and liability depends ultimately on what the reasonable man would have foreseen, which in turn may depend upon what particular knowledge and experience, if any, is to be attributed to him, and also to the state of knowledge at the relevant time (see *Roe v Minister of Health* (CA, 1954)).

However, although a defendant is not negligent if the consequences of his or her conduct were unforeseeable, it does not necessarily follow that such a defendant will be liable for all foreseeable consequences. In practice, the courts evaluate the defendant's behaviour in terms of risk, so that he or she will be adjudged negligent if the claimant is exposed to an unreasonable risk of harm. Note that this can shade into assessing what aspects of harm are to be attributed to the defendant in terms of causation and remoteness. However if the only harm in question is the allegedly unforeseeable one, the case is more likely to be dealt with in terms of breach.

Risk-balancing factors

The defendant's behaviour is evaluated in terms of risk and the following factors must be weighed in the balance to determine if the claimant was exposed to an unreasonable risk of harm:

- the magnitude of the risk;
- the social utility or desirability (if any) of the activity in question; and
- the cost and practicability of precautionary measures to minimise or eliminate the risk.

In performing this balancing act the court will decide what weight is to be given to each of these factors and will make a value judgment as to what the reasonable man would have done in the circumstances.

Compensation Act 2006

A perception that society is becoming "risk averse" and concerns about the emergence of a "compensation culture" led to a fear that many worthwhile activities would be curtailed because of the deterrent effect of potential liability. One of the aims of the **Compensation Act 2006** is to address this concern and to serve as a reminder to judges to consider carefully the impact which decisions about potential negligence liability might have in deterring the organisation and pursuit of worthwhile activities.

LEGISLATION HIGHLIGHTER

Section 1 of the Compensation Act deals with the deterrent effect of potential liability and provides:

"A court considering a claim in negligence or breach of statutory duty may, in determining whether the defendant should have taken particular steps to meet a standard of care (whether by taking precautions against a risk or otherwise), have regard to whether a requirement to take those steps might—

(a) prevent a desirable activity from being undertaken at all, to a particular extent or in a particular way, or

(b) discourage persons from undertaking functions in connection with a desirable activity."

Magnitude of the risk

The degree of care which the law exacts must be commensurate with the risk created. Two factors are involved here, namely the likelihood that harm will be caused and the potential gravity of that harm should the risk materialise. The following cases will illustrate that even where some precautions are required the standard of care that can reasonably be expected will vary according to the magnitude of the risk, the purpose of the defendant's activity and the practicability of precautions.

KEY CASE

Bolton v Stone (1951)

The claimant was standing in a quiet road when she was struck by a cricket ball which had been driven from the defendants' cricket ground. It was rare for balls to be hit out of the ground; this has only happened on about six occasions in 28 and no injury had resulted. Even though the risk of such an accident was foreseeable the chance that it would actually occur was very small, and it was likely that injury would not be severe.

Held: (HL) The defendants were not liable because in the circumstances it was reasonable to ignore such a small risk. [1951] A.C. 850.

Comment

(1) In *Miller v Jackson* (CA, 1977) cricket balls were hit out of their ground eight or nine times a season and, on several occasions, had damaged the claimant's property. The risk of harm was so great that a majority of the Court of Appeal held that the defendants were liable. Lord Denning took the view that the playing of cricket was of such public value that it should outweigh the private interests of the claimants.

(2) In *Haley v London Electricity Board* (HL, 1965) during excavation of a hole in the street the safety precautions taken by the defendant were adequate for sighted persons, but not for the claimant who was blind and fell into the hole. The defendants were held liable; the presence of blind persons on the pavement was foreseeable and adequate precautions would have been simple to take.

Gravity of that harm to a particular *claimant*
The relevance of the potential gravity of the consequences to a particular claimant is illustrated in *Paris v Stepney BC* (HL, 1951), where a one-eyed garage worker became totally blind after being struck in the eye by a metal chip which flew from a bolt which he was trying to hammer loose. The defendant employers were held liable for failing to provide him with safety goggles, even though they were justified in not providing such equipment to a person with normal sight. Although the risk was small, the injury to this particular claimant was very serious. Note that today the obligation to provide safety equipment is much more extensive, and would apply to all persons working in these circumstances.

Where the claimant consents to injury, for example, by an opponent in a boxing ring, he does not consent to injury resulting from inadequate safety arrangements by the sport's governing body after being hit. In *Watson v British Boxing Board of Control* (CA, 2001), the Board was found to have breached its duty by failing to inform itself adequately about the risks inherent in a blow to the head and by failing to require resuscitation equipment to be provided at the ringside with persons capable of operating it.

A similar approach has been taken in cases involving alleged negligence by referees. In *Smoldon v Whitworth* (CA, 1997), applying the test for the level of care adopted in *Condon v Basi* (Ch.5), the referee of a colts rugby match was held liable to the claimant, who was injured as the result of a collapsed scrum. Here one can see that a high standard can be demanded because the players are young, inexperienced, and particularly susceptible to injury. In *Vowles v Evans* (CA, 2003) the court held the threshold of referee liability in an adult game at a high level to be a high one and the standard of care required depended on all the circumstances of the case. The referee allowed a player to deputise for an injured front row player. Only experienced front row players should be allowed to play if the scrummage is contested. However, if the scrummage is uncontested, league points will not be awarded. The substitute had played for some 60 minutes without incident. Another player was injured when a scrum collapsed at the end of the game. It was however held that the referee was in breach of duty because he was ultimately responsible for safety issues.

Social utility

The purpose to be served, if sufficiently important or desirable, may justify the assumption of what might otherwise be regarded as an abnormal risk.

KEY CASE

Watt v Hertfordshire County Council (1954)
The claimant was a fireman called out to an emergency where a woman was trapped under a lorry. A heavy lifting jack was urgently required but, since a vehicle designed to carry this was not available, the lifting jack was loaded onto a lorry which was not equipped to secure it. On the way to the scene of the accident the lorry had to brake suddenly and the claimant was injured when the jack slipped.

Held: (CA) The fire authorities had not been negligent. The risk had to be balanced against the end to be achieved and the saving of life or limb justifies taking considerable risk.

Comment
Lord Denning took the view that if the accident had happened in a commercial venture without any emergency the claimant would have succeeded, but "the commercial end to make profit is very different from the human end to save life or limb." Note again that standards of health and safety have developed since then. On the same facts the authority might be held to be in breach. They are also likely to be in breach of statutory duty. The principle that an emergency may justify the taking of risks remains valid but its application will be different.

On the other hand, the laudable object of saving human life or limb has its limits and is plainly self-defeating if the danger risked is too great, so that a fire authority has been held negligent where a fire engine passed through a red traffic signal on its way to a fire and caused a collision (*Ward v L.C.C.* (HC, 1938)). However we see emergency vehicles today routinely using their lights and sirens to obtain the right-of-way. Provided the driver is taking reasonable care and keeping a lookout at intersections, this would seem to be acceptable behaviour. It should also be noted here that standards of health and safety have evolved, and older cases might not be decided the same way today.

Cost of precautions

The risk has to be weighed against the cost and practicability of minimising or overcoming it. In *Latimer v A.E.C. Ltd* (HL, 1953) a factory floor became slippery with oil and water after a heavy rainfall caused flooding. Despite taking such steps as they were able, the defendants could not entirely eradicate the danger and the claimant slipped and was injured. The defendants were held not liable because the risk was not so great as to require the drastic step of closing the factory until the floor dried out. The same "health warning" about changing standards applies here to.

CHARACTERISTICS OF THE DEFENDANT

It has already been noted that the legal standard generally takes no account of the personal characteristics of the particular defendant, and a defendant cannot therefore claim to have done his or her incompetent best. Inexperience, lack of intelligence or slow reactions provide no defence to a charge of negligence. Nor, for that matter, will a defendant be able to avail himself of some lower standard of care on account of a physical disability. A partially sighted driver (but one who has been assessed and allowed to drive by the DVLA) owes the same duty as one with normal sight, and the fact that he or she has a reduced field of vision merely imposes an obligation to proceed with greater caution.

> **CHECKPOINT**
>
> *What is reasonable varies according to the circumstances*
> The "reasonable man" is expected to know those things that common experience teaches and, in appropriate cases, can be expected to anticipate that others may be careless. This is normally assessed by reference to the ordinary average man or woman if the activity in question is one which anyone could undertake: *Wells v Cooper* (CA, 1958). Two types of defendant, children and those professing a particular skill (below) require special mention.

Children

As far as children are concerned, there is no defence of minority as such and a child is in principle as responsible for its torts (through its litigation friend) as a person of full age. Thus, a boy of 16 has been held negligent in the use of an air rifle (*Gorely v Codd* (HC, 1967)). However, as in cases of contributory negligence, it was held in *Mullin v Richards* (CA, 1998) that the standard of care is that which can reasonably be expected of an ordinary child of the defendant's age.

Parents and teachers have a responsibility for children

Those who have taken on the responsibility of looking after children assume a legal duty of care to ensure that they do not harm others.

> **KEY CASE**
>
> CARMARTHENSHIRE COUNTY COUNCIL V LEWIS (1955)
> This case concerned a young child who ran from his nursery school onto a nearby busy road. The claimant's husband swerved his lorry to avoid hitting the child and was himself killed when his lorry hit a lamp-post.
>
> **Held:** (HL) The defendants were liable in negligence on the ground that where a young child does cause injury by conduct which in an adult would be classed as negligent then, more often than not, a parent or other responsible person, such as a teacher, will be liable. This is not vicarious liability but a primary liability arising from a failure to exercise proper supervision and control. Here it was probably the absence of what we would today call a proper risk assessment of the ease with which a child could leave the premises which was the crucial factor.

Professionals

Persons holding themselves out as having a particular skill or profession must attain the standard of the reasonably competent person exercising that skill or profession. The level of skill demanded, however, will vary according to the extent of the risk. For example, the do-it-yourself enthusiast fixing a door handle in his home must reach the standard of a reasonably competent carpenter doing that type of work, but not of a professional working for reward (*Wells v Cooper* (CA, 1958)). If, however, the work is of a technical or complex nature, and there is a risk of serious injury should it not be properly done, the defendant may be expected either to employ an expert or to display the same degree of skill.

A member of a profession discharges their duty by conforming to the standards of a reasonably competent member of that profession. Thus, a doctor must act in accordance with a practice accepted as proper by a body of responsible and skilled medical opinion, and is not negligent merely because there is a body of opinion which would take a contrary view. This certainly applies to the process of diagnosis, selection of treatment options and the actual treatment. However the aspect of the duty relating to advising the patient on the advantages and risks of the various treatment options is subject to a slightly different test.

In the case of professionals the standard is essentially set by the profession itself in most respects.

BOLAM V FRIERN HOSPITAL MANAGEMENT COMMITTEE (1957)

The claimant agreed to undergo electro-convulsive therapy (ECT) during which he suffered a fracture to the pelvis. The issue was whether the doctor was negligent in failing to give a relaxant drug before the treatment, or in failing to provide means of restraint during the procedure. Evidence was given of the practices of various doctors in the use of relaxant drugs before ECT treatment. One body of medical opinion favoured the use of relaxant drugs, but another body of opinion took the view that they should not be used because of the risk of fractures.

Held: (HC) The appropriate test for judging the standard of professional behaviour is not that of the ordinary man; the defendant is judged by the standard of the ordinary skilled person exercising and professing to have that special skill. The action failed because the defendant had acted in accordance with a practice accepted at the time as proper by a responsible body of professional opinion skilled in the particular form of treatment.

Comment

In *Bolitho v City and Hackney HA* (HL, 1997) although the issue was one of causation, the medical experts had disagreed as to whether a doctor ought to have intubated the claimant. The court said that whether it would have been a breach of duty not to intubate had to be decided by applying the *Bolam* test. However, the House of Lords emphasised that ultimately it was for the court, and not for medical opinion, to decide the standard of care required in each case. The court had to be satisfied that the medical opinion had a logical basis, which would involve the weighing of risks against benefits, in order to reach a defensible conclusion.

In *Wilsher v Essex HA* (HL, 1988) it was held that a doctor occupying a particular role was obliged to meet the standard appropriate to the role. His personal inexperience, or indeed the fact that he was covering for a more senior clinician, was irrelevant. This reflects the objective nature of the standard required. The hospital authorities are also responsible for ensuring that they have a suitable team of professionals in place: *Cassidy v Ministry of Health* (CA, 1953).

Although the Bolam test applies to professions generally, it has on occasions been suggested, in relation only to the medical profession, that practitioners themselves are the final arbiters in determining standards of professional competence. In *Bolitho v City and Hackney HA* (HL, 1997) (above) the House of Lords made it clear, however, that this is not so, holding that a doctor could be liable for negligent treatment or diagnosis despite a body of professional opinion supporting his conduct. The court had to be satisfied that that body of opinion was reasonable or responsible in that it could stand up to logical analysis, although their Lordships accepted that, in the vast majority of cases, the fact that acknowledged experts in the field were of a particular opinion would demonstrate its reasonableness. It remains the case that the effect of the *Bolam* test is to make proof of professional negligence extremely difficult where the defendant has followed an accepted practice. An error of judgment by a professional may or may not be negligent, depending upon whether it was such as a reasonably competent practitioner might make: *Whitehouse v Jordan* (HL, 1981).

The *Bolam* test applies in a modified form to the disclosure of information by doctors to patients about risks of proposed procedures.

KEY CASE

SIDAWAY V BETHLEM ROYAL HOSPITAL GOVERNORS (1985)

The claimant agreed to undergo an operation to her spine in order to relieve pain in her right arm and shoulder. She was not informed that the operation carried a risk (of less than 1 per cent) that she would suffer damage to the spine. The operation was performed without negligence but unfortunately the risk materialised and the claimant became severely disabled. She sued the defendants on the ground that the surgeon had failed to inform her of the risk.

Held: (HL) The defendants were not liable; the surgeon had followed approved practice of neurosurgeons in not disclosing the risk of damage to the spinal cord and was therefore not negligent. There was a minority judgement to the effect that the standard in this respect should be based on what the doctor should have told a reasonable patient to enable her to make an informed decision.

Comment

(1) The contention that the standard of care ought to be what the reasonable patient would want to know, rather than what the reasonable doctor was prepared to tell, was rejected by a majority in the House of Lords. In failing to adopt the doctrine of "informed consent" which operates in other jurisdictions and allows the patient access to

full and frank information about treatment and prognoses the English courts left discretion to the professional judgment of the doctor regarding the disclosure of information. However in later cases such as *Pearce v United Bristol Healthcare NHS Trust* (CA, 1999) and *Chester v Afshar* (HL, 2004) it has been made clear that the touchstone for liability in respect of this aspect of the duty has shifted, so the test is now one of the prudent patient. In effect, the minority opinion in *Sidaway* has now become the accepted norm in the light of developing medical standards and approaches. This also means that English law is now more consistent with the common law in other jurisdictions.

(2) A doctor who fails to give proper warning to his patient about a risk inherent in surgery may be held to have caused the injury if the risk materialises, even where the surgery is performed without negligence: *Chester v Afshar* (HL, 2004). The majority judgment was that this departure from ordinary rules of causation was necessary to justly compensate the claimant for the breach of duty in failing to provide appropriate information. The minority considered that the failure to inform was quite separate. Some compensation was due in order to vindicate the right of the patient to be treated as a responsible adult with full autonomy. With respect, the minority view is the preferable one. The claimant was just as likely to suffer the injury whenever the operation was performed. Indeed it was perfectly possible that the injury occurred to 1% of patients because of some peculiarity of their anatomy. In that case the claimant was bound to suffer the injury if she undertook the operation.

What is reasonable is judged by the standards at the relevant time, not later knowledge. It is part of the professional's duty to keep abreast of new developments and techniques, as what is reasonably foreseeable may depend upon the state of existing knowledge within that profession at the time. A defendant is not expected to have anticipated future developments in knowledge or practice but will be judged by reference to the state of knowledge at the time of the event.

KEY CASE

ROE V MINISTRY OF HEALTH (1954)

The two claimants entered hospital for minor surgery and emerged permanently paralysed from the waist down. Anaesthetic which was injected spinally during the course of the operation had, according to the evidence accepted by the judge, become contaminated by seepage through invisible cracks in the glass. At the time of the accident in 1947 the risk of this seepage occurring was not known.

Held: (CA) It was not negligent for the defendant not to have known of the danger. Denning L.J. warned that it is so easy to be wise after the event and said: "We must not look at the 1947 accident with 1954 spectacles." Subsequent research has indicated that the actual cause is likely to have been contamination caused by the failure to remove a cleaning agent from a sterilising vessel. If this is the case that failure was the result of a breach of duty by a theatre nurse. Had that evidence been before the court, the claimants would probably have succeeded, since this would have been a fairly obvious breach.

EVIDENCE OF NEGLIGENCE

It is for the claimant to prove, on a balance of probabilities, that the defendant was negligent, subject to the proviso that proof that a person stands convicted of an offence is conclusive evidence in civil proceedings that he or she did commit it unless the contrary is proved (Civil Evidence Act 1968, s.11). The effect of this provision is to shift the burden of proof where the claimant proves that the defendant has been convicted of an offence involving conduct complained of as negligent, such as careless driving.

In order to discharge the burden of proof, the claimant must usually prove particular conduct on the part of the defendant which can be regarded as negligent. The claimant will not be able to do so, however, if he or she does not know how the accident was caused and, in such a case, the maxim res ipsa loquitur (the thing speaks for itself) may be relied on. This is simply a rule of evidence by which the claimant, who is unable to explain how the accident happened, asks the court to make a prima facie finding of negligence which it is then for the defendant to rebut if he or she can. After a long history of uncertainty on the issue, the Privy Council has now held that there is no shift in the legal burden of proof (*Ng Chun Pui v Lee Chuen Tat* (PC, 1988)).

With regard to the first requirement, if the cause of the accident is known then the doctrine does not apply because all that need then be done is to decide whether, on the facts, negligence is proved (*Barkway v South Wales Transport Co Ltd* (HL, 1950)). The operation of the second requirement is illustrated in *Easson v L.N.E.R.* (CA, 1944) where it was held that the doors of a long distance express train could not be said to be under the continuous control of the defendants, so that a child who fell out of the train could not rely on the maxim. Control by the defendant depends on the probability of outside interference. If the facts establish that such interference was improbable, the defendant will be regarded as being in control.

Res ipsa loquitur

Whether the accident is such as would not ordinarily have happened without negligence is to be judged in the light of common experience. Thus res ipsa loquitur has been applied:

- where a claimant went into hospital with two stiff fingers and came out with four stiff fingers (*Cassidy v Ministry of Health* (CA, 1951);
- where there was no evidence of negligence for a plane crash in which the appellant's husband was killed, the Privy Council said that the aircraft was airworthy when it took off and held that the doctrine of res ipsa loquitur applied to her claim. The maxim of res ipsa loquitur was said to be potentially of great importance in plane crashes because of the difficulty of proof of negligence in these cases (*Emad v Eagle Air Services Ltd* (PC, 2009).

If the maxim applies (and it need not be specifically pleaded) the defendant may be able to rebut the inference of negligence if it can be shown how the accident actually occurred, and that explanation is consistent with no neg-ligence on the defendant's part, or a defendant may be able to provide a reasonable explanation of how the accident could have happened without negligence, in which case one of the essential conditions for the application of the maxim is not satisfied.

Figure 13: res ipsa loquitur (the thing speaks for itself)

---

res ipsa loquitur (the thing speaks for itself)

Three conditions are necessary for the application of the doctrine, according to *Scott v London and St. Katherine Docks Co* (1865):

1. there must be an absence of explanation as to how the accident happened

2. the "thing" which causes the damage must be under the control of the defendant (or someone for whose negligence he is responsible)

3. the accident must be such as would not ordinarily occur without negligence.

You should now understand:

- ☐ The second step in a claim in negligence is for the claimant to show (on the balance of probabilities) that the defendant has breached his duty of care and fallen below the standard of care required in the circumstances.

- ☐ The standard of care in negligence is objectively assessed—the standard is measured against that of the *reasonable man*.

- ☐ The *reasonable man* test is modified in the case of professionals; the standard applied to doctors is set down in the *Bolam* test.

- ☐ The balancing factors which judges use to determine the standard of care required in the circumstances and attempts to address the deterrent effect of potential liability in setting the standard of care too high.

QUESTION AND ANSWER

QUESTION

Emad, a voluntary youth leader at the Hermitage hiking club, organised a late October trip to take a group of teenagers to climb a local mountain range. Although the start of the climb was scheduled for 10.00am, one member of the party was delayed in traffic so the group did not set out on the climb until 11.30am. The day was bright and clear until the party stopped for lunch at 1.30pm. However, soon after lunch the temperature dropped rapidly and visibility became very poor so the group decided to return to their minibus.

Emad had forgotten to bring with him his map and compass, and as dusk began to fall the group became hopelessly lost. Some of the teenagers had mobile phones but it was impossible to obtain a signal on the mountain so they could not raise the alarm. After rambling aimlessly for some considerable time they took shelter in a clearing to wait for the rescue services. As dusk began to fall Rex, one of the group members, missed his footing and fell over a ledge. Rex suffered a broken leg.

Rex will argue that he is owed a duty of care by Emad (the "three stage" test in *Caparo* (1990), based on *Donoghue v Stevenson* (1932)—the neighbour principle. This is routinely applied in personal injury cases.). Once the existence of a duty of care is established, the second step in a claim in negligence is for Rex to show that Emad has breached that duty. In establishing a breach of duty the court considers the standard of care required of Emad and whether he acted reasonably in all the circumstances: *Blyth v Birmingham Waterworks Co* (1856). The standard of care is that of the hypothetical, reasonable man: *Glasgow Corp v Muir* (1943). The weather conditions which occurred were foreseeable in the month of October and Emad ought reasonably to have foreseen the risk of harm to the teenagers in these circumstances. *Bolton v Stone* (1951) held that precautions required to meet the standard of care required will in each case vary according to the magnitude of the risk, the purpose of the defendant's activity and the practicability of precautions. In the context of the potential severity of the injury in the present circumstances, and the fact that the precautions (taking a map, compass, and mobile phone) were very easy to do and entailed no real cost it would seem that Emad is in breach of duty.

We are told that Emad is acting in a voluntary capacity. In determining the standard of care, the Compensation Act 2006 provides that whether by taking precautions against risk or otherwise, the court should have regard to whether a requirement to take those steps might prevent a desirable activity from being undertaken at all, or discourage persons from undertaking a desirable activity. In *Cole v Davis-Gilbert* (2007) the Court of Appeal said there was a danger in setting too high a standard of care as it could lead to inhibiting consequences. Therefore factors such as whether Emad or Hermitage is insured, who can best bear the loss and the implications for society as a whole of a finding of liability on Emad will be considered. Young people need not be wrapped in cotton wool, but activities must be properly risk-assessed and effectively managed.

Negligence: Causation and Remoteness of Damage

INTRODUCTION

The issues of causation and remoteness are relevant to the law of tort generally but are dealt with in the context of negligence because that is where most of the problems have arisen. Unless the claimant can prove that the defendant's tort in fact caused the loss suffered, the action will fail or, in the case of torts actionable per se, only nominal damages will be recovered. This is essentially a question of fact, although in a few particularly complex areas, issues of policy also arise. Even if the claimant can prove a sufficient causal connection in fact, the claim will still fail if the defendant's breach is not a cause in law of the damage or, to put the matter another way, if the damage is too remote. This is a question of law, or legal policy. The courts are setting appropriate limits to the scope of liability.

CHECKPOINT

Causation in fact
The claimant must show that, as a matter of fact, that defendant's breach of duty caused the harm. This element is known as causation in fact. If "but for" the defendant's negligent conduct the damage would not have happened then that negligence is the cause of the damage.

Causation in law
Where causation is in fact established, the question of remoteness of damage then arises. This is known as causation in law and liability may still be avoided if the defendant can show that the damage suffered was too remote a consequence of the breach of duty, either because harm of that type was not reasonably foreseeable, or because it would not be reasonable to impose liability for that kind of harm.

FACTUAL CAUSATION

It must first be established that the breach was a cause of the damage, not necessarily the sole or principal cause provided it at least "materially contributed" to the damage (*Bonnington Castings Ltd v Wardlaw* (HL, 1956)). In determining this issue it is usual to employ the "but for" test, the function of which is not to allocate legal responsibility, but merely to eliminate those factors which could not have had any causal effect.

> "If the damage would not have happened but for a particular fault then that fault is the cause of the damage; if it would have happened just the same, fault or no fault, the fault is not the cause of the damage" per Denning L.J. in *Cork v Kirby Maclean Ltd* (CA, 1952).

In other words, the test is used to distinguish between those events which are part of a chain of cause and effect, and those which are coincidental. Take the case of Mustapha, who was involved in a car accident. There is clear evidence that he has suffered head and neck injuries. Shortly after the accident he complains of deafness. However tests show that the deafness results from a medical condition unrelated to the accident. The head and neck injuries are part of the chain of cause and effect, but the deafness is merely co-incidental, so it cannot be included in Mustapha's claim.

KEY CASE

Barnett v Chelsea and Kensington Hospital Management Committee (1968)

The claimant's husband was one of three night watchmen who went to the defendant's hospital complaining of vomiting after drinking some tea. The nurse on duty consulted the casualty doctor by telephone and was instructed by him to tell the three men to go home to bed and to call their own doctors. Soon afterwards the claimant's husband died of arsenical poisoning. It was discovered that arsenic had been put into the tea of the workmen by persons unknown. There was no dispute that in failing to examine the claimant the doctor was negligent. The issue to be decided was whether the doctor's breach of duty had caused the man's death.

Held: (HC) The claim failed. The question was whether the harm would not have occurred "but for" the defendant's breach of duty. The hospital was able to produce evidence to show that even if the deceased had been examined and treated with proper care, he would still have died. Since the death would have occurred in any event the defendant's breach of duty was not a factual cause.

Comment

(1) This case established what is known as the "but for" test. Even though the test is widely applied it is not always adequate as, for example, where there are multiple causes of the claimant's damage.

(2) The "but for" test was applied in *Robinson v Post Office* (1974). The claimant sought medical treatment following a leg injury sustained through the defendant's negligence. During the treatment he suffered a serious reaction to an anti-tetanus vaccination which was administered by a doctor who omitted to test for the allergy. The defendant was held liable for this injury also; the doctor was not liable for his omission to test for an allergic reaction because the vaccination was urgently needed and the test would not have revealed the allergy in time.

The "but for" test in action

The "but for" test will not always solve the problem as is apparent where two simultaneous wrongs are done to the claimant, each of which would in itself be sufficient to cause the damage. In this case the test leads to the absurd result that neither breach is a cause of the damage, whereas in practice both will be held to have caused it. The classic example is where the claimant is injured by a bullet from one or other of two guns. In the Californian case of *Summers v Tice* (1948) it was held that as each shooter was in breach of duty, each should be held liable. The Canadian case of *Cook v Lewis* (1951) reached the same conclusion. In *Fitzgerald v Lane* (HL, 1989) where a pedestrian was hit in quick succession by two negligently driven cars, each was held liable for all the injuries as it could not be established which caused what harm.

Industrial disease cases often involve multiple defendants, all of whom have either negligently or in breach of statutory duty exposed the defendant to dust, chemicals, noise or unsafe machinery. Many diseases are cumulative, the longer the exposure the worse the condition. This is the case for silicosis and similar dust-related lung diseases, industrial deafness and "vibration white finger" among others. Applying the "but for" test results in each defendant being liable for a proportionate part of the total loss: *Holtby v Brigham & Cowan* (CA, 2000). The same principle applies where there is one defendant, but some of the exposure to the noxious agent is legal, but some is in breach of duty, as in *Bonnington Castings v Wardlaw* (HL, 1956).

Bonnington Castings Ltd v Wardlaw (1956)

The defendant's breach of duty was not the sole or principal cause of the damage, but it "materially contributed" to the development of the claimant's illness. The claimant, a steel worker who had been exposed to noxious dust over a period of years as the result of his employer's negligence, contracted a progressive disease. However, some of the exposure was from a "non-negligent" source and there was no evidence of the proportions of negligent and non-negligent exposure to the dust, so the "but for" test could not be satisfied.

Held: (HL) In these circumstances causation could be established because the employer's act or omission made a "material contribution" to the harm and this constituted an application of, or an exception to, the but for test.

Further difficulties may also arise where the disease is not cumulative. It is known that it is caused by a particular noxious agent, but it is caused by a specific exposure at some point in time. Usually that point cannot be established. If there is only one defendant, and all the exposure is in breach of duty, this does not matter, as the breach has, somehow, caused the disease. However, when only some of the exposure is in breach of duty, or there are multiple defendants, there is a problem. In the first case the claimant cannot show which part of the exposure caused the disease, so cannot show that it would not have happened "but for" the breach In the second each defendant can say—"prove it was my dust not his"—and of course the claimant cannot.

The first situation was addressed in *McGhee v National Coal Board* (HL, 1972), where the claimant contracted dermatitis as a result of exposure to abrasive dust at work.

McGhee v National Coal Board (1973)

The claimant, as stated above, contracted dermatitis as a result of exposure to abrasive dust at work. His employers were not at fault for exposing him to this during the normal course of his work, but were in breach of statutory duty in failing to provide washing facilities with the result that he was caked in dust for longer than necessary as he cycled home.

The medical evidence was unable to show that had washing facilities been provided the claimant would have escaped the disease.

Dermatitis results from a single episode where the dust reacts with a susceptible area of skin, which produces an immune reaction. This could have been in the first minutes of exposure, or at a later stage if his skin became damaged and susceptible. Although it was uncertain exactly when and how the dermatitis was caused, the evidence did show that the provision of showers would have materially reduced the risk of contracting the condition, by reducing the time of exposure.

Held: (HL) The claimant succeeded on the ground that it was sufficient to show that the defendants' breach materially increased the risk of injury. If the claimant cannot positively prove that the defendant's breach of duty caused the damage, it is sufficient to show that the defendant's negligence made the injury more probable. Here, the defendants were liable on the ground that it was sufficient for the claimant to show that the defendants' breach of duty made the risk of injury more probable, even though medical knowledge was unable to establish the breach as the probable cause.

The second situation arose in *Fairchild v Glenhaven Funeral Services Ltd* (HL, 2002), a case of mesothelioma. This is a cancer of the lining of the lungs or abdomen almost exclusively caused by industrial exposure to asbestos. All experts agree that it is not the result of cumulative exposure. It seems that a single asbestos fibre must make contact with a cell which is defective, and this triggers the cell into becoming cancerous, although the process may be more complex. As the cancer may only develop many years later, it is quite impossible to identify when the initial process occurs.

KEY CASE

FAIRCHILD V GLENHAVEN FUNERAL SERVICES LTD (2002)

Fairchild was exposed to asbestos by a number of employers, all of whom were in breach of statutory duty. He then developed mesothelioma. While the link between asbestos and mesothelioma is well-established, the exact causation of the disease is still unclear.

Each employer denied liability on the basis that the claimant could not prove it was "their" asbestos which made the critical contact. It could not be proved which breach of duty was the actual cause of the disease so the claimant was unable to prove, on the balance of probabilities, that any particular defendant's breach of duty was the cause of the mesothelioma, so satisfying the "but for" test. The High Court and Court of Appeal dismissed the action by applying the "but-for" test.

The question for the House of Lords was whether in these circumstances the claimant needed to satisfy the "but for" test.

Held: (HL) The House of Lords applied and extended *McGhee* which had varied the ordinary "but for" approach to causation. On the balance of probabilities each defendant's wrong-doing had materially increased the risk of the claimant contracting the disease. It was sufficient to show that the asbestos exposure for which any one defendant was responsible had contributed materially to the risk which in fact materialised.

Comment
These appeals raised conflicting policy considerations but their Lordships found the injustice of denying a remedy to employees who had suffered grave harm to outweigh the potential unfairness in imposing liability on successive employers who could not be proved to have caused the harm. According to Lord Nicholls:

"The present appeals are another example of such circumstances, where good policy reasons exist for departing from the usual threshold "but for" test of causal connection. Inhalation of asbestos dust carries a risk of mesothelioma. That is one of the very risks from which an employer's duty of care is intended to protect employees. Tragically, each claimant acquired this fatal disease from wrongful exposure to asbestos dust in the course of his employment. A former employee's inability to identify which particular period of wrongful exposure brought about the onset of his disease ought not, in all justice, to preclude recovery of compensation".

Their Lordships pointed out that each defendant was under a duty to protect the claimant from, inter alia, mesothelioma, and were in breach of duty. Policy demanded, as in the shooting cases, that each should be held liable, as each had increased the risk. Although the appeal raised conflicting policy considerations, the injustice of denying a remedy to employees who had suffered grave harm outweighed the potential unfairness of imposing liability on successive employers who could not be proved to have caused the harm.

Barker v Corus UK (HL, 2006) also concerned exposure to asbestos on three separate occasions. Here the circumstances differed from *Fairchild* in that the negligence for one of these exposures was that of the claimant himself during short periods when he worked as a self-employed plasterer. The question arose as to whether the *Fairchild* principle could apply in this situation and whether the defendant was liable for all the damage suffered by the claimant or only for its contribution to the risk that materialised. The House of Lords partially reversed the ruling in *Fairchild* and held that although a defendant could still be liable without proof of causation, his liability only extended to the relative proportion to which he could have contributed to the chance of the outcome. This decision was seen as a victory for employers' insurers but it met with strong resistance from trade unions and victim groups. The Government responded by introducing the **Compensation Act 2006** to restore the *Fairchild* approach to liability in cases of mesothelioma. Section 3 sets out the provisions for dealing with cases where the victim has contracted mesothelioma as a result of exposure to asbestos.

LEGISLATION HIGHLIGHTER

Section 3(1) of the **Compensation Act 2006** was interpreted in *Sienkiewicz v Greif (UK) Ltd.* (SC, 2009) where an office employee, who had been exposed to asbestos dust in the factory where she worked for 18 years, died of mesothelioma. Although there was only one employer, the woman had also been exposed to asbestos dust in the environment of the town where she lived. The trial judge said that since there was another potential cause which did not arise from the tort of the employer, the claimant should have to prove causation on the normal balance of probabilities test and he found that she failed to discharge this test. The Court of Appeal allowed the claimant's appeal and said that in mesothelioma cases a claimant could establish causation by showing that the workplace exposure to asbestos had materially increased the *risk* of the employee developing the disease. The court further said the intention of Parliament was to reflect the common law requirements of causation in mesothelioma cases, which exceptionally required proof of causation by reference to a material increase in risk.

Increasingly, the courts are applying the "material increase in risk" test to medical cases where clinical negligence and some other cause (which may also be another episode of clinical negligence) appear to be collectively responsible for the claimant's condition. In *Wright v Cambridge Medical Group* (CA, 2011) a general practitioner's negligent delay in referring a child to hospital was compounded by a further delay by the hospital in diagnosing and treating the child. As a result of the negligence of both parties the child suffered a permanent disability. The Court of Appeal held the general practitioner's negligence was a cause of the child's injury which was separately quantifiable from that caused by the hospital's negligence. Therefore, both the doctor and the hospital were jointly and severally liable. In *Bailey v*

Ministry of Defence (CA, 2008) the question was whether the damage suffered was the result of the claimant's state of weakness because of the negligence in her post-operative care at the MoD's hospital or a non-negligent cause, each of which had made a material contribution to her overall weakness. The Court of Appeal held that it was enough for a patient to establish that, on the balance of probabilities, a lack of post-operative care and what flowed from that made a material contribution, namely something greater than negligible, to the overall weakness of her condition and the resulting brain damage. The court said that if the evidence demonstrated on a balance of probabilities that the injury would have occurred as a result of the non-negligent cause, the claimant would have failed to establish causation.

Multiple independent causes

Another area which requires further consideration is where there are multiple potential causal factors, but these are independent of each other. In other words, it is either cause A or cause B, but not both. These may operate simultaneously, but more often consecutively.

The leading case on simultaneous alternative causes is *Wilsher v Essex Area Health Authority* (HL, 1988). Here a premature baby developed an eye condition, retrolental fibroplasia (RLF). He was suffering from a number of conditions, apnoea, hypercarbia, intraventricular haemorrhage and patent ductus arteriosus, all of which were associated with RLF. However, he was also given excess oxygen as a result of clinical negligence. Excess oxygen is also associated with RLF.

KEY CASE

WILSHER V ESSEX AREA HEALTH AUTHORITY (1988)
It is known that excessive oxygen given to premature babies can lead to blindness and the claimant alleged that this was the cause of his blindness. But there were up to five possible causes of the claimant's injury, any one of which might have caused his blindness.

Held: (HL) As the causes were alternatives, the onus was on the claimant to prove, on the balance of probabilities, that it was the negligent administration of oxygen which was that cause. Material contribution and material increase in risk only applied to "single agent" cases, not to alternative causes. Showing the defendant's negligence to be one out of five possible causes of the claimant's blindness was not acceptable evidence that it was the cause. In *McGhee* the claimant had established his disease was caused by the brick dust; the only question was whether the additional period of exposure to the brick dust had contributed to his dermatitis.

When there is a sequence of incidents affecting a claimant, his situation must be evaluated at each stage. There may be successive torts, a tort preceded by a non-tort or a tort succeeded by a non-tort. *Hotson v East Berkshire Area Health Authority* (HL, 1987) was a case where the claimant fell from a tree and injured himself. He went to hospital and was initially treated negligently. He actually suffered an avascular necrosis of the femoral epiphysis, a very serious soft tissue injury to the hip. The issue in the case was whether this was the inevitable result of the fall from the tree, or whether proper treatment would have resulted in a lesser level of injury (in this respect the case is just like *Barnett*). The trial judge determined that there was a 25 per cent chance that a patient with this history would have a lesser level of injury with proper initial treatment. The House of Lords ruled that any particular claimant would either be seriously injured or not, but on the balance of probabilities, the claimant was seriously injured before he went to the hospital, so the medical negligence did not cause this serious injury.

In *Gregg v Scott* (HL, 2005) the misdiagnosis of the appellant's medical condition by a doctor had reduced his chances of surviving for more than 10 years from 42 per cent to 25 per cent, but his claim was dismissed because the delay had not deprived him of the prospect of a cure on the balance of probabilities; at the time of his misdiagnosis, the appellant had less than a 50 per cent chance of surviving more than 10 years anyway. This decision was upheld in the Court of Appeal and the House of Lords where it was held that liability for loss of chance of a more favourable outcome should not be introduced into personal injury claims.

Jobling v Associated Dairies (HL, 1982) was a case where the claimant suffered a tortious injury which injured his back. It then emerged that he was suffering from a medical condition which would have led to disability within seven years in any event. Bizarrely, the House of Lords treated this disease as a subsequent event—in reality it was something which preceded the tort. However, they reached the right result, that what the tortfeasor had caused was a seven year acceleration of disability, so that was the extent of his liability.

Baker v Willoughby (HL, 1970) was a case where the claimant suffered a tortious leg injury. He was then caught up innocently in a robbery, and shot in his bad leg, which had to be amputated. Although the House of Lords made heavy weather of the case, and the reasoning is somewhat difficult to follow, they again reached the right conclusion—that the original defendant remained liable for the consequences of the injury he caused. The amputation did not mean that the claimant now had a good leg.

Hotson establishes that there is no recovery for "loss of chance" in tort, at least for personal injuries, and this is confirmed by *Gregg v Scott*. The claimant has to prove his case on the balance of probabilities. A given person is either injured or not, he is not x% injured. Had the claimant been able to show that it was more likely than not that he was uninjured, their Lordships made it clear that there was no principle of law which would have justified a discount from the full measure of damages, incidentally demonstrating that, ignoring any possibility of contributory negligence, the claimant's claim is determined on an "all or nothing" basis.

Oddly, if a negligently inflicted injury carries a statistical risk of a future complication, damages are assessed taking account of this possibility.

However, loss of chance can be claimed in a different class of case, those involving negligent advice. In *Allied Maples v Simmons & Simmons* (CA, 1995) solicitors negligently failed to advise clients of a risk associated with the contract they entered into. If they had done so, it was possible that the deal would have been renegotiated. Damages were awarded for the loss of the chance to do so. Some commentators think that this principle is an aspect of the law on pure economic loss, others that the chance must be related to the decisions of a third party.

In terms of proving causation, it has been held by the House of Lords that a doctor who failed to warn a patient of a small risk inherent in surgery, was liable to the claimant when that risk eventuated. The decision in favour of the claimant could not be based on conventional causation principles because the risk of which she should have been warned was not created or increased by the failure to warn and the operation had not been performed negligently. However, the claimant satisfied the test for causation in negligence as she could prove that, had she been properly informed, she would not have consented to the operation at that particular time but would have obtained further advice before making her decision (*Chester v Afshar* (2004)).

KEY CASE

CHESTER V AFSHAR (2004)

Following an elective surgical procedure on her spine, the claimant suffered paralysis and brought an action against the defendant neurosurgeon in negligence. The operation had not been negligently performed so there was no breach of duty in respect of the procedure. The issue was one of causation; the claimant argued that she had not been given adequate warning of a 1–2 per cent risk of paralysis before she consented to the operation. Had she been aware of the risks of the proposed surgery she would not have consented to the operation taking place so soon and also, before deciding what to do, she would have sought a second or possibly even a third opinion.

Held: (HL) There was a sufficient causal link between the defendant's failure to warn of the risk in the surgical procedure and the damage sustained by the claimant. That link was not broken by the possibility that the claimant might have consented to surgery in the future. Where a risk that eventuates falls within the scope of a duty to warn, the "but for" test of causation may be satisfied on grounds of policy. In such circumstances the injury may be regarded as having been caused, in the legal sense, by the breach of that duty.

Comment

The House of Lords (majority) decision in favour of the claimant could not be based on conventional causation principles because the risk of which she should have been warned was not created or increased by the failure to warn. Nevertheless, the "but for" test was satisfied on the ground that the claimant would not have had the operation when she did if the warning had been given. This case demonstrates judicial recognition that rights need to be vindicated and a remedy provided when the duty to warn patients of risks associated with procedures has been breached. Despite the fact that the claimant might well have gone on to have the surgery in the future when the risk would still have existed, a majority ruled in her favour on grounds of policy. According to Lord Steyn:

"Standing back from the detailed arguments, I have come to the conclusion that, as a result of the surgeon's failure to warn the patient, she cannot be said to have given informed consent to the surgery in the full legal sense. Her right of autonomy and dignity can and ought to be vindicated by a narrow and modest departure from traditional causation principles."

According to the minority, there was no need to interfere with the ordinary rule. The negligence was essentially failing to give the information to allow the patient to make a fully informed decision. The harm resulted from a side-effect of a non-negligent procedure. The claimant would run the same risk whenever she had the operation so the negligence did not cause the harm. They would still have awarded damages to reflect the fact that because of the surgeon's negligence she had not been given the opportunity to make an informed choice.

REMOTENESS OF DAMAGE

It is not for every consequence of the defendant's wrong that the claimant is entitled to compensation. In order to contain the defendant's liability within reasonable bounds a line must be drawn, and those consequences which fall on the far side of that line are said to be too remote or, to put the matter another way, are regarded as not having been caused in law by the defendant's breach of duty.

All that is required is that the damage of a certain kind is reasonably foreseeable. Normally the courts take a fairly broad view of what constitutes a particular kind of damage. It is certainly not necessary to foresee exactly how the damage will occur.

- In *Hughes v Lord Advocate* (HL, 1963), post office employees negligently left a manhole uncovered with a canvas shelter over it, surrounded by paraffin lamps. The claimant, aged eight, took one of the lamps into the shelter and knocked it into the manhole. By an unusual combination of circumstances there was a violent explosion in which the boy was badly burned. Although the explosion was unforeseeable, the defendants were held liable because burns from the lamp were foreseeable, and it was immaterial that the precise chain of events leading to the injury was not. In this case the type of damage was personal injury through burning.

By contrast:

- In *Doughty v Turner Manufacturing Co Ltd* (CA, 1964), the defendants' employee dropped an asbestos cover into a vat of molten liquid which, due to an unforeseeable chemical reaction, erupted and burned a fellow worker standing nearby. It was held that, even if injury by splashing were foreseeable (which was doubted), the eruption was not, and the claimant failed. This case is clearly at odds with *Hughes*, because if it is accepted that some injury by burning was foreseeable, then it ought not to matter that the way in which it occurred was not. On the balance of authority, *Hughes* is to be preferred.

Type of damage

The precise nature of the damage need not be foreseeable, provided it is of a type which could have been foreseen. The difficulty in defining damage "of a type" is illustrated by two contrasting cases. In *Bradford v Robinson Rentals Ltd* (HC, 1967), a van driver sent on a long journey in an unheated vehicle in severe weather was able to recover for frostbite because, although not in itself foreseeable, it was within the broad class of foreseeable risk arising from exposure to extreme cold. In *Tremain v Pike* (HC, 1969), the defendant's alleged negligence caused his farm to become rat-infested with the result that the claimant contracted leptospirosis by contact with rat's urine. It was held that, even if negligence had been proved, the claimant could not succeed because although injury from rat bites or food contamination was foreseeable, this particularly rare disease was entirely different in kind. The decision in *Bradford* is a more accurate reflection of the current tendency to adopt a liberal approach to this issue. Indeed there have subsequently been many successful claims for leptospirosis.

Extent of damage; the "eggshell skull" rule

Subject to what has been said above, it matters not that the actual damage is far greater in extent than could have been foreseen. Thus, in *Vacwell Engineering Co Ltd v BDH Chemicals Ltd* (CA, 1971) the claimants purchased a chemical manufactured and supplied by the defendants, who failed to give warning that it was liable to cause a minor explosion upon contact with water. The claimants' employee placed a large quantity of the chemical in a sink whereupon an explosion of unforeseeable violence extensively damaged the premises. Since the explosion and consequent damage were foreseeable, even though the magnitude and extent thereof were not, the defendants were held liable.

A similar rule operates where the claimant suffers foreseeable personal injury which is exacerbated by some pre-existing physical or psychic abnormality.

CHECKPOINT

The "eggshell skull" principle
The so-called "eggshell skull" principle means that a defendant must take his victim as he finds him. Liability is imposed upon the defendant for harm which is not only greater in extent than, but which is of an entirely different kind to, that which is initially foreseeable, as long as this is foreseeable in the context of the incident. In *Smith v Leech Brain & Co Ltd* (HC, 1962) a workman who had a predisposition to cancer received a burn on the lip from molten metal due to a colleague's negligence. The defendants were held liable under the "eggshell skull" principle for his eventual death from cancer triggered off by the burn. In *Corr v IBC Vehicles* (HL, 2008) physical injury led to depression, and, in turn, to suicide. This chain of developments was foreseeable, at least in outline.

The principle applies equally to:
- a claimant who suffers from nervous shock (*Brice v Brown* (HC, 1984)); and
- a claimant with an "eggshell personality" (*Malcolm v Broadhurst* (HC, 1970)).

In *Robinson v Post Office* (CA, 1974), the principle was applied to a claimant who suffered serious damage due to an allergy to medical treatment, which was foreseeably required as a result of an injury caused by the defendants' negligence. According to *Liesbosch Dredger v S.S. Edison* (HL, 1933) the "eggshell skull" rule does not apply where the claimant's loss is aggravated by his own lack of financial resources. However, this decision was the subject of strong criticism and it has now been disapproved by the House of Lords. In *Lagden v O'Connor* (HL, 2004), the defendant negligently drove into the 10-year-old car of the claimant, who did not have the financial resources to pay for a hire car while his car was off the road so he entered into a credit agreement which involved greater expense. The court found that this additional expense was at least broadly foreseeable and, in stating that the wrongdoer must take his victim as he finds him, Lord Hope said: "The rule applies to the economic state of the victim in the same way as it applies to his physical and mental vulnerability." However, it is unclear whether the decision in *Lagden* is restricted to consumers, or applies also to commercial operators.

INTERVENING CAUSES

In some cases the claimant's damage is alleged to be attributable not to the defendant's breach of duty, but to some intervening event which breaks the chain of causation. Such an event is called a novus actus interveniens and is usually dealt with as part of the issue of remoteness because even though the damage would not have occurred "but for" the defendant's breach, it may still be regarded in law as falling outside the scope of the risk created by the original fault.

Claimant's intervention

These are cases where damage is caused by a combination of the claimant's own act and the defendant's breach.

> **KEY CASES**
>
> - In *McKew v Holland & Hannen & Cubitts (Scotland) Ltd* (1969), as a result of an injury caused by the defendants' negligence, the claimant's leg would give way without warning. Whilst descending a steep flight of steps without assistance or support, his leg gave way and he fell and fractured his ankle. The defendants were held not liable for this further injury because, although foreseeable, the claimant's conduct was so unreasonable as to amount to a novus actus.

- In *Sayers v Harlow UDC* (CA, 1958), a faulty lock on the door of a public lavatory cubicle caused the claimant to become trapped inside. She fell and injured herself when the toilet-roll holder onto which she had climbed in order to get out gave way, and damages were reduced under the **Law Reform (Contributory Negligence) Act 1945** (see Ch.5) for the unreasonable manner in which she had attempted her escape.

These two cases illustrate the different approach that may be taken where the damage is caused by a combination of the claimant's own act and the defendant's breach. Whether the issue is seen as one of novus actus or of contributory negligence (which is the more common approach) will depend upon the nature and quality of the claimant's conduct, and it may be that a positive act is more likely to break the causal chain than a mere omission (cf. *Knightley v Johns* (CA, 1982); see below).

On any view of the matter *McKew* seems to be a harsh decision. In *Spencer v Wincanton Holdings Ltd* (CA, 2009), the employer admitted liability for the first injury but sought to rely on *McKew*, arguing there was no liability to pay damages for a second accident which resulted in the employee becoming wheelchair dependent, because it had been caused by his own unreasonable conduct when he pulled into a petrol station to fill his car with petrol without wearing his artificial leg or using his sticks. The Court of Appeal held that there was no novus actus that broke the chain of causation: the employee's contributory conduct towards the second accident had been below the standard of unreasonableness required to break the chain of causation and contributory negligence was available to deal with the sharing of responsibility.

CHECKPOINT

There may be instances where even a deliberate act by the claimant will not relieve the defendant of responsibility

- In *Pigney v Pointer's Transport Services Ltd* (HC, 1957), the defendants were held liable to a claimant whose husband committed suicide as a result of mental depression brought on by an injury caused by the defendants' negligence.
- In *Corr v IBC Vehicles* (HL, 2008), following a near-fatal accident at work as a result of the defendant's negligence, the claimant's husband suffered ongoing physical and psychological problems. In these circumstances the suicide is merely the culmination of the depression and the damage flowing from the injury and the chain of causation had not been broken by the intentional act of suicide.

Corr v IBC Vehicles (2008)

The claimant's husband was injured at work. He suffered disfiguring injuries and had to undergo extensive reconstruction surgery. As a result he suffered ongoing physical and psychological problems. He had no history of previous psychiatric illness, but developed severe reactive depression. Eventually this drove him to commit suicide. The question for the House of Lords was whether his suicide was a novus actus interveniens *or* whether it was a reasonably foreseeable consequence of the injury at work and his subsequent depression.

Held: (HL) The suicide was reasonably foreseeable, and should be regarded as within the risk created by the defendant. Depression as a result of the accident was within the compensable damage flowing from the injury and the chain of causation had not been broken by the intentional act of suicide.

Comment

In *Pigney v Pointers Transport* (HC, 1957) a depressive mental illness which resulted from a negligently inflicted head injury had affected the deceased's capacity for rational judgment. His suicide was therefore held not to break the chain of causation. This decision reflects an outdated view of suicide. *Corr* now provides a more appropriate solution to this type of case.

In any event, the above decisions are presumably justifiable on the basis of the "eggshell skull" principle (see also *Reeves v Commissioner of Police of the Metropolis* (HL, 1999), Ch.5).

As far as rescuers are concerned (see Ch.5), there is generally no question of categorising the claimant's conduct as a novus actus: *Haynes v Harwood* (CA, 1935), unless the danger has passed, in which case it is arguable that a duty is no longer owed (see *Cutler v United Dairies (London) Ltd* (CA, 1933)). It makes no difference in principle whether the rescuer acts on impulse or after conscious reflection: *Haynes v Harwood*, per Greer L.J..

Intervention of third party

According to Lord Reid in *Dorset Yacht Co Ltd v Home Office* (HL, 1970), the intervention of a third party must have been something very likely to happen if it is not to be regarded as breaking the chain of causation. However, this dictum should be interpreted in the light of its proper context, namely the potential liability of a defendant for the criminal act of another, because a less stringent test may be applied in the case of non-wilful intervention by the third party.

Negligent conduct in the intervening act of a third party is more likely to break the chain of causation than non-negligent conduct.

KEY CASE

KNIGHTLEY V JOHNS (1982)

The defendant negligently caused a crash on a dangerous bend in a one-way tunnel. The police inspector at the scene of the accident forgot to close the tunnel to oncoming traffic as he ought to have done in accordance with standing orders, so he ordered the claimant officer to ride back on his motorcycle against the flow of traffic in order to do so, and the claimant was injured in a further collision. The order to ride back against the flow of traffic was a quite extraordinary one. It broke a number of rules and procedures.

Held: (CA) In considering whether the intervening act of a third party breaks the chain of causation, the test is whether the damage is reasonably foreseeable in the sense of being a "natural and probable" result of the defendant's breach. A deliberate decision to do a positive act is more likely to break the chain than a mere omission; so too, tortious conduct is more likely to break it than conduct which is not. In this case the inspector's errors amounted to tortious negligence which could scarcely be described as the natural and probable consequence of the original collision, and the defendant was therefore not liable.

It must be decided in each case whether the nature of the intervening actor's conduct was such as to eclipse the causative effect of the original wrong. In *Rouse v Squires* (CA, 1973), the negligence of the first defendant in causing a motorway crash was held to be an operative cause of the death of the claimant who, whilst assisting at the scene of the accident, was run down by the negligent driving of the second defendant. By contrast, in *Wright v Lodge* (CA, 1993) the defendant's negligence caused a lorry driver to collide with his car, as a result of which the lorry was involved in a further collision. It was found that the lorry driver had driven recklessly (not merely carelessly), and his driving was therefore held to be the sole legal cause of the damage arising from the second accident. If the lorry driver had merely been driving negligently, it is unlikely that the second accident would have occurred at all.

A question which as yet remains unresolved is the extent to which negligent medical treatment or diagnosis may break the chain of causation, although the answer will no doubt depend upon the extent to which the practitioner has departed from the requisite standard of care. In *Prendergast v Sam & Dee Ltd* (HC, 1988), the negligent misreading by a pharmacist of a doctor's prescription did not relieve the doctor of his duty to write in a reasonably legible hand, and liability was apportioned between them.

In *Hogan v Bentinck West Hartley Collieries* (HL, 1949) it was said that unreasonable medical treatment, including clear negligence, would break the chain, but the defendant should remain liable for the consequences of normal treatment. However cases such as *Wright v Cambridge Medical Group* (CA, 2011), and *Bailey v MoD* (CA, 2008) suggest that the modern approach is to treat the negligence as a concurrent cause where appropriate. This is consistent with the approach in *Spencer v Wincanton* (CA, 2009) although the context is different; contribution between tortfeasors and/or contributory negligence allow for a more precise allocation of responsibility.

We have seen in *Bonnington Castings Ltd. v Wardlaw* (HL, 1956) and *Wilsher v Essex Area Health Authority* (HL, 1988) that where a breach of a duty of care is proved or admitted, the burden still lies on the claimant to prove that the breach in question caused the injury suffered. In all cases the key question is one of fact: did the wrongful act cause the injury? However, in cases where the breach of duty consists of an omission to do an act which ought to be done (e.g. the failure by a doctor to attend a patient) that key question involves an element of hypothesis. In *Bolitho v City and Hackney Health Authority* (HL, 1997) a two-year-old boy suffered catastrophic brain damage as a result of cardiac arrest induced by respiratory failure. It was admitted that the doctor's failure to attend the child constituted a breach of duty so whether her failure to attend caused the child's damage depended on what she would have done had she turned up.

KEY CASE

BOLITHO V CITY AND HACKNEY HEALTH AUTHORITY (1997)

The claimant, a two-year-old patient in the defendant's hospital, suffered respiratory failure and cardiac arrest from which he subsequently died. It was accepted that, having been called on more than one occasion by a nursing sister, a doctor was in breach of her duty by failing to attend the child. The issue before the court was causation; did this breach of duty cause the claimant's injuries? Whether the doctor's failure to attend caused the claimant's damage depended on what she would have done had she turned up. If the claimant had been intubated (to provide an airway) the respiratory difficulties would not have resulted in cardiac arrest. However, the doctor who failed to respond said that even if she had attended she would not have intubated, and therefore the cardiac arrest would have occurred in any event (no "but for" causation). Both the claimant and the defendant called distinguished medical experts in determining whether the professional standard of care required any doctor who attended the claimant to intubate.

Held: (HL) The action failed because the House of Lords accepted that even if the doctor had attended she would not have intubated. This approach was supported by a responsible body of professional opinion and therefore it was not negligent. It was also the case that this body of opinion could be seen to be founded on a logical footing.

Comment

In assessing the whether the treatment has been negligent the court has to be satisfied that the professional opinion is capable of logical analysis. However, in a rare case where professional medical opinion does not withstand logical analysis it is open to the court to hold that it cannot be relied on to assess the doctor's conduct.

CHECKPOINT

Intervening conduct in the context of the risk created by the defendant's negligence

In dealing generally with the question of what amounts to a novus actus, the answer is sometimes to be found by considering whether the intervening conduct was within the ambit of the risk created by the defendant's negligence. For example, an incursion of squatters is not one of the risks attendant upon undermining the foundations of a building (*Lamb v Camden LBC*); but the act of a rescuer who goes to assist another put in peril by the defendant's negligence clearly is within the risk created by that negligence and is not therefore a novus actus: *Haynes v Harwood* (CA, 1935); (see Ch.5).

Intervening natural force

The defendant will not normally be liable for damage suffered as the immediate consequence of a natural event which occurs independently of the breach. In *Carslogie Steamship Co Ltd v Royal Norwegian Government* (HL, 1952), the defendants were held not liable for storm damage suffered by a ship during a voyage to a place where repairs to collision damage caused by the defendants' negligence were to be done, even though that voyage would not have been undertaken had the collision not occurred. This is clearly a case of coincidence rather than cause and effect.

It will be apparent from the foregoing discussion that, in the case of intervening acts, foreseeability may be a rough guide in assessing relative degrees of responsibility but it can never be the sole criterion of liability. A number of the cases evince a notable lack of consistency of approach and precision in the use of language, which serves only to mask the policy factors at play in the judicial process.

• •

QUESTION AND ANSWER

• •

QUESTION

Dave was negligently driving a minibus when it crashed into a wall. A number of passengers were injured and Dave immediately phoned the emergency services. He was told that an ambulance was on the way. Reena, one of the passengers, was uninjured but she wished to leave the scene of the accident to go to her home close by. Against Dave's advice Reena attempted to climb out of the minibus. She used the rear door, which had a very high step down to the ground, because the passenger door was unusable, but she fell as she was stepping down and suffered a broken hip.

The condition of Ariel, one of the injured minibus passengers, began to deteriorate. Dave became very concerned and rang the ambulance again to stress the emergency of the situation. The ambulance did not arrive for 40 minutes and when Ariel reached the hospital there was a further delay in diagnosing her spinal injury. Ariel is now permanently disabled but if she had been treated promptly she would have made a full recovery from her injuries.

ANSWER

Reena

Reena will need to show, firstly, that it was Dave's breach that caused the damage to her leg using the "but for test" (*Barnett v Kensington and Chelsea* (1963)). Secondly, Reena will argue that the damage she suffered as a result of Dave's breach is of a foreseeable kind and not too remote (*The Wagon Mound* (1956)). Applying the "but for" test, in respect of Reena's broken leg, Dave would be liable unless he could claim that her refusal to follow his instruction to remain in the minibus until the ambulance arrived constituted a *novus actus interveniens* thereby breaking the chain of causation between his negligence and Reena's injury. Dave would rely on *McKew v Holland* (1969) and say that Reena's own unreasonable conduct broke the chain of causation and he is therefore not liable for her injury. The key question then is whether she acted unreasonably is disobeying Dave's instruction. Contrast the decision in *Wieland v Cyril Lord Carpets* (1969) where the defendants were found liable because the claimant had not acted unreasonably. Alternatively, Dave may seek to argue contributory negligence on Reena's part. The principle of contributory negligence is that a person has responsibility for his actions and it is just and equitable that the reduction in damages should take account of the relative blameworthiness of the claimant's conduct. This appears to be the preferred method for the courts to deal with these cases today: *Spencer v Wincanton* (2011).

Ariel

Ariel may wish to make a claim against Dave, the ambulance service and the hospital. If a defendant has injured someone who conse-quently requires medical attention, he is likely to be liable for the consequences of that treatment, even if unforeseeable: *Robinson v Post Office* (1974). On this basis Dave would remain liable for Reena's injuries but the delay in the arrival of the ambulance or the hospital delay in diagnosing Ariel's condition may amount to a novus actus interveniens which breaks the chain of causation between Dave's breach and Ariel's injury: *Knightley v Johns* (1982). Ariel would need to know that for policy reasons there have been difficulties in bringing negligence actions against public bodies so that at the third stage of the *Caparo* test it has been found that it is not fair, just or reasonable to impose liability. However, in *Kent v Griffiths* (2000) the acceptance of the call created a duty of care on the ambulance service and they were liable to the claimant for injuries resulting from the late arrival of the ambulance. The question of whether the delayed diagnosis caused Ariel's harm and amounted to a novus actus interveniens will be determined by establishing whether there was a breach of duty (see *Bolam v Friern Hosp Management Committee* (1957)), whether that breach actually on balance caused all or part of her injuries (see *Hotson v East Berkshire AHA* (1987)), and whether it is seen as a separate or a cumulative cause (see *Wright v Cambridge Medical Group* (2011) and *Bailey v Ministry of Defence* (2008) for cases on each side of this divide).

In this situation, asking whether Ariel's disability would have occurred "but for" the hospital's breach as in *Barnett v Chelsea & Kensington Hospital Management Committee (1969)* leads to the answer "no" because there are two possible connected causes of this damage. On the facts it is impossible to know whether it was the ambulance delay or the hospital's delayed diagnosis which caused Ariel's disability or the extent to which it was caused by the connected factors. In relation to the late arrival of the ambulance, applying *McGhee v National Coal Board* (1972) it would be sufficient to show that the ambulance service's and the hospital's breach of duty had made her disability more probable even though it could not be shown that being late was the actual cause. Alternatively, if the evidence supports it, this issue between the ambulance service and the hospital could also be resolved by treating the two causes as cumulative: *Bailey v Ministry of Defence* (2008).

Defences to Negligence: Contributory Negligence, Volenti Non Fit Injuria and Ex Turpi Causa

CONTRIBUTORY NEGLIGENCE

At common law a claimant whose injuries were caused partly by his own negligence could recover nothing. To succeed in this defence it was not necessary for the defendant to prove that the claimant owed a duty of care as such, but simply that the claimant "did not in his own interest take reasonable care of himself and contributed, by this want of care, to his own injury" (per Lord Simon in *Nance v British Columbia Electric Ry* (PC, 1951)). Since the **Law Reform (Contributory Negligence) Act 1945**, contributory negligence is no longer a complete bar to recovery but, in accordance with s.1(1) of the Act, will result in a reduction of damages.

LEGISLATION HIGHLIGHTER

Section 1(1) of the Law Reform (Contributory Negligence) Act 1945 provides:

> "Where any person suffers damage as the result partly of his own fault and partly of the fault of any other person or persons, a claim in respect of that damage shall not be defeated by reason of the fault of the person suffering the damage, but the damages recoverable in respect thereof shall be reduced to such extent as the court thinks just and equitable having regard to the claimant's share in the responsibility for the damage."

The Act applies where the damage is attributable to the fault of both parties, and "fault" is defined in s.4 to mean "negligence, breach of statutory duty or other act or omission which gives rise to a liability in tort or would, apart from this Act, give rise to the defence of contributory negligence". Note that contributory negligence does not apply to the trespass torts (see *CWS v Pritchard* (CA, 2011)).

Causation

The damage suffered must be caused partly by the fault of the claimant and it is therefore immaterial that the claimant's fault was nothing to do with the causation of the accident. Thus, reductions have been made for failing to wear a seat belt or a crash helmet, and for travelling in a vehicle with a drunk driver. To put the matter another way, a claimant's damage must be within the foreseeable risk to which he or she unreasonably exposed themselves. In *Jones v Livox Quarries Ltd* (CA, 1952) the claimant, contrary to instructions, stood on the rear towbar of a vehicle and was injured when another vehicle ran into the back of it.

KEY CASE

JONES V LIVOX QUARRIES LTD (1952)
This case shows that the injury sustained must be within the scope of the risk created by the claimant's negligence. The claimant argued that his contributory negligence should not count against him because the obvious danger arising from riding on the towbar was being thrown off, not being run into from behind and crushed by another vehicle.

Held: (CA) The risk of being run into from behind was also one to which the claimant had exposed himself and his damages were reduced accordingly.

Comment
Lord Denning said that the claimant's carelessness would have been irrelevant if, instead of being hit by another vehicle, he had been struck in the eye by a shot fired by a negligent sportsman.

CHECKPOINT

Damage must be caused partly by the fault of the claimant
- In *Badger v Ministry of Defence* (HC, 2006), the deceased's lung cancer was caused by asbestos fibres to which he been exposed during his employment, however, his failure to stop smoking despite warnings about the risk of cancer constituted contributory negligence.

On the other hand:

- In *Westwood v Post Office* (HL, 1974), the premises where W worked contained a machine room. There was a notice prohibiting access to the room, except for technicians, but in practice employees use the room to get access to the roof to take rest breaks. W fell through a defective trapdoor in the room. There was nothing to suggest that there was anything wrong with the trapdoor. The prohibition of access was because of the lift machinery. W was not contributorily negligent in relation to his fall; there was nothing to suggest that he should have been aware that he was running this particular kind of risk.
- A claimant who has been injured, and who then takes insufficient care of himself, as a result of which he suffers further injury, may be held to be contributorily negligent in relation to this want of care (see *Spencer v Wincanton* (CA, 2011)).

Standard of care

The claimant is expected to show an objective standard of reasonable care in much the same way as the defendant must to avoid tortious negligence. A claimant who ought reasonably to have foreseen that, if he or she did not act as a "reasonable man" they might be hurt themselves, is guilty of contributory negligence. Similar factors to those determining whether the defendant is in breach of duty (see Ch.3) are therefore relevant here.

Particular cases

1. Children

As a matter of law there is no age below which it can be said that a child is incapable of contributory negligence, but the degree of care to be expected must be proportioned to the age of the child, and all the circumstances. In *Gough v Thorne* (CA, 1966), a 13-year-old girl who was knocked down by a negligent motorist when she stepped past a stationary lorry whose driver had beckoned her to cross, was held not guilty of contributory negligence. According to Lord Denning: "A very young child cannot be guilty of contributory negligence." However, this is too wide. In *Morales v Eccleston* (CA, 1991), an 11-year-old who was struck by the defendant driver while kicking a ball in the middle of a road with traffic passing in either direction had his damages reduced by 75 per cent. The point is that even a child ought to appreciate the dangers of playing in the road, while it is not negligent to rely on a responsible adult.

YACHUK V OLIVER BLAIS CO LTD (1949)
In the case of children, age is a circumstance which must be considered in deciding if there has been contributory negligence. The defendants (acting in breach of a statutory prohibition) supplied a nine-year-old boy with a pint of petrol. He had falsely stated that his mother wanted the petrol for her car. When he used the fuel to make a burning torch for the purposes of a game he suffered severe injury.

Held: The defendants were liable in negligence for supplying petrol to so young a boy and he had not been guilty of contributory negligence for he neither knew nor could be expected to appreciate the danger.

2. Old or infirm persons

It seems that some latitude may be given to such persons in assessing whether they are guilty of contributory negligence. Thus, an elderly person who is unable to move quickly enough to get out of the path of a motorist who drives close by in the expectation that he is able to do so may not be penalised (*Daly v Liverpool Corp* (HC, 1939)). But note that this case precedes the reform of contributory negligence. It might be a sympathetic decision which would not be followed today.

3. Rescuers

It is not often that a rescuer will be found guilty of contributory negligence, bearing in mind that, in the face of imminent danger, his reaction is usually instinctive. Thus, in *Brandon v Osborne, Garrett & Co Ltd* (HC, 1924) the defendants negligently allowed a sheet of glass to fall from their shop roof and the claimant, believing her husband to be in danger, tried to pull him away and injured her leg. It was held that she was not contributorily negligent. A similar principle applies where the claimant is injured in trying to extricate him or herself from a perilous situation in which the defendant's negligence has placed them, even though with hindsight the claimant is shown to have chosen the wrong course of action (*Jones v Boyce* (1816), cf. *Sayers v Harlow UDC* (CA, 1958)). That a rescuer may be contributorily negligent, however, is illustrated by *Harrison v British Railways Board* (HC, 1981), although in this case the claimant was plainly at fault in not following an established work procedure designed to deal with the particular emergency in question. Again the more recent decisions are to be preferred. They reflect the ability to allocate responsibility proportionately under the 1945 Act.

4. Workers

In relation to actions for breach of statutory duty, this issue is dealt with in Ch.9. It seems clear from *Westwood v Post Office* (HL, 1974) that the more lenient approach towards employees is appropriate only where the action is founded upon the employer's breach of statutory duty and not upon ordinary negligence.

5. Car passengers

For instance, failure to wear a seat belt can result in a finding of contributory negligence.

KEY CASE

FROOM V BUTCHER (1976)

The claimant's carelessness need not be a cause of the accident but it is essential to show that it contributed to the damage suffered. In this case the claimant was involved in a collision caused by the defendant's negligence. He was not wearing a seat belt but if he had been wearing a belt the head and chest injuries which he sustained in the accident would have been avoided.

Held: (CA) The standard of care is objective. In failing to wear a seat belt the claimant failed to take reasonable precautions for his own safety and his damages were reduced accordingly.

Comment

(1) The negligence of the claimant did not contribute to the accident happening, but his failure to take precautions increased the risk of harm. He was more likely to suffer more serious injury.

(2) Froom had made a conscious decision not wear a seat belt because of the risk of becoming trapped in an accident. However, in *Condon v Condon* (1978) a claimant who suffered from a seatbelt phobia was held not to be contributorily negligent for failing to do so. It was reasonable not to wear a seatbelt because of the phobia.

It was suggested that ordinarily there should be:

- a reduction of 25 per cent in respect of injuries which would have been avoided altogether; and
- a reduction of 15 per cent in respect of those injuries which would have been less severe.

Although these figures are guidelines only, they should, according to *Capps v Miller* (CA, 1989), generally be followed. So, too, a motor-cyclist who fails to wear a crash helmet will have his damages similarly reduced (*O'Connell v Jackson* (CA, 1972)), although failure to fasten a helmet properly has been held to merit a slightly smaller reduction (*Capps v Miller*).

Even though there is no legal requirement to wear a cycling helmet, contributory negligence was argued in *Smith v Finch* (HC, 2009) where a cyclist sustained serious head injuries in a road accident caused by the defendant. The court concluded that the judgment and observations of Lord Denning MR in *Froom v Butcher* should apply to the wearing of helmets by cyclists (however, contributory negligence failed here because the defendant was unable to show that a helmet would have prevented the claimant's serious head injuries or made them less severe).

It is also clear that to ride in a car in the knowledge that the driver has been drinking constitutes contributory negligence, even though the passenger himself is so intoxicated as not to appreciate that the driver is unfit to drive (*Owens v Brimmell* (HC, 1977)).

Apportionment

Apportionment is on a just and equitable basis according to the 1945 Act and, in assessing the claimant's reduction, the court may take into account both the causative potency of his act and the degree of blameworthiness (i.e. the extent to which the claimants conduct fell below the requisite standard of care) to be attached to it. There seem to be no hard and fast rules, however, and a good deal of judicial discretion is exercised in the matter. The Court of Appeal has held that no apportionment should be made unless each of the parties is at least 10 per cent to blame (*Johnson v Tennant Bros Ltd* (CA, 1954)), although the case seems to have been decided on the ground that the defendant's breach was not a cause of the damage (see *Capps v Miller* (CA, 1989)).

CHECKPOINT

The Law Reform (Contributory Negligence) Act 1945 provides that there must be fault on the part of both parties.
In *Jayes v IMI (Kynoch) Ltd* (CA, 1985), the claimant was adjudged 100 per cent contributorily negligent, but such a finding is illogical according to *Pitts v Hunt* (CA, 1990) because the 1945 Act does not apply unless both parties were at fault. The earlier case can presumably be explained on the basis that the claimant was solely to blame for the damage.

Where the same accident involves two or more defendants, any contributory negligence must be assessed by comparing the claimant's conduct with the totality of the defendants' negligence. The issue of the extent to which each defendant contributed to the damage should thereafter be dealt with in contribution proceedings (*Fitzgerald v Lane* (HL, 1988)).

One final point to note is that a defendant who seeks to rely on the defence must plead it (*Fookes v Slaytor* (CA, 1978)).

VOLENTI NON FIT INJURIA

This maxim embodies the principle that a person who expressly or impliedly agrees with another to run the risk of harm created by that other cannot thereafter sue in respect of damage suffered as a result of the materialisation of that risk. The defence is commonly called consent or voluntary assumption of risk and, if successful, is a complete bar to recovery.

For the defence to apply, the defendant must have committed what would, in the absence of any assumption of risk, amount to a tort. The defendant must prove not only that the claimant consented to the risk of actual damage, but also that he or she agreed to waive their right of action in respect of that damage. The application of the defence is most straightforward in the case of intentional torts, as, for instance, where each party to a boxing match consents to being struck by the other, provided that the blow is struck fairly, or at least within the spirit of the rules of boxing. Most of the problems in the past have arisen in negligence where the alleged assumption of risk is as to the possibility of damage rather than a certainty, but in view of the power to apportion responsibility by a finding of contributory negligence, the defence is rarely successful today.

Knowledge of the risk

Mere knowledge of the risk does not amount to consent. It must be found as a fact that the claimant freely and voluntarily, with full knowledge of the nature and extent of the risk, impliedly agreed to incur it (*Osborne v L. & N. W. Ry.* (HC, 1888)). The claimant must therefore have genuine freedom of choice which requires the absence of any feeling of constraint (*Bowater v Rowley Regis Corp* (CA, 1944)). One explanation for the lack of success of this defence to a negligence action is that, since the alleged consent usually precedes the defendant's breach of duty, the claimant cannot be said in these circumstances to have full knowledge and appreciation of the risk (*Wooldridge v Sumner* (CA, 1963), per Diplock L.J.).

Agreement

It has been suggested that an appreciation of, and willingness to take, the risk will not satisfy the requirements of the defence; there must, in addition, be evidence that the claimant has expressly or impliedly agreed to waive his or her right of action (see, e.g. *Nettleship v Weston* (CA, 1971) per Lord Denning where the argument failed in relation to the supervisor of a learner driver). On the other hand the defence may apply where the claimant consciously assumes the risk of an existing danger created by the defendant, independently of any agreement (*Titchener v British Railways Board* (HL, 1983). This case concerned a teenage trespasser on the railway. She admitted that she was well aware of the dangers, and in the circumstances it was held that she was *volens* to the risk of being hit by a train while trespassing.).

LEGISLATION HIGHLIGHTER

An express antecedent agreement to relieve the defendant of liability for future negligence operates in effect as an exclusion notice and is therefore subject to the Unfair Contract Terms Act 1977.

Section 2(1) renders void any purported exclusion of liability for death or personal injury caused by negligence and, in the case of other loss or damage, s.2(2) subjects such an exclusion to a test of reasonableness.

Section 2(3) further provides that a person's agreement to, or awareness of, such a notice is not of itself to be taken as indicating his voluntary acceptance of any risk.

It should be noted, however, that the above provisions only apply to business liability. In respect of employers' liability, in *Johnstone v Bloomsbury Health Authority* (CA, 1991), it was considered that, on the assumption that reliance on an express contractual term amounted to a plea of volenti, it could fall within the ambit of s.2(1) of the Act (see further Ch.8).

LEGISLATION HIGHLIGHTER

Section 149 of the Road Traffic Act 1988 makes the following provision:

Avoidance of certain agreements as to liability towards passengers

(1) This section applies where a person uses a motor vehicle in circumstances such that under section 143 of this Act there is required to be in force in relation to his use of it such a policy of insurance or such a security in respect of third-party risks as complies with the requirements of this Part of this Act.

(2) If any other person is carried in or upon the vehicle while the user is so using it, any antecedent agreement or understanding between them (whether intended to be legally binding or not) shall be of no effect so far as it purports or might be held—

(a) to negative or restrict any such liability of the user in respect of persons carried in or upon the vehicle as is required by section 145 of this Act to be covered by a policy of insurance, or

(b) to impose any conditions with respect to the enforcement of any such liability of the user.

(3) The fact that a person so carried has willingly accepted as his the risk of negligence on the part of the user shall not be treated as negativing any such liability of the user.

(4) For the purposes of this section–

(a) references to a person being carried in or upon a vehicle include references to a person entering or getting on to, or alighting from, the vehicle, and

(b) the reference to an antecedent agreement is to one made at any time before the liability arose.

The effect of this section is to remove the possibility of a defence of volenti in relation to a passenger on a motor vehicle in all normal circumstances.

In some circumstances the conduct of the parties may enable an inference to be drawn that the claimant has impliedly agreed to waive his legal rights in respect of future negligence. For example, in *Morris v Murray* (CA, 1990) the defence applied when, in poor weather conditions, the defendant, who to the claimant's knowledge was extremely drunk, offered the claimant a ride in his aircraft. The aircraft crashed during takeoff. In relation to light aircraft there is no statutory equivalent to section 149 of the **Road Traffic Act 1988**. That was the claimant's bad luck.

1. *Sporting events*

Sporting events can give rise to specific problems in relation to assumption of risk. The general position is that a spectator injured by a participant in a sporting event does not consent to negligence, or assume on himself the risk of injury, whether this is caused by the participants or by the organiser, though he may be defeated by a valid exclusion notice (*White v Blackmore* (CA, 1972); note however that this case precedes the Unfair Contract Terms Act. Any exclusion notice would now have to comply with the Act.). A spectator may be taken to have accepted those risks ordinarily incidental to the game (e.g. being hit by a cricket ball struck into the crowd), but in this case there is no negligence and volenti is therefore irrelevant. The potential liability of the participants depends upon the standard and scope of the duty of care owed and, in *Wooldridge v Sumner* (CA, 1963), this was expressed by Diplock L.J. as a duty not to act with reckless disregard for the spectator's safety. This was criticised, however, in *Wilks v Cheltenham Home Guard Motor Cycle & Light Car Club* (CA, 1971) where it was said that the proper standard was one of reasonable care in all the circumstances, which might include the fact that the defendant is involved in a fast-moving, competitive sport in an all-out effort to win. It will in any event be a relatively low standard.

CHECKPOINT

Approach adopted to incidents between one player and another at sporting events:
- In *Condon v Basi* (CA, 1985), a "reckless and dangerous" tackle in a local amateur football match was held to be negligence. It has to be accepted that participants in sport will sometimes be unskilful, or overexuberant. This is an inherent risk, and does not amount to a breach of duty. However, serious foul play goes beyond the inherent risks. It will therefore be actionable. Inevitably, the courts will have to decide on which side of this line the defendant's behaviour falls in any particular case.
- In *Watson v British Boxing Board of Control* (CA, 2001), it was pointed out that where the claimant consents to injury by an opponent in a boxing ring he does not consent to injury resulting from inadequate safety arrangements by the sport's governing body after being hit.

2. Employees

In relation to claims by employees against their employer, volenti or consent will not apply where the claimant has no choice but to accept the risk; knowledge of the risk does not necessarily imply consent.

Smith v Charles Baker & Sons (HL, 1891) held that a plea of volenti by an employer in an action by his employee for common law negligence is almost bound to fail because the unequal nature of the relationship is such that the employee does not exercise complete freedom of will.

KEY CASE

SMITH V CHARLES BAKER & SONS (1891)

The defendant will not be liable if the claimant voluntarily assumed to take the risk involved, but knowledge of the danger does not necessarily imply consent. In this case the claimant was employed drilling holes in a rock cutting over which a crane often swung heavy stones while he was working. He was aware that there was a risk of the stones falling and he had complained to his employer about the dangerous practice. When he was injured by a falling stone he brought an action against his employers, who pleaded volenti non fit injuria.

Held: (HL) Volenti was rejected; even though the claimant had knowledge of the danger and continued to work, he had not voluntarily undertaken the risk.

Comment

As noted above, the defence will rarely be successful in an action by an employee against an employer. The employee is not in a position where he is freely accepting the risk. Any argument that he is being paid "danger money" will be met by saying that that payment is to get him to work in these conditions in the first place. It is not a means of buying out his right of action if he is injured by the employer's negligence.

It will only be in exceptional circumstances that this general assumption will not apply. One such case is *Imperial Chemical Industries Ltd (ICI) v Shatwell* (1965). The claimant, in defiance of his employer's orders and statutory safety regulations, went to test some detonators without taking the required safety precautions. During the testing an explosion occurred and the claimant was injured. His employer was not liable because the claimant was held to have consented to and fully appreciated the risk of injury. However it is important to bear in mind that the claimant, and his brother, who actually caused the explosion, were both shotfirers. As such they were quite senior safety officials, and personally responsible for compliance with the regulations. In addition, they were working in circumstances where there was no other senior manager who could control what they were doing. It is therefore a fairly extreme case and not likely to be a general precedent.

In *Johnstone v Bloomsbury Health Authority* (CA, 1991), an express term in the contract of employment of a junior doctor required the claimant to work 40 hours per week and to "be available" for a further average 48 hours per week overtime at the employer's discretion. In an action for breach of the employer's common law duty to take reasonable care for the claimant's health and safety, Leggatt L.J. took the view that the express term could not be overridden by the implied duty, and Browne-Wilkinson VC would have agreed if the term had imposed an absolute obligation to work those further hours, as opposed to giving a discretion. If this view is correct it would appear to undermine the proposition that volenti ought not, in principle, to afford a defence to the employer. However, the case must be seen in its context. Historically junior doctors have been expected to work lengthy on-call periods and this case amounted to a challenge to historic custom and practice.

3. Car passengers

A car passenger who accepts a lift with a driver who, to his or her knowledge, is inexperienced or whose ability to drive safely is otherwise impaired (e.g. through drink) cannot be held volenti to the risk, because s.149 of the Road Traffic Act 1988, as set out above, prohibits any restriction on the driver's liability to his passenger as is required to be covered by insurance (*Pitts v Hunt* (CA, 1990); there is no such statutory intervention in relation to travelling in a light aircraft with a drunken pilot (see *Morris v Murray* (CA, 1990)). Taking a lift with an inebriated car driver is, however, likely to amount to contributory negligence (*Owens v Brimmell* (HC, 1977)).

4. Rescuers

If the defendant's negligence endangers the safety of others such that a rescue attempt is reasonably foreseeable, a duty is owed to the rescuer (see *Haynes v Harwood* (CA, 1935)). It makes no difference that the person imperilled is actually the defendant rather than a third party (*Harrison v British Railways Board* (HC, 1981)), and the duty owed is wholly independent of any duty owed by the defendant to those who are rescued (*Videan v British Transport Commission* (CA, 1963)). Nor is there any rule of law to prevent a claim by a professional "rescuer", so that a fireman injured whilst fighting a negligently-started fire may recover (*Ogwo v Taylor* (HL, 1988)). In these situations volenti clearly does not apply. In the first place the rescuer acts under moral compulsion and does not therefore exercise freedom of choice, and secondly, since the defendant's negligence precedes the rescue the claimant cannot be said to consent to it and may not even be aware of it at the time (*Baker v T. E. Hopkins & Son Ltd* (CA, 1959)).

KEY CASE

BAKER V HOPKINS (1959)

The doctrine of the assumption of risk does not apply to a rescuer when the emergency was created by the defendant's negligence. The defendant employer in this case had adopted a dangerous system of working by lowering a petrol engine down into the inside of a well. The engine discharged poisonous emissions and two of the workmen were overcome by the fumes. The claimant, a doctor, had volunteered to go down the well to rescue the workmen. He too was overcome by the fumes and was killed.

Held: (CA) Volenti was inapplicable because the claimant's actions as a rescuer were not truly voluntary, rather they were motivated by humanitarian concerns. This decision can also be explained on policy grounds as it is against the public interest to deter rescue.

In *Chadwick v British Transport Commission* (HC, 1967) a rescuer who assisted at the scene of a train crash and who suffered nervous shock as a result of what he saw was held entitled to recover. There was no reference in the case to the fact that he was running significant risk of physical injury. The court considered that his status as a rescuer justified recovery. Subsequent developments in relation to liability for psychiatric harm (see Ch. 2) appear to suggest that for a rescuer to recover in respect of psychiatric injury he must satisfy the normal criteria. *Chadwick* may well be correctly decided, but this depends on his being a primary victim, i.e. someone at risk of injury.

EX TURPI CAUSA

Where the alleged wrong occurs while the claimant is engaged in criminal activity, the claim may be barred because ex turpi causa non oritur actio (no action can be founded on an illegal act).

In *Gray v Thames Trains Ltd* (HL, 2009) (below), Lord Hoffman said the maxim expresses not so much a principle as a policy; that policy is not based upon a single justification but on a group of reasons, which vary in different situations:

> "The wider and simpler version was that you could not recover for damage which was the consequence of your own criminal act. In its narrower form [as applicable in this case], it was that you could not recover for damage which was the consequence of a sentence imposed upon you for a criminal act."

This principle may also apply where the claimant's conduct is immoral (*Kirkham v Chief Constable of Greater Manchester* (CA, 1990)). The difficulty is in determining which types of non-criminal conduct are considered sufficiently heinous for the purposes of the defence. Some cases have said that it will apply where it would be impossible to determine an appropriate standard of care (e.g. *Pitts v Hunt* (CA, 1990), a case where a drunken motorcyclist gave a lift to an equally drunk passenger. The driver was showing off by driving recklessly and the passenger was encouraging him). Others have suggested that the claimant ought not to succeed if to permit him to do so would be an "affront to the public conscience" (*Kirkham v Chief Constable of Greater Manchester*).

In *Clunis v Camden and Islington Health Authority* (CA, 1998), the claimant, who had a long history of mental illness, was convicted of manslaughter and ordered to be detained in a secure hospital. He sued the defendant for negligence for failing to take reasonable care to provide him with after-care services following his discharge from hospital where he had been detained under the Mental Health Act 1983. It was held that, despite a successful plea of diminished responsibility at the criminal trial, his action was barred on grounds of public policy since he was directly implicated in the illegality and must be taken to have known that what he was doing was wrong (cf. *Meah v McCreamer* (HC, 1985), a case where Meah developed a personality disorder following injury in a road accident. Under the influence of this he committed serious criminal offences. Since he had recovered compensation for his injuries, his victims sued him. In turn he attempted to recover additional damages to cover this. His claim failed for similar reasons to those in *Clunis*).

In *Vellino v Chief Constable of Greater Manchester Police* (CA, 2001), the claimant suffered brain damage when he attempted to escape from police custody by jumping from a window of his second floor flat. He claimed negligence on the part of the arresting officers, alleging that they had stood idly by and let him jump. The Court of Appeal held that the maxim ex turpi causa made the claim untenable because the defendant had to rely on his own criminal conduct in escaping lawful custody to found his claim.

In *Gray v Thames Trains Ltd* (HL, 2009), as the result of a serious rail crash caused by the defendant's negligence, the claimant suffered severe psychological depression which led to his conviction for killing a man. His claim in damages for loss of earnings after he committed the manslaughter was allowed by the Court of Appeal on the ground that it was not defeated by ex turpi causa because the damages were not inextricably bound up with or linked to his criminal conduct. However, on appeal the House of Lords ruled that Gray's conviction for manslaughter precluded a claim for loss of earnings during his detention by reason of the public policy expressed in the doctrine of ex turpi causa.

KEY CASE

GRAY V THAMES TRAINS LTD [(2009)

At the criminal trial for this offence Gray's plea of guilty to manslaughter on the ground of diminished responsibility was accepted and he was ordered to be detained in a mental hospital under the Mental Health Act 1983. Thames Trains Ltd appealed against the decision that

Gray's claim was not defeated by ex turpi causa arguing that a claimant cannot recover compensation for loss which has been suffered in consequence of his own criminal act.

Held: In allowing the appeal the House of Lords ruled that Gray's conviction for manslaughter precluded a claim for loss of earnings during his detention by reason of the public policy expressed in the doctrine of ex turpi causa.

Both the degree of moral turpitude and the closeness of the causal connection between it and the claimant's damage are relevant factors. In *Joyce v O'Brien* (CA, 2013) the principle of ex turpi causa provided a defence to an action by a party involved in a joint criminal enterprise. During the course of making their get-away from the scene of the crime, the claimant suffered serious injury caused by his co-conspirator's negligent driving. In contrast, the ex turpi causa principle did not apply in *Delaney v Pickett* (CA, 2011) a case which also concerned a claimant who sustained a serious injury in a car crash driven by his co-conspirator. The criminal conspiracy in this case related to drugs. There were actually drugs in the car. However, the Court of Appeal held that in this case the accident did not happen because of the joint criminal activity; the accident was caused by negligent driving and the drugs were purely coincidental. (Although not defeated by ex turpi causa, the claim failed on other grounds.)

The principle was applied to a claimant who, having gone drinking with the defendant, then rode as a pillion passenger on the defendant's motorcycle and encouraged him to drive in a reckless manner, in the knowledge also that the defendant did not hold a licence and was uninsured (*Pitts v Hunt* (CA, 1990)).

KEY CASE

PITTS V HUNT (1990)

In this case the defence of volenti non fit injuria, was raised but in circumstances where insurance is compulsory (as it is with motor insurance) this defence is excluded under the Road Traffic Act 1988. However, the courts will not assist a claimant who has been guilty of illegal conduct as here where he encouraged the defendant to drive his motorbike in a reckless and dangerous fashion which led to the accident. The defendant was killed and the claimant, who was a pillion passenger, was badly injured.

Held: (CA) The defendant's own criminal and disgraceful conduct gave rise to a successful defence of the ex turpi causa.

In *Kirkham* (above) the defence was held not to apply to a claim based directly on the suicide of a man who was mentally disturbed, though it was considered that the position might be otherwise where the suicide was entirely sane; the same conclusions were reached in relation to the application of the volenti defence. This reflects the common law classification of suicide as a crime. However suicide has now been decriminalised and this logic does not apply. It has subsequently been held that the defence cannot apply even where the suicide was of sound mind, provided that the defendant was under a duty of care to prevent a suicide attempt; nor can the claimant's conduct be regarded as a novus actus interveniens (see Ch.4) (*Reeves v Commissioner of Police of the Metropolis* (HL, 1999)).

According to Lord Denning a burglar bitten by a guard dog may be defeated by the maxim (*Cummings v Granger* (CA, 1977)), as may one who instigates an affray and gets "more than he bargained for" (*Murphy v Culhane* (CA, 1977)), though these decisions must now be read in the light of *Revill v Newbery* (CA, 1996); see Ch.6. In *Rance v Mid-Downs Health Authority* (HC, 1991), the claimant alleged that the defendants negligently failed to detect a foetal abnormality during pregnancy and to advise her of her right to terminate it, with the result that she gave birth to a seriously handicapped child. It was held that even if the defendants were negligent, they could not be liable because the pregnancy was so far advanced by the time of the alleged negligence that, as the law then stood, abortion would have been a criminal offence.

One somewhat unusual claim in tort is that available to the victim of anti-competitive behaviour. This claim is based on art.101 of the Treaty on the Functioning of the European Union. There have been cases where the anti-competitive behaviour involves a major company imposing anti- competitive terms in an agreement with a small business. One example is restrictive conditions in the tenancy of a public house. Strictly, the tenant, by agreeing to the terms, is a party to the illegality. Nevertheless the European Court of Justice has ruled that the party in the weaker position may be able to bring a claim for breach of statutory duty notwithstanding the fact that they are technically parties to the illegality: *Courage v Crehan* (2001).

REVISION CHECKLIST

You should now understand:

- ☐ **The conditions within which the three general defences apply in tort and the overlap between the defences.**
- ☐ **Volenti is a complete defence and contributory negligence is preferred because it is more flexible.**

- ☐ Volenti is not easily established—the defendant must show that the claimant had full knowledge and consented to the nature and the extent of the risk.

- ☐ Ex turpi causa prevents a claimant engaged in illegal activity from obtaining damages.

QUESTION AND ANSWER

QUESTION

To what extent is a defendant in a tort action liable to a claimant who was engaged in an illegal activity at the time the injury was sustained?

APPROACH TO THE ANSWER

Outline the effect of ex turpi causa (the claim is barred because no action can be founded on an illegal act) and the policy reasons underlying the defence—per Lord Hoffman in *Gray v Thames Trains Ltd* (2009).

Discuss the factors taken into account in determining which types of conduct are considered sufficiently heinous for the defence to be established: *Pitts v Hunt* (1990) and considerations such as:

(a) where it is impossible for the court to determine the appropriate standard of care in a particular case (e.g. of one sado-masochist to another).

(b) the closeness of the connection required between the illegal activity of the claimant and the damage suffered—the damage must be a direct result of the illegal activity. In *Joyce v O'Brien* (2013) the principle of ex turpi causa provided a defence in a joint criminal enterprise where the accident happened in the course of the get-away from the scene of the crime. However the principle did not provide a defence in *Delaney v Pickett* (2011) where the accident did not happen because of the joint criminal activity (transporting illegal drugs) but was caused by negligent driving.

(c) where to permit the claimant to succeed would be an affront to the public conscience.

Occupiers' Liability

....

THE OCCUPIERS' LIABILITY ACTS 1957 AND 1984

Introduction

The liability of occupiers towards persons injured on their premises is largely governed by two statutes. The Occupiers' Liability Act 1957 is concerned with liability to lawful visitors but the 1957 Act did not deal with trespassers so a subsequent statute, the Occupiers' Liability Act 1984 was enacted to govern the duty of an occupier to persons other than visitors (e.g. trespassers). The liability of an occupier in respect of loss or injury suffered by those who come lawfully upon his premises is primarily governed by the 1957 Act. The main object of the 1957 Act was to simplify the law. The nature of the duty varied according to the status of the visitor, and these distinctions were removed; henceforth there was one category of lawful visitor, and one duty owed. Although it is clear that the duty imposed by the Act arises where damage results from the static condition of the premises, there is some doubt as to whether it applies where the claimant is injured in consequence of an activity conducted upon the premises (see *Revill v Newbery* (CA, 1996)). The balance of authority would suggest that it does, at least where the activity in question is an integral purpose of the occupation, rather than being merely ancillary to it. In any event, the point is largely academic, as liability for activities is covered by common law negligence in any event. Occupiers liability is actually one of the long established duty situations, so is essentially a branch of negligence with some statutory modifications.

CHECKPOINT

An illustration of how the general law of negligence applies to an activity on the premises at common law is provided in *Slater v Clay Cross Co Ltd* (CA, 1956) by Denning L.J.:

"If a landowner is driving his car down his private drive and meets someone lawfully walking upon it, then he is under a duty to take reasonable care so as not to injure the walker and his duty is the same, no matter whether it is his gardener coming up with his plants, a tradesman delivering his goods, a friend coming to tea, or a flag seller seeking a charitable gift."

Section 2(1) of the Act provides:

"An occupier owes the same duty, the "common duty of care" to all his visitors, except in so far as he is free to and does extend, restrict, modify or exclude his duty to any visitor or visitors by agreement or otherwise."

In any event, since this statutory duty is to take reasonable care, there is little or no difference between an action under the Act and one for breach of the common law duty of care.

The occupier

The Act contains no definition of "occupier" which is simply a term of convenience to denote a person who has a sufficient degree of control over premises to put him under a duty of care towards those who come lawfully on to the premises (*Wheat v Lacon & Co Ltd* (HL, 1966)). Control is thus the decisive factor, and it is immaterial that the occupier has no interest in the land. He may be an owner in occupation, a tenant, a licensee or any person having the right to possession and to permit others to enter the premises. There may be more than one occupier, and each may be responsible for different aspects. For example, in *AMF International Ltd v Magnet Bowling Ltd* (HC, 1968), building contractors were held to be joint occupiers along with the building owners. But a landlord who lets a flat by a formal lease to a tenant is not the occupier of the flat for the purposes of the Act, though he remains the occupier of those parts of the premises excluded from the lease, such as an entrance hall or common staircase in a block of flats (*Moloney v Lambeth London BC* (HC, 1966)).

KEY CASE

WHEAT V LACON (E) & CO LTD (1966)

The 1957 Act does not define "occupier" but provides that the rules of the common law shall apply. An occupier is one who has sufficient control over the premises so as to be under a duty of care towards lawful entrants. This case, where the defendant brewing company were owners of a pub which was run by a manager, shows that there can be more than one occupier of the same premises at any one time. The brewing company granted the manager a licence to use the top floor of the premises for his private accommodation. His wife took in paying guests and one evening as it was getting dark a guest fell down the back staircase in the private portion of the premises and was killed.

The handrail on the stairs was too short and did not stretch to the bottom of the staircase and someone had removed the light bulb from the top of the stairs.

Held: (HL) There may be two or more occupiers at any one time. Although the grant of a licence to occupy had been made to the manager the defendants remained occupiers and under a duty of care in relation to the premises as a whole; the manager was the occupier of his flat, and responsible for things like the safety of floor coverings and light bulbs. However, on the facts of the case the duty to the deceased had not been broken and the defendants were not liable.

Comment
In *Harris v Birkenhead Corp* (CA, 1976) the local authority acquired a house from the owner under a compulsory purchase order. The house was occupied by a tenant, who then moved out, leaving the property vacant. Before the local authority moved in to have the property boarded up, a child got in and was injured. The local authority argued that before it could be an occupier there had to be an actual or symbolic taking of possession on its behalf. The Court of Appeal held that because the local authority had the legal right to control the state of the property it had become an occupier when the tenant vacated the premises.

The premises
By s.1(3)(a) of the Act, the statutory provisions extend to any fixed or movable structure, including any vessel, vehicle or aircraft. This is apt to include not only structures of a permanent nature but temporary erections such as ladders and scaffolding.

LEGISLATION HIGHLIGHTER

With regard to "vessels, vehicles and aircraft" the Act would appear to apply only to the structural state of the premises, so that where injury is caused to a passenger by, say, negligent driving, the appropriate cause of action is negligence at common law

Visitors
The statutory duty is owed only to visitors who, by s.1(2), are those who would, at common law, have been either invitees or licensees. The common law distinction between these two categories of entrant is thereby abolished and the remaining vital distinction (which remains unaffected by the Act) is

that between the visitor and the trespasser. No difficulty arises where the occupier expressly invites or permits another to enter or use his premises, bearing in mind that such invitation or permission may legitimately be limited either to a particular part of the premises or for a specified purpose. It may be alleged, however, that the occupier has impliedly sanctioned the entry, so that the person in question becomes a visitor rather than a trespasser, and whether this is so is a question to be decided on the facts of each case. A tradesman, for example, has an implied licence to walk along a garden path to the front door for the purpose of promoting his business with the occupier, unless of course he has been clearly forbidden to do so. For a licence to be inferred there must be evidence that the occupier has permitted entry as opposed to merely tolerated it, for there is no positive obligation to keep the trespasser out. Moreover, repeated trespass of itself confers no licence (*Edwards v Railway Executive* (HL, 1952)).

CHECKPOINT

In some cases the courts have been at pains to infer the existence of an implied licence

In *Lowery v Walker* (HL, 1911), members of the public had for many years used the defendant's field as a short cut to the railway station. The defendant had from time to time objected to them so doing, however, the defendant was a local shopkeeper and was not particularly keen to upset his customers by continual objections. Eventually, the defendant pastured a horse in the field. The horse proved to be of a fairly violent disposition. The animal attacked and injured the claimant, who succeeded in his action on the basis that he was an implied licensee, not a trespasser. However, this and other cases were decided at a time when trespassers were afforded little or no protection and, in view of the more favourable treatment which they now receive (see later in this Chapter), the courts may be less favourably inclined to find an implied licence in a case such as *Lowery*.

Three further types of entrant must now be considered. First, those who enter premises for any purpose in the exercise of a right conferred by law are, by s. 2 (6) of the Act, treated as having the occupier's permission to be there for that purpose (whether they in fact have it or not) and are therefore owed the common duty of care. Secondly, s. 5 (1) provides that where a person enters under the terms of a contract with the occupier there is, in the absence of express provision in the contract, an implied term that the entrant is owed the common duty of care and, according to *Sole v W. J. Hallt Ltd* (HC, 1973), he may frame his claim either in contract or under the 1957 Act. It is further provided by s. 3 (1) that where a person contracts with the occupier on the basis that a third party is to have access to the premises, the duty owed by the occupier to such third party as his visitor cannot be reduced by the terms of the contract to a level lower than the common duty of care. Conversely, if the contract imposes upon the occupier any obligation which exceeds the requirements of the statutory duty, then the third party is entitled to the benefit of that additional obligation. Thirdly, those who use public (*Greenhalgh v British Railways Board* (CA, 1969)) or private (*Holden v White* (CA, 1982)) rights of way are not visitors for the purposes of the 1957 Act, though the user of a private right of way is now owed a duty under the Occupiers' Liability Act 1984 (see later in this Chapter). An owner of land over which a public right of way passes may be liable for misfeasance, but not negligent nonfeasance (*McGeown v Northern Ireland Housing Executive* (HL, 1994)).

Exclusion of the duty

It has already been seen that the duty owed to a contractual entrant is governed by the terms of the contract and that a person who enters under a contract to which he is not a party is owed, as a minimum, the common duty of care. In the case of non-contractual entrants, at common law, an occupier can exclude or limit his liability by notice, provided that reasonable steps were taken to bring it to the visitor's attention and that, upon its proper construction, it was clear and unambiguous. Such was the decision in *Ashdown v Samuel Williams & Sons* (CA, 1956), where it was held that the claimant, who was injured by the negligent shunting of a railway wagon upon the defendant's premises, was defeated in her claim by exclusion notices erected by the defendant stating that persons entered at their own risk and that no liability would be accepted for injury or damage, whether caused by negligence or otherwise.

KEY CASE

ASHDOWN V SAMUEL WILLIAMS & SONS LTD (1956)
The liability of occupiers under s.2(1), above) can be excluded "by agreement or otherwise", but the ability of business occupiers to exclude liability has been severely restricted by the Unfair Contract Terms Act 1977. However, private occupiers, within certain limits, still have freedom to exclude liability. Here, the second defendants occupied industrial premises surrounded by land owned by the first defendants. Access to the defendant's land was by two roads, one of which was safe. The other road, a short cut, could be used at the user's risk and notices to that effect had been posted on the land. The

claimant was taking a short cut when she was injured by the negligent shunting of railway trucks.

Held: (CA) The defendants, who had taken all reasonable steps to bring to the claimant's attention the conditions attached to their permission to enter, were not liable.

Comment
Even though this was a pre-Occupiers' Liability Act 1957 decision it is still good law, indeed s. 2(1) closely reflects it. In *White v Blackmore* (1972) a majority in the Court of Appeal concluded that it was an effective defence. The claimant's husband was killed at a jalopy race when a car's wheel became entangled in the safety ropes and he was catapulted 20 feet through the air. A notice had been posted at the entrance to the course, and at other points about the field, absolving the defendants of all liability arising from accidents. The deceased was held to have entered subject to these conditions.

LEGISLATION HIGHLIGHTER

Despite the criticisms of the defeat of the claim by exclusion notices in *Ashdown*, s.2(1) of the 1957 Act clearly envisages the possibility of an exclusion of the duty and, as seen above, the decision was followed by a majority in *White v Blackmore* (CA, 1972). The principle is said to rest upon the basis that if an occupier can prevent people from entering his premises, then he can equally impose conditions, subject to which entry is permitted. However under the Unfair Contract Terms Act 1977 it is not possible to exclude the common duty of care in relation to business liability in cases of personal injury: s. 2 (1), and any exclusion in relation to property damage or loss must satisfy the requirement of reasonableness: s. 2 (2).

The operation of s.2 of the 1977 Act is confined to those situations where there is "business liability" which is defined in s.1(3) as liability for breach of duty arising from things done in the course of a business or from the occupation of premises used for the business purposes of the occupier. There is no exhaustive definition of "business", though s.14 provides that it includes a profession and the activities of any government department or local or public authority. It should also be noted that s.1(3) has been modified by s.2 of the Occupiers' Liability Act 1984 which enables a business occupier to exclude liability to those whom he allows on to his land for recreational or educational purposes, provided that it is not part of his business to grant access for such purposes. This could apply to a sports and social club operated by an employer for the benefit of employees, or to students on field trips.

As a result of these provisions *Ashdown* would be decided differently today. But whether or not *White v Blackmore* (CA, 1972) is similarly affected is debatable, because in that case private land was used to stage a fundraising event for charity, and it is not certain whether that would be classed as a business activity.

The common duty of care

LEGISLATION HIGHLIGHTER

The common duty of care is defined in s.2(2) as:

"a duty to take such care as in all circumstances of the case is reasonable to see that the visitor will be reasonably safe in using the premises for the purposes for which he is invited or permitted to be there".

The duty is to ensure that the visitor will be reasonably safe. It is not a duty to make the premises safe. Clearly if the premises are safe, the visitor will be safe. However the visitor can be rendered safe in other ways. If effective steps are taken to exclude the visitor from dangerous areas this will suffice. Equally a notice alerting the visitor to a danger may also enable the visitor to be safe. The duty may extend to taking steps to see that one visitor does not deliberately harm other visitors by foreseeably likely misconduct (*Cunningham v Reading Football Club Ltd* (HC, 1991)). The standard is that of reasonable care. In *Sutton v Syston Rugby Club* (CA, 2011) a player who gashed his knee on a plastic object embedded in the rugby pitch claimed that the rugby club was negligent in failing to carry out a sufficiently thorough inspection of the pitch in advance of the match. The judge rejected the suggestion that a quick walk over inspection of the rugby pitch was sufficient to discharge a club's duty to take such care as was reasonable. In allowing the club's appeal the Court of Appeal held that a "reasonable walk over of the pitch" was sufficient. It was unlikely that any such object would be present, anything more than a reasonable visual inspection went beyond what a reasonable occupier would regard as necessary. Another factor that influenced the court is that games of rugby are desirable activities within the meaning of section 1 of the **Compensation Act 2006**.

There is no obligation to take precautions in respect of an obvious danger which the claimant is perfectly capable of recognising and protecting himself against. In *Staples v West Dorset DC* (HC, 1995) the defendant was occupier of the celebrated harbour feature known as the Cobb in Lyme Regis. The seaward end of the Cobb is partly submerged by the tide; as a result it is covered by slippery seaweed. The claimant slipped and fell on the seaweed. He complained that there was no notice warning of this danger. The court took the view that the danger was obvious. The risk of slipping was one which the claimant had to deal with. *Darby v National Trust* (CA, 2001) is to similar effect. The claimant's husband drowned while swimming in a pond on the National Trust's Hardwick Hall estate. She alleged that there was a breach of duty because there were no signs prohibiting swimming. The court took the view that the risks of swimming were obvious. If a sign was required for this pond, it would be required for every bathing beach and this was absurd. Those using premises are expected to use reasonable care for their own protection, and cannot rely on the occupier to guard against every conceivable hazard.

Whether the occupier has complied with the common duty of care depends upon the facts, taking into account such matters as the nature of the danger, the purpose of the visit and the knowledge of the parties. In particular, there is express provision in the Act relating to children, those with special skills, warning notices and independent contractors, and these will now be considered in turn.

1. Children

LEGISLATION HIGHLIGHTER

The Act provides that the amount of care, or of lack of it, which the occupier may expect in the visitor is a relevant consideration, so that, by s. 2(3)(a), the occupier must be prepared for children to be less careful than adults.

In *West Sussex CC v Pierce* (CA, 2013) the Court of Appeal considered the application of this test in the context of a school. The claim related to a thumb injury sustained by a child on a drinking fountain which had recently been installed at the school in question. The accident occurred during horseplay when the claimant was trying to punch his brother. Over 70,000 drinking fountains of this kind had been installed up and down the United Kingdom and there had been no previous incident reported. Bearing in mind that children do not behave like adults, so any risk assessment should take account of their behaviour, the question was whether visitors to the school were reasonably safe in using the premises; the answer was yes. There was no possible basis for suggesting that the decision to install this particular design of drinking fountain created any significant risk. The accident resulted from the actions of the claimant, not from any danger for which the defendant could be held responsible.

At common law, where a child was injured by some especially attractive but potentially dangerous object which had allured him on to the land, the occupier could not be heard to say that the child was a trespasser in relation to the very thing which had attracted him in the first place. This remains the case under the 1957 Act.

KEY CASE

GLASGOW CORP V TAYLOR (1922)

Section 2(3)(a) provides that an occupier must be prepared for children to be less careful than adults. Common law principles provide guidance in interpreting the section. In this case a seven-year-old child died from eating poisonous berries which he had picked from a shrub in a public park. The berries looked like cherries or large blackcurrants. The shrub was not. It was alleged that the local authority knew of the poisonous nature of the berries but the shrub was not fenced off in any effective way, nor was any warning of the danger given.

Held: (HL) The defendants were liable. The tempting-looking berries constituted an "allurement" to children. The children were lawful visitors and there was a responsibility to protect them against what were fairly obvious dangers.

Comment

(1) In *Latham v Johnson & Nephew* (CA, 1913) the court said that there is a duty not to lead children into temptation. But an object such as a pile of stones against a wall could not possibly constitute a trap and did not amount to an allurement.

(2) In *Jolley v Sutton LBC* (HL, 1998) a derelict boat constituted an allurement and a trap but these were not the causes of the accident. The immediate cause was that the claimant, a 14-year-old boy, and a friend decided to repair the boat and jacked it up with a car jack. The Court of Appeal had ruled that, even making full allowance for the unpredictability of children's behaviour, it was not reasonably foreseeable that the boys would work under a propped up boat; it was too remote because it occurred in an unforeseeable manner. Allowing the appeal, the House of Lords approached the question of what risk was foreseeable in much wider terms and said that the trial judge had been correct to consider the reasonable forseeability of the wider risk that children would meddle with a dilapidated boat and be at risk of physical injury.

In *Phipps v Rochester Corp* (HC, 1955) two very young children were playing on a building site. One of them fell into a trench. The trench would have been an obvious hazard to an adult, or to an older child. It was held that the children were too young to be allowed to go to this location unsupervised.

The court considered that it was proper to have regard to the habits of prudent parents who will, where appropriate, either take steps to satisfy themselves that the place holds no danger for children, or not permit the child to wander without supervision. In the circumstances the occupier was entitled to expect that children of this age would be supervised.

Phipps was followed in *Simkiss v Rhonnda BC* (CA, 1983) and, although decided prior to the 1957 Act, is clearly consonant with the provisions of the 1957 Act which state that, in determining whether the occupier has discharged his duty, regard is to be had to all the circumstances. One of those circumstances must be what the occupier is reasonably entitled to expect of a young child's parents.

In *Bourne Leisure Ltd v Marsden* (CA, 2009), the question was whether a holiday site owner was liable for the drowning of a child in a pond, by failing to warn of the dangers and bring the pond's location to the parent's attention. The Court of Appeal held that although an occupier ought reasonably to anticipate that small children might escape the attention of parents and wander into places of danger, it does not follow that the occupier is under a duty to take precautions against such dangers.

KEY CASE

KEOWN V COVENTRY HEALTHCARE NHS TRUST (2006)

Although an occupier must be prepared for children to be less careful than adults, the extent of the occupier's liability is a question of fact and degree and depends on the particular circumstances of the case. When the claimant was 11 years old he climbed the underside of the defendant's fire escape when he fell to the ground and was injured. The trial judge acknowledged that the claimant had not only appreciated that there was a risk of falling but also that what he was doing was dangerous and that he should not have been climbing the fire escape. However, he found that the fire escape, which could be climbed from the outside, constituted an inducement to children habitually playing in the grounds of the hospital.

Held: (CA) Allowing the defendant's appeal, the Court of Appeal said that it would not be right to ignore a child's choice to indulge in a dangerous activity in every case merely because he was a child. In this case it could not be said that the risk arose not out of the state of the premises but out of what the claimant chose to do.

Comment

According to Lewison J.:

"In the present case there was nothing inherently dangerous about the fire escape. There was no physical defect in it: no element of disrepair or structural deficiency. Nor was there any hidden danger. The only danger arose from the activity of Master Keown in choosing to climb up the outside, knowing it was dangerous to do so."

The remarkable aspect of this case is that despite making these findings, the judge nevertheless was prepared to hold the defendant in breach of duty. It is unfair to judge on a four line extract from the judgment, but there is nothing here to suggest a breach of the common duty of care.

2. Special skills

LEGISLATION HIGHLIGHTER

Section 2(3)(b) provides that:

"an occupier may expect that a person, in the exercise of his calling, will appreciate and guard against any special risks ordinarily incident to it, so far as the occupier leaves him free to do so".

Thus, in *Roles v Nathan* (CA, 1963) the defendant was held not liable for the death of two chimney sweeps killed by carbon monoxide fumes while sealing up a flue in the defendant's boiler. Had they suffered injury by falling through a rotten floorboard the position would, of course, have been otherwise (see *Woollins v British Celanese Ltd* (CA, 1966)). In *Salmon v Seafarer Restaurants Ltd* (HC, 1983), a fireman was entitled to recover damages when it was reasonably foreseeable that he would be injured while fighting a blaze caused by the occupier's negligence, despite the exercise of his special skills (approved in *Ogwo v Taylor* (HL, 1988), although it is noteworthy that the Occupiers Liability Act 1957 is nowhere referred to in the speeches in the House of Lords. The House approved *Salmon*, not the application of the Act).

KEY CASE

ROLES v NATHAN 1963

Section 2(3)(b) of the 1957 Act provides that an occupier may expect that a person, in the exercise of his calling, will appreciate and guard against special risks ordinarily incident to it. Here, two chimney sweeps were called to clean an old coke-burning boiler which smoked badly. They were warned by an expert that the sweep-hole and inspection chamber should be sealed before the boiler was lit. They disregarded the warning and died when they were overcome with the fumes.

Held: (CA) The occupier was not liable. His duty had been discharged by warning the sweeps of the particular risks, and also, he could reasonably expect a specialist to appreciate and guard against the dangers arising from the very defect that he had been called to deal with.

Comment
Lord Denning said:

> "If it had been a different danger, as for instance if the stairs leading to the cellar gave way, the occupier might no doubt be responsible."

3. Warnings

LEGISLATION HIGHLIGHTER

Section 2(4)(a) of the Act, provides that an occupier may discharge his duty by warning his visitor of the particular danger, provided that the warning is sufficient to enable the visitor to be reasonably safe.

The occupier may, in accordance with s.2(4)(a) of the Act, discharge his duty by warning his visitor of the particular danger, provided that the warning is sufficient to enable the visitor to be reasonably safe. The warning may exclude the visitor from a dangerous area. "Keep out" may be sufficient. "Danger! High voltage" may be more effective. Regard must be had to those who are likely to come in contact with the notice. Children may not be able to read or understand warnings. In a location such as an airport, many of those present may not understand English, and warnings should be graphic rather than in words. It is a question of context. Even informal warnings can be effective. "Duck or Grouse" displayed on the low beam of a country pub may be perfectly effective. The crucial question is whether it enables the visitor to be safe. Simply warning that there is a danger will not count if the visitor has to encounter the danger. A notice to the effect that a pathway is slippery is of little use, if the visitors still have to use the pathway. A notice warning that a particular path is slippery, but advising an alternative route will be effective. Warning notices should be distinguished from exclusion notices. By giving a sufficient warning the occupier discharges his duty, whereas an exclusion purports to take away the right of recovery in respect of a breach. To be effective a warning must sufficiently identify the source of the danger and be brought adequately to the visitor's notice. Mere knowledge of the nature and extent of the risk is not necessarily a bar to recovery, though it may go towards establishing a defence of volenti non fit injuria or, more likely, contributory negligence (*Bunker v Charles Brand & Son Ltd* (HC, 1969); see Ch.5).

4. Independent contractors

Where a visitor suffers damage due to faulty construction, maintenance or repair work by an independent contractor employed by the occupier, s.2(4)(b) provides that the occupier will not be liable if it was reasonable to entrust the work to a contractor and he took such steps (if any) as he reasonably ought to see that the contractor was competent and had done the work properly. Assuming, therefore, that the occupier reasonably entrusted the work to a contractor whom he had checked to see was suitably qualified to do the job, he will not be liable for that contractor's defaults provided that he took reasonable steps, where necessary, to satisfy himself that the work was properly done.

CHECKPOINT

No liability if the occupier acted reasonably in entrusting the work to an independent contractor
The occupier is not necessarily expected to check work of a technical nature (e.g. lift maintenance as in *Haseldine v Daw & Son Ltd* (CA, 1941)), but in the case of a complex project he may be under a duty to have the contractor's work supervised by a qualified specialist such as an architect or surveyor (*AMF International Ltd v Magnet Bowling Ltd* (HC, 1968); it is a question of fact and degree since the occupier cannot be expected to multiply checks). Where the work is of a routine nature requiring no particular skill or expertise, the occupier may himself be expected to check it and will be liable for failing to do so (*Woodward v Mayor of Hastings* (CA, 1944)).

On a point of interpretation it was held in *Ferguson v Welsh* (HL, 1987) that the word "construction" in s. 2 (4)(b) was wide enough to embrace demolition and that the provision protected an occupier from liability for injuries to visitors not only after completion of the work, but also during its execution. The majority also held that where an occupier had notice of an unsafe system of work adopted by the contractor, he could be liable to an employee of the contractor injured thereby, although two of their Lordships thought that any such liability would be as joint tortfeasor rather than occupier.

KEY CASE

FERGUSON V WELSH (1987)

Occupiers will not normally be expected to supervise the contractor's activities to ensure that they operate a safe system of work for the employees. Competent contractors can be presumed to have safe systems as here where a tender awarded by a district council for the demolition of a building stipulated that the work must not be sub-contracted without the council's consent. The claimant was the employee of a sub-contractor who had been carrying out the work without the council's consent. He suffered serious injury as a result of the sub-contractor's unsafe system of work. When it was discovered that neither the main contractor nor the sub-contractor were covered by insurance, he sued the local authority as occupiers of the premises.

Held: (HL) The district council was not liable. It would not ordinarily be reasonable to expect an occupier, having engaged a contractor whom he has reasonable grounds for regarding as competent, to supervise the contractor's activities in order to ensure that he was discharging his duties to his employees to observe a safe system of work.

Occupier's duty to check on the competency of contractors

In *Bottomley v Tordmorden Cricket Club* (CA, 2003), the defendant club had allowed independent contractors to carry out a pyrotechnic display on its land. The claimant (an unpaid assistant of the independent contractors) suffered severe burns and other injuries during the display, and although the case was not about a risk caused by the state of the premises under the Occupiers Liability Act 1957, the defendant occupier, along with the contractors (who had no public liability insurance) was liable in common law negligence. The club had allowed the dangerous event to take place without proper safety precautions.

In *Naylor v Payling* (CA, 2004), the claimant suffered severe injuries whilst being forcibly ejected from a nightclub by a door attendant employed by the independent contractor responsible for security at the nightclub. The independent contractor had no public liability insurance and the claimant sued the defendant nightclub owner for failing to ensure that the independent contractor was insured. In this case, the defendant had not acted negligently in selecting the independent contractor and, it was held that, save in special circumstances, there was no free-standing duty to take reasonable steps to ensure that the independent contractor was insured.

Damage

In *AMF International Ltd v Magnet Bowling Ltd* (HC, 1968), it was held that financial loss consequential upon damage to property is also recoverable. The ordinary principles of causation and remoteness (see Ch.4) apply, so that a negligent occupier will not be liable if the accident was of an unforeseeable kind.

Defences

The provisions of the **Law Reform (Contributory Negligence) Act 1945** apply and s.2(5) of the 1957 Act provides that an occupier is not liable in respect of risks which the visitor willingly accepts, thus allowing for the defence of volenti non fit injuria (see Ch.5). However, where there is business liability within the meaning of the **Unfair Contract Terms Act 1977**, s.2(3) of that Act provides that a person's agreement to or awareness of a notice purporting to exclude liability for negligence is not of itself to be taken as indicating his voluntary acceptance of any risk.

THE OCCUPIERS' LIABILITY ACT 1984

Persons to whom the 1984 Act applies

The 1984 Act governs the liability of an occupier to "persons other than his visitors" in respect of injury suffered by them on the premises due to the state of the premises or to things done or omitted to be done upon them. For the position with regard to activities on the premises see *Revill v Newbery* (CA, 1996).

The terms "occupier" and "premises" have the same meanings as for the purposes of the **Occupiers' Liability Act 1957**. The expression "persons other than his visitors" includes trespassers and persons exercising private rights of way, but those using public rights of way are specifically excluded.

LEGISLATION HIGHLIGHTER

The scope of the duty

Section 1(3) of the 1984 Act provides that the occupier owes a duty if:

(a) he is aware of the danger or has reasonable grounds to believe that it exists;

(b) he knows or has reasonable grounds to believe that the non-visitor is in the vicinity of the danger concerned or that he may come into the existence of the risk vicinity of the danger; and

(c) the risk is one against which, in all the circumstances of the case, he may reasonably be expected to offer the non-visitor some protection.

The test is therefore an objective one. The first two elements relate to the existence of the risk. The third element is somewhat different. A duty will only be imposed if in all the circumstances it is reasonable to do so, and to the extent it is reasonable to do so. It will not normally be reasonable to require the occupier to take precautions against an obvious danger which the claimant should be expected to protect himself against.

CHECKPOINT

The scope of section 1(3) of the 1984 Act is not far removed from the common law duty of "common humanity" which took into account, along with the occupier's skill and resources, his actual knowledge of the trespasser's presence or of the likelihood of it. This duty was established in *British Railways Board v Herrington* (HL, 1972)). Although it seems, from the objective wording of paragraph (c), that the individual occupier's skill and resources no longer come into the equation, the position is not entirely clear as regards what knowledge is required. In particular the mere fact that an occupier has been particularly prudent will not necessarily result in liability being imposed. One example is the case of *White v St Albans City Council* (CA, 1990). There was a trench on the defendant's land. The defendant fenced it off. The claimant managed nevertheless to fall into the trench. It was held that in all the circumstances the defendant did not have reasonable grounds to believe that the claimant would get into the trench.

Where the duty arises s.1(4) states that the duty is to take such care as is reasonable in all the circumstances of the case to see that the non-visitor does not suffer injury on the premises by reason of the danger concerned.

This is the usual standard in negligence generally, and whether the occupier has discharged his duty will depend upon the circumstances in which the claimant has entered the premises, the age of the claimant, and the extent of the risk, including the burden that would be imposed upon the occupier in eliminating it.

The principle of "individual responsibility"

We have already seen that lawful visitors are expected to take reasonable precautions against obvious dangers (see *Staples v West Dorset DC* and *Darby v National Trust*). As might be expected, the same principle applies to non-visitors, and in respect of them the onus on the occupier is even lower.

KEY CASE

TOMLINSON V CONGLETON BOROUGH COUNCIL (2004)
Where the risk is obvious, an occupier is under no liability under s. 1(3) Occupiers' Liability Act 1984 for a claimant's injuries. In this case, on a hot day, the 18-year-old claimant went to a popular park with some friends. Ignoring the warning signs around a shallow lake, he dived into the water from a standing position. The stretch of water into which he dived was shallow and he struck his head and suffered appalling personal injury. The claimant accepted that on entering the water he ceased to be a visitor and became a trespasser but he claimed that the council was in its breach of duty to persons other than visitors under s.1 (3) Occupiers' Liability Act 1984. The defendants were aware of the danger and the claimant argued that the warning notices and other precautionary measures taken by the council were shown to be ineffective and did not discharge the council's duty under s. 1 (3).

The trial judge dismissed his claim but the Court of Appeal held that on account of: the attraction of the lake to swimmers; the frequency of exposure to danger; and the relatively inexpensive and simple deterrents available to reduce the risk of persons entering the lake, the council's duty had not been discharged by its notices, oral warnings and the safety leaflets issued by its employees. In other words they recognised that the council was aware of a risk, and concluded that it must therefore be liable.

Held: (HL) The House of Lords allowed the council's appeal and held that no duty of care was owed. There was no risk to the claimant from the state of premises or from anything done or omitted to be done on them. The risk of striking the lake bottom from diving into shallow water was perfectly obvious and not a risk against which the defendant might reasonably have been expected to offer the claimant some protection under s.1 (3) of the Act. Judicial concern about the effect of liability preventing desirable activities being undertaken can be seen in the comments of Lords Scott and Hoffman:

Lord Scott:

> "And why should the council be discouraged by the law of tort from providing facilities for young men and young women to enjoy themselves in this way? Of course there is some risk of accidents arising out of the joie-de-vivre of the young. But that is no reason for imposing a grey and dull safety regime on everyone."

Lord Hoffmann:

> "Mr Tomlinson was a person of full capacity who voluntarily and without any pressure or inducement engaged in an activity which had inherent risk. The risk was that he might not execute his dive properly and so sustain injury. Likewise, a person who goes mountaineering incurs the risk that he might stumble or mis-judge where to put his weight. In neither case can the risk be attributed to the state of the premises. The risk of striking the bottom of the lake by diving into shallow water was perfectly obvious and it was his own misjudgement which had caused his injury. .... A duty to protect against obvious risks or self-inflicted harm exists only in cases in which there is no genuine and informed choice, as in the case of employees, or some lack of capacity, such as the inability of children to recognise danger (*British Railways Board v. Herrington* (HL, 1972)) or the despair of prisoners which may lead them to inflict injuries on themselves (*Reeves v Commissioner of Police* (HL, 2000))."

Comment

(1) This is simply one of a number of cases involving swimming acci-dents. All have been decided against the claimant. In *Ratcliff v McConnell* (CA, 1997) (below) a student chose to trespass in the compound containing the College swimming pool, which was closed for the winter, and to dive in without checking the water level. This was

held to be an obvious danger. In *Rhind v Astbury Water* (HC, 2003) a trespasser dived into a lake and was injured, not on the lake bed as Mr Tomlinson was, but by an object lying on the bed. Again this was held not to be within any duty of care owed by the occupier. It was a risk associated with diving, not with the state of the premises.

(2) In *Mann v Northern Electric Distribution Ltd* (CA, 2010) a trespasser aged 15 was electrocuted when he climbed into an electricity substation and suffered devastating injuries. The question was whether the unauthorised access was reasonably foreseeable and whether the security precautions taken by the occupier were sufficient to keep the reasonable trespasser out. In a decision consistent with precedent limiting the imposition of liability on occupiers where claimants have acted carelessly, the Court of Appeal found that the occupier had discharged the burden of showing that it had done what was reasonably practicable to prevent unauthorised access.

(3) This approach has been carried forward into cases under the 1957 Act. This is hardly surprising; the principle that there is no liability in respect of obvious dangers was first developed in relation to lawful visitors. *Tomlinson* was applied in *Trustees of the Portsmouth Youth Activities Committee v Poppleton* (CA, 2008). Here, the claimant suffered serious injuries as the result of an accident which occurred as he was engaged in simulated rock climbing at the defendant's indoor climbing premises. He claimed for damages on the grounds that the defendant had failed to provide sufficient supervision and was in breach of its duty of care to him by failing to warn him of the nature of the risks involved. The Court of Appeal, applying *Tomlinson*, held that there was an inherent risk in the activity that the claimant voluntarily undertook and the law did not require the defendant to prevent him from engaging in that activity. Judicial concern in *Tomlinson* about the deterrent effect of liability can be seen in the comments of May L.J.:

> "If the law required training or supervision in this case, it would equally be required for a multitude of other commonplace leisure activities which nevertheless carry with them a degree of obvious inherent risk—as for instance bathing in the sea."

It is to be noted that the statutory duty under the 1984 Act applies only to personal injury or death. Liability for loss of, or damage to, property is expressly excluded by s.1(8).

Defences

Warnings

> ### LEGISLATION HIGHLIGHTER
>
> Section 1(5) of the Act provides that the occupier may, in appropriate cases, discharge his duty by taking reasonable steps to warn of the danger or to discourage persons from incurring the risk.

Whether a warning is effective will depend, among other things, upon the nature of the risk and the age of the entrant. What is adequate for an adult may not be so for a child, particularly if the danger is an allurement.

The defence of volenti non fit injuria is preserved by s. 1(6) of the Act. It remains to be seen whether it will be more readily available as against trespassers, though there seems no reason why it should be. In any event the indication in *Titchener v British Railways Board* (HL, 1983) is that it will normally be limited to dangers arising from the state of the premises. The claimant was held to have willingly accepted the risk as his within the meaning of s.1(6) in *Ratcliffe v McConnell* (CA, 1997) (above) where, having drunk about four pints of beer, he agreed to go swimming with two friends and climbed over the gate of a college open-air swimming pool which was closed for the winter. Although aware to some extent that there were warnings about the dangers of the pool, he took a running dive into the pool and suffered injuries which led to tetraplegia when he struck his head. The Court of Appeal rejected the claimant's claim for damages on the ground that he was aware of the risk and had willingly accepted it. This was an additional ground, since the court also held that the risk was an obvious one, and therefore one the claimant was well able to guard against.

> ### CHECKPOINT
>
> *Can ex turpi causa act as a defence to an action by a trespasser?*
> As far as the defence of *ex turpi causa* is concerned, it was held in *Revill v Newbery* (CA, 1996) that the fact that the claimant was a burglar did not take him outside the protection of the law, so that he was held entitled to succeed in negligence when the defendant shot him (cf. Lord Denning in *Cummings v Granger* (CA, 1977); see Ch.5). There was, however, a substantial reduction of damages for contributory negligence. The court in *Revill* took the view that, since the discharge of the gun was an activity unconnected with the defendant's status as occupier, the 1984 Act was not strictly relevant, but nevertheless thought that the common law principles applicable were analogous to the relevant statutory provisions.

It is unclear whether the above case is authority for the proposition that ex turpi can never be a defence to an action by a trespasser, at least where the defendant is actively instrumental in causing the injury (cf. *Murphy v Culhane* (CA, 1977); see Ch.5). The actual decision may well have been quite different had the claimant been injured by some defect in the premises (e.g. by falling through a hole in the floor), or had the defendant not reacted so vehemently; in either case there may have been no duty, having regard to the requirement in s. 1(3)(c) of the 1984 Act.

Exclusion notices

> **LEGISLATION HIGHLIGHTER**
>
> By virtue of s. 1 (5) of the 1984 Act it is possible to exclude liability by means of an appropriate notice or other warning:
>
> "Any duty owed by virtue of this section in respect of a risk may, in an appropriate case, be discharged by taking such steps as are reasonable in all the circumstances of the case to give warning of the danger concerned or to discourage persons from incurring the risk."

Furthermore the provisions of the **Unfair Contract Terms Act 1977** do not apply to the duty under the 1984 Act. Trespassers do of course pose particular problems because, depending upon the point at which they enter the premises, they may be less likely to see a notice than a lawful visitor. There is as yet no case law on the point, but it would seem that as long as notices are deployed at reasonable points, the occupier will have fulfilled the duty.

Liability of an independent contractor to a trespasser

At common law, the liability of a contractor to the trespasser rests upon ordinary negligence principles. The fact that the claimant is a trespasser in relation to the occupier is not relevant except in so far as the trespasser's presence may be less foreseeable. Thus in *Buckland v Guildford Gas Light and Coke Co* (HC, 1949), the defendants, who had erected electricity cables on a farmer's land close to the top of a tree, were held liable for the death of a young girl who climbed the tree and was electrocuted. This decision is unaffected by the 1984 Act, but there are indications in *Herrington* that no distinction should be drawn in this respect between occupiers and non-occupiers, in which case the defendants in *Buckland* would now owe the duty of common humanity.

You should now understand:

☐ The scope of an occupier's liability and range of potential defendants including landlords, occupiers, and those involved in the construction process.

☐ The duty of care owed by occupiers to lawful visitors under the Occupiers' Liability Act 1957 (covers personal injury and damage to property).

☐ The duty of care owed by occupiers to trespassers under the Occupiers' Liability Act 1984 (imposes liability only for personal injury).

☐ The Occupiers' Liability Act 1957 is silent on the meaning of "occupier", "premises", and "lawful visitors" so these terms are interpreted by reference to the common law.

QUESTION AND ANSWER

QUESTION

Button Builders took over an office block for redevelopment. They immediately erected a prominent notice outside the entrance to the premises stating: "Keep out—No admission to unauthorised persons".

Haris, a car salesman, misread his map and mistakenly drove his car onto the premises and parked close to the building. A pallet of bricks fell onto his car and seriously damaged it. When Clive, a surveyor from the Council, called at the premises to inspect the work in progress he realised that he had forgotten his safety helmet. Although aware of the risk of injury, Clive decided to proceed with the inspection anyway. He suffered severe head injuries when a piece of scaffolding which had been negligently erected by Scaffkwik, contractors engaged by Button Builders, fell on him. Olga took her eight-year-old son, Danny, to play in the park which adjoined the premises. As Olga was checking her emails on her mobile phone Danny slipped away and wandered into the premises. He suffered a leg injury when he fell through a broken floor.

Advise the parties as to the principal issues of law which will arise under the Occupiers' Liability Acts of 1957 and 1984 if they attempt to recover their losses.

This question requires a discussion of the duty of care owed by occupiers to lawful visitors under the Occupiers' Liability Act 1957 (which covers personal injury and damage to property) and the duty of care owed by occupiers to trespassers under the Occupiers' Liability Act 1984 (which imposes liability for personal injury only). Each potential claimant should be considered separately:

Haris: He actually has no authority to be on the premises. He is not a "visitor" for the purposes of the 1957 Act. It is probable that as a trespasser (a trespass to land depends on the fact of unauthorised presence, not Haris's state of mind), Haris is a person who is "other than a visitor". If so, his situation is governed by the Occupiers' Liability Act 1984. Section 1(3) of the 1984 Act provides that the occupier owes a duty to a trespasser if: (a) he is aware of the danger or has reasonable grounds to believe that it exists; (b) he knows or has reasonable grounds to believe that the non-visitor is in the vicinity of the danger concerned or that he may come into the vicinity of the danger; and (c) the risk is one against which, in all the circumstances of the case, he may reasonably be expected to offer the non-visitor some protection. This depends on whether it was foreseeable that trespassers would enter these premises in these circumstances. The duty owed by Button Builders was to take such care as is reasonable in all the circumstances to see that Haris did not suffer injury on the premises by reason of the danger concerned. Whether Button Builders has discharged its duty would depend upon the extent of the risk of the bricks falling and the burden that would be imposed in eliminating it. However, liability under the 1984 Act applies only to personal injury or death so liability for the broken windscreen (property damage) suffered by Haris is expressly excluded by section 1(8). Note also that the duty can be performed by giving an effective warning, so even if Haris suffered personal injury, the notice here may achieve this: s 1(5).

Clive: as a lawful entrant the liability of Button Builders would be governed by the Occupiers' Liability Act 1957. Section 2(3)(b) provides that "an occupier may expect that a person, in the exercise of his calling, will appreciate and guard against any special risks ordinarily incident to it, so far as the occupier leaves him free to do so". Button Builders may deny liability on this ground and seek to argue that as a surveyor from the Council, Clive should have appreciated and guarded against the risk of injury associated with his surveying work by wearing his safety helmet. (see *Roles v Nathan* (1963)). Button Builders may also argue that the actual fault is that of the contractors. Under s 2(4)(b) of the Act, the occupier is not liable (although Scaffkwik may be) where 'in all the circumstances he had acted reasonably in entrusting the work to an independent contractor and had taken such steps (if any) as he reasonably ought in order to satisfy himself that the contractor was competent and that the work had been properly done." It may not be reasonable to check complex technical work (see *Haseldine v Daw* (1941), but each case turns on its own facts: *Woodward v Mayor of Hastings* (1945).

Danny: In some cases children have been deemed to be implied licensees at common law, and therefore visitors within the 1957 Act, rather than trespassers. However, there must normally be some specific "allurement", and some evidence of toleration of the children (see *Addie v Dumbreck* (1929)). Note that in *Glasgow Corporation v Taylor* (1922) the claimant was a lawful visitor, so the allurement there simply related to the danger. If Danny is deemed to be a visitor section 2(3)(a) of the 1957 Act provides that the occupier must be prepared for children to be less careful than adults. However, the extent of the occupier's liability for children is a question of fact and degree and much depends on the particular circumstances of the case. Since Danny is a young child the court would consider whether Olga had taken proper steps to supervise him and prevent him wandering without supervision (*Phipps v Rochester Corp* (1955); *Simkiss v Rhondda BC* (1983); *Bourne Leisure Ltd v Marsden* (2009)). This places the onus firmly on the parent or carer, rather than the occupier. Today the courts seem less willing to treat children as not being trespassers where they have no actual permission, so the same considerations will apply as for Haris.

Liability for Dangerous Products

INTRODUCTION

Part I of the Consumer Protection Act 1987, which has been in force since 1988 was enacted to give effect to an EC Directive requiring the harmonisation of law on product liability throughout the European Union. Subject to certain defences, the Act creates a regime of strict liability, although existing common law rights remain unaffected so that if, for some reason, the Act does not apply a claimant may still be able to sue in negligence. You should note that, since s.1 of the Act makes it clear that the Act is intended to give effect to the requirements of EU law, it must be interpreted consistently with the Directive. It is therefore necessary to look at the Directive if the Act is not easily interpreted, since the Directive may clarify the position.

STRICT LIABILITY UNDER THE 1987 ACT

Although a successful claim under the Act is not dependent upon proof of negligence, the claimant will have to prove that he or she suffered damage caused wholly or partly by a defect in a product.

Parties to the action and the meaning of "product"
No mention is made in the Act of who may be able to sue, so anyone who suffers damage would appear to be covered, whether a user of the product in question or not. As far as potential defendants are concerned, s.2(2) provides that the following are liable for the damage:
  (a) the producer of the product;
  (b) any person who holds himself out as producer by putting his name or trade mark or other distinguishing mark on the product;
  (c) an importer of the product into a Member State from a place outside the EC in order to supply it to another in the course of his business.

- "Producer" is defined in s.1(2) to mean either the manufacturer, or the person who won or abstracted the product (which is intended to cover mining and other extraction of natural raw materials and also the production of agricultural produce, meat or fish) or, where the product has not been manufactured, won or abstracted but the essential characteristics of which are attributable to an industrial or other process having been carried out (for example agricultural produce which has been processed in some way, e.g. milling corn into flour), the person who carried out that process. The underlying intention is that the producer should be liable. However, for policy reasons it is important to have an available defendant within the European Union. Under the Brussels Regulation, there are rules enabling legal action to be brought conveniently against the defendant within the European Union. If the producer is based elsewhere these rules would not apply. Extending primary liability to someone who "own brands" a product is specifically intended to encourage these undertakings to take full responsibility for these products. The obvious example of this is supermarket own brand goods. Furthermore, by s.2(3), the supplier (e.g. retailer) is liable if he fails within a reasonable time to comply with the claimant's request to identify one or more of the persons to whom s.2(2) (see above) applies, or to identify his own supplier. This again is intended to ensure that the claimant is not frustrated by inability to identify the relevant defendant. The object is not that there should be actions against suppliers, but that the threat of action will induce the supplier to identify his own source of supply. The underlying Directive makes this rather clearer than the Act does.

- "Product" is defined in s.1(2) as any goods or electricity and, although the definition of "goods" in a later part of the Act is wide enough to cover fixtures in buildings and component parts of the building itself, there is no liability under this legislation where goods are supplied by virtue of the creation or disposal of an interest in land. So the producer of a central heating system which is fitted into an existing property is potentially liable, but the Act will not apply if a property is sold with the central heating system already installed. Component parts and raw materials also fall within the definition of "product" as distinct from the overall product in which they are comprised.

Thus, where X manufactures a product containing a defective component manufactured by Y which causes damage (e.g. a car with faulty brakes), both X and Y are jointly and severally liable. However, s.1(3) in effect provides that the mere supplier of a product containing component parts will not, by reason only of that supply, be treated as supplying those components. This means that liability under s.2(3) in respect of a product containing a defective component will only arise for failure to identify the producer or supplier of the finished product. The dealer who sells a car such as the one discussed above will therefore have satisfied his obligations under the Act if he identifies the manufacturer of the car.

It has been noted that, where the essential characteristics of a product are attributable to an industrial or other process having been carried out, the processor may be liable as a producer within the meaning of s.1(2). The failure of the legislature to define "essential characteristics" or "industrial or other process" may present difficulties of interpretation, particularly with regard to foodstuffs. The essential difficulty is determining whether responsibility for the defect rests with the farmer who produced the agricultural raw material, or with the undertakings which processed the raw material and subsequently incorporated it into foodstuffs. There may be several steps in this chain. One example would be where a farmer grows corn, this is then milled into flour, the flour is incorporated into pastry, the pastry is sold to a baker who then incorporates it into a pie. A defect could be incorporated at any stage. The original corn could be mouldy, impurities could be introduced in the milling process or in the production of pastry, and the final pie could be stored in unhygienic conditions.

The meaning of "defect"

According to s.3(1) a product is defective if its safety is not such as persons generally are entitled to expect. In *Tesco Stores v Connor Fredrick Pollard* (CA, 2006), a small child suffered injury after swallowing detergent from a bottle which was supposed to have a child resistant cap. The cap was found to provide the level of protection that persons generally would be entitled to expect because the resistance required to open it was significantly more than a child could be expected to apply. The "safety" of a product expressly includes safety "with respect to products comprised in that product" (i.e. components and raw materials), and a product may be unsafe not only if there is a risk of personal injury but also if it poses a risk of damage to property.

LEGISLATION HIGHLIGHTER

In determining what persons generally are entitled to expect, s.3(2) provides that account shall be taken of all the circumstances including the following specific matters:

(a) the way in which and the purposes for which the product has been marketed, its get-up, and warnings and instructions for use accompanying it;

(b) what might reasonably be expected to be done with or in relation to the product;

(c) the time when the product was supplied by its producer to another.

The reference in (a) to the purposes for which the product has been marketed may indicate that a balance has to be struck between known risks associated with a product and the benefits which it seeks to confer. Adopting this interpretation in the case of drugs, for example, a product which produces harmful side-effects is not necessarily defective if its disadvantages are outweighed by the long-term benefits. With regard to (b), a product which is clearly intended for a particular use may not be defective if it causes damage when put to an entirely different use. Similarly, where the defendant reasonably contemplates that something would be done to the product before use (e.g. testing), he may argue that there is no defect if that thing is not done (cf. *Kubach v Hollands* (HC, 1937), which is of course a decision at common law, but the reasoning is persuasive).

KEY CASE

KUBACH V HOLLANDS (1937)

This case illustrates that a warning of danger, provided it is adequate in the circumstances, may absolve the defendant. Here, a manufacturer sold a chemical to the second defendants (retailers) and an accompanying invoice expressly stated, inter alia, that the chemical must be "examined and tested by user before use". The retailer failed to observe the manufacturer's instructions to test the product before labelling it and sold it to a science teacher. The chemical was used in a school experiment and it exploded, injuring a schoolgirl and her father.

Held: (HC) The retailer was liable but the manufacturers were not. They had given an adequate warning and the retailer had ignored it. Liability would of course now depend on compliance with the Act. Many products need to be "handled with care". This does not mean that they are necessarily defective. Accurate, comprehensible instructions will

> enable users to avoid harm. If the instructions are incomplete or themselves defective in some way, this will render the product defective.

The provision of appropriate warnings and instructions is clearly relevant in cases of this kind. The manufacturer can argue that when he supplied the product it was not defective because it came with appropriate instructions. He can also argue that it was reasonable to assume that it would be handled in accordance with the instructions. Furthermore the defect of which the claimant complained was that the product as supplied had not been tested. All this occurred after the manufacturer had parted with the product and any control over it. Alternatively, it might be argued that if the product is dangerous, the producer is responsible for ensuring that clear warnings and instructions are given at all stages.

The concluding words of s.3(2) provide that the mere fact that a product supplied after that time is safer than the product in question does not require the inference that there is a defect. This clearly makes allowance for the fact that improved safety standards are constantly being developed, so that what is considered safe, say, in 2008, will not necessarily be so in 2014.

Fault based arguments against liability are not relevant in a "no-fault" regime

In *A v National Blood Authority* (HC, 2001), the claimants had been infected with hepatitis C through blood transfusions which had used blood products obtained from infected donors. It was held that, in relation to blood products, persons generally were entitled to expect that they were entirely safe, in the absence of any public warnings to the contrary. This was so, even though there was no means to test the product for contamination, so the defendant had done all it could. This decision would suggest that liability under the statute is considerably stricter than the common law.

KEY CASE

IDE V ATB SALES LTD (2008)
The claimant was injured in a cycling accident. The accident was not witnessed, and the claimant had no recollection. The left side of the handlebar had snapped, but it was not clear if this had caused the accident, or if the claimant had lost control, and the handlebar fractured when the bike hit the ground. There was evidence that the handlebar was not as strong as others of the type, and some evidence of developing cracks. This was consistent either with a manufacturing defect or a lack of durability. Both would make the bike defective. The

judge rejected the hypothesis that the fall caused the crash. Therefore the defect caused the crash.

Held: (CA) Since the claim was under the Consumer Protection Act it was not strictly necessary to make any finding as to the *specific* nature of the defect and the claimant was entitled to succeed. Per Thomas L.J.:

"Moreover as this was a claim under the Consumer Protection Act, it was, in my view, unnecessary to ascertain the cause of the defect. The issue was simply was the fall caused [by loss of control] or was there a defect."

Damage

Section 5(1) defines damage for the purposes of Part I as "death or personal injury, or loss of or damage to property (including land)". Claims for property damage are, however, limited in several important respects. First, the defendant will not be liable for damage to the defective product itself, nor for damage to any product supplied with a defective component comprised in it (s.5(2)). A parallel may be drawn here with the common law, where such claims are regarded as being concerned essentially with the quality of the product so that, in the absence of a contract, there is generally no liability in tort on the ground that the loss is purely economic (see *Muirhead v Industrial Tank Specialities Ltd* (CA, 1986); see Ch.2). Secondly, there is no liability unless, at the time of the damage, the property was "of a description of property ordinarily intended for private use, occupation or consumption" and was intended by the claimant mainly for such purposes (s.5(3)). A person who suffers damage to his business property must therefore sue in negligence. This definition does leave a grey area. Most stand-by generators are bought by businesses, but a minority are bought for private use. What level of secondary use will count as making the product one "ordinarily intended" for private use? Finally, no claim will lie where the value of the property does not exceed £275, excluding interest (s.5(4)).

Defences

The Act provides specific defences:

LEGISLATION HIGHLIGHTER

Section 4(1), paras (a)–(f), provides for the following defences:
(a) The defect is attributable to compliance either with a domestic enactment or with Community law.
(b) The defendant did not at any time supply the product to another. A broad definition is given to "supply" in a later Part of the Act to include not only the usual types of supply contract, but also gifts.

(c) The defendant supplied the product otherwise than in the course of his business and either he does not fall within s.2(2) (i.e. he is not a producer, "own-brander" or importer) or he does so only by virtue of things done otherwise than with a view to profit. Thus, for example, the producer of home-made wine who gives a bottle to a friend (or, indeed, who charges simply to cover the costs of his production) will be protected.

(d) The defect did not exist at the relevant time. By s.4(2) the "relevant time" means, in relation to electricity, the time at which it was generated; as far as all other products are concerned it means, in the case of the defendant to whom s.2(2) applies, the time when he supplied the product to another and, in the case of a supplier, the time of the last supply by a person who is within the ambit of that section.

(e) The state of scientific and technical knowledge at the relevant time was not such that a producer of products of the same description as the product in question might be expected to have discovered the defect if it had existed in his products while they were under his control. This is the so-called "development risks" or "state of the art" defence which has provoked considerable controversy, not least because it would appear to offer a wider protection than the corresponding provision of the Directive which it seeks to implement. Whereas art.7(e) of the Directive would only allow the defence if the state of scientific and technical knowledge was not such as to enable the existence of the defect to be discovered, s.4(1)(e) of the Act talks in terms of what might be expected to have been discovered by a producer of products of the same description as the product in question. The statutory language may thus lead to the inference that the defendant is to be judged by the standards of the hypothetical, reasonable producer of the same, or similar, products, which is tantamount to saying that the defendant will not be liable in the absence of negligence. The apparent discrepancy between the Directive and the Act was, however, referred to the European Commission, and the issue was taken to the European Court of Justice, who concluded that there was nothing to suggest that s.4(1)(e) could not be interpreted so as to achieve the purpose of art.7(e) of the Directive. "Relevant time" bears the same meaning as in (d) above and will normally be the time of supply of the product by a person to whom s.2(2) applies. Remember of course that the Act is intended to give effect to the Directive, and should therefore be interpreted accordingly.

(f) The defect constituted a defect in a product containing the defendant's component part (or raw material) and was wholly attributable to the design of the overall product or to compliance by the defendant with instructions given by the producer of the overall product. This will not affect the liability of the producer of the overall product.

Apart from the above defences, the effect of s.6(4) is to preserve the claimant's contributory negligence as a partial defence to a claim against any person under the Act.

It has been noted that the claimant must prove that the damage was caused wholly or partly by the defect. It seems clear that there can be no question of categorising the damage as too remote but if, for example, the claimant seriously misuses the product, or an intermediary fails to follow clear instructions (e.g. to test before use), it is unlikely that the product would be found to be defective. Once it has been categorised as defective, however, failure by an intermediary to examine it will not defeat the action on grounds of causation.

Three final points are worthy of note:

(1) Although there is a limitation period of three years, this is subject to an overall long-stop period of 10 years from the relevant time (see above), after which no claim may be brought. Thus, for example, where a product manufactured and distributed in 2003 causes damage in 2015, a claim against the manufacturer will lie only in negligence.

(2) Section 7 of the Act prevents the defendant from limiting or excluding his liability, either contractually or otherwise.

(3) Section 1(1) states that the purpose of Part I of the Act is to give effect to the Directive and that it should be construed accordingly. Any ambiguity in the Act should therefore be resolved, wherever possible, by reference to the Directive and not merely in accordance with traditional canons of construction.

COMMON LAW NEGLIGENCE

Where the **Consumer Protection Act** does not apply, the claimant must rely upon existing common law remedies. If the claimant acquires defective goods under a sale or similar supply contract the first line of attack is to sue the supplier in contract for breach of implied undertakings relating to quality. Although these contractual obligations are generally imposed as statutory implied terms only upon those who supply in the course of a business, they are strict and entitle the claimant to recover both in respect of goods which simply fail to work or which are less valuable than those contracted for, and where the defect causes personal injury or damage to property. If the claimant does not have a contract, however, or indeed where an action against the supplier is not viable (e.g. the supplier is in liquidation), an action in tort may be pursued.

The manufacturer's duty

The source of the duty owed by a manufacturer to the ultimate consumer is to be found in the so-called narrow rule in *Donoghue v Stevenson* (HL, 1932), expressed by Lord Atkin as follows:

> "A manufacturer of products, which he sells in such a form as to show that he intends them to reach the ultimate consumer in the form in which they left him with no reasonable possibility of intermediate examination, and with the knowledge that the absence of reasonable care in the preparation or putting up of the products will result in an injury to the consumer's life or property, owes a duty to the consumer to take that reasonable care."

The term "products" includes not only food and drink, but such diverse items as lifts, hair-dye, motor vehicles, chemicals and underpants. The essential point is that these will be consumed, applied to the body or directly used, so can cause harm. The manufacturer's duty extends to the packaging of the product and to any labels, warnings or instructions for use which accompany it (e.g. *Vacwell Engineering Co Ltd v B.D.H. Chemicals Ltd* (HC, 1971)). If the manufacturer of a finished product incorporates a component made by another, he is under a duty to check on its suitability and may be liable for failure to do so should it turn out to be defective (*Winward v TVR Engineering* (CA, 1986)). Where products are already in circulation when the defect is discovered the manufacturer must take reasonable steps to warn of the danger or to recall the products (*Walton v British Leyland (UK) Ltd* (HC, 1978)).

Manufacturer and ultimate consumer

The term "manufacturer" has been judicially interpreted to include any person who actively does something to the goods to create the danger, such as assemblers, servicers, repairers, installers and erectors. In *Malfroot v Noxal Ltd* (HC, 1935), an assembler was held liable when the side-car which he had negligently fitted to a motor-cycle came adrift and injured the claimant. In *Stennett v Hancock and Peters* (HC, 1939) a vehicle repairer was liable when the repair failed within hours.

Apart from the end user of the product, an "ultimate consumer" is any person who may foreseeably be affected by it. In *Stennett v Hancock and Peters* the claimant was a pedestrian who was struck by a part which fell off the lorry in question.

KEY CASE

STENNETT V HANCOCK AND PETERS (1939)
A manufacturer has been given a wide interpretation by the courts and extended beyond the maker of a product. Mere distributors or suppliers and repairers of goods may incur liability. Here, the claimant pedestrian was injured when he was struck by a flange which had come off one of the wheels of the first defendant's lorry. The wheel had earlier been repaired by the second defendants and the cause of the accident was found to be the careless reassembly of the wheel by one of the second defendant's employees.

Held: (HC) The claim against the first defendant failed but the second defendant (the repairer) was held liable under the principle of *Donoghue v Stevenson*.

Comment
This principle has been extended to:
(i) suppliers: liability can arise in circumstances where a supplier would normally be expected to check for safety before selling the goods. In *Andrews v Hopkinson* (HC, 1957), a second-hand car dealer was held liable because defective steering on an 18-year-old car could easily have been discovered by a competent mechanic;
(ii) distributors: in *Watson v Buckley, Osborne, Garrett & Co* (HC, 1940) the distributors who failed to test a hair dye for themselves before they advertised it as harmless were held to be negligent.

Breach of duty

The duty is one to take reasonable care. Sometimes a very high standard is imposed, as in *Grant v Australian Knitting Mills* (PC, 1935), where the presence of a contaminant on one of many thousands of products was held to be sufficient evidence of breach. In other cases the defendant has satisfied the judge that he has done all he reasonably could, as in *Daniels v White and Tarbard* (HC, 1938), where the judge was very impressed with the "state of the art" and "foolproof" systems in place. This can lead to uncertainty. The defendant will no longer necessarily escape liability, however, merely by showing that he had a "foolproof" system of manufacture and quality control, because the very fact of the defect may be interpreted as evidence of negligence in the operation of the system by a servant for whom the defendant is vicariously liable (*Hill v J. Crowe (Cases) Ltd* (HC, 1978)).

Intermediate examination and causation

The normal rules of causation and remoteness apply (see Ch.4) and, as elsewhere in negligence, difficulties may arise where the negligence of two or more defendants causes indivisible damage. According to Lord Atkin's formulation of the rule, the duty only arises where there is "no reasonable possibility of intermediate examination", which would suggest that there is no duty where such a possibility exists. From a conceptual point of view, however, it is perhaps preferable to deal with the issue of intermediate examination in terms of causation. Thus, failure by an intermediary to make an examination reasonably expected of him, may either break the chain of causation (assuming that the examination would, or should, have revealed the defect) or, given that the manufacturer originally created the danger, both manufacturer and intermediary will be liable, as in the Irish case of *Power v Bedford Motor Co* (1959). What is clear is that, if the intermediary's failure to examine is to be regarded as severing the causal chain, it must at least have been likely that an examination would be made, so that a mere foreseeable possibility of inspection will not suffice (*Griffiths v Arch Engineering Co Ltd* (HC, 1968)).

KEY CASE

GRIFFITHS V ARCH ENGINEERING CO (1968)

The claimant was injured by a portable grinding tool which he borrowed from the first defendants but which was actually owned by the second defendants. It was lent by the first defendants without further inspection and without knowledge that it had been made dangerous by an employee of the second defendants.

Held: (HC) A mere opportunity for intermediate examination will not exonerate the defendant; there must be a reasonable probability of intermediate inspection. The first defendants were liable because they had an opportunity to examine the tool and failed to do so. The second defendants were equally liable because they had no reason to suppose that such an examination would be carried out.

Comment

A manufacturer who has no reason to believe that an intermediate inspection will take place, whether by a third party or the consumer, will be liable. The product need not reach the ultimate consumer in a sealed package for the duty to arise; in *Grant v Australian Knitting Mills* (PC, 1935) the Privy Council stated that for the rule to apply, "the customer must use the article exactly as it left the maker, that is in all material features, and use it as it was intended to be used".

If, of course, the intermediary acquires actual knowledge of the defect and fails to withdraw the product from circulation, the manufacturer will probably escape liability (*Taylor v Rover Co Ltd* (HC, 1966)), just as he will where the intermediary ignores a clear warning to test the product before use (*Kubach v Hollands* (HC, 1937)).

CHECKPOINT

Apart from anything that the intermediary may do in relation to the product, regard must equally be had to what the consumer himself does.

Failure by the claimant to conduct an expected examination or a continued use of the product after discovery of the defect, may produce one of two consequences, depending upon the degree of fault:

- either the chain of causation will be broken (see, e.g. *Farr v Butters Bros* (CA, 1932)); or
- the loss may be apportioned under the Law Reform (Contributory Negligence) Act 1945.

The claimant will not be barred from recovery, however, where he has no effective choice in assuming a risk created by a defect of which he is aware (*Denny v Supplies and Transport Co Ltd* (CA, 1950)).

Proof of negligence and damage

The burden rests upon the claimant as in any other negligence action; however, despite judicial reluctance to allow the application of res ipsa loquitur (see Ch.3), damage caused by a defect in manufacture, as distinct from a defect in design, may easily give rise to an inference of negligence (*Grant v Australian Knitting Mills Ltd* (PC, 1936)). On the other hand, if it is equally probable that the defect arose after the manufacturing process and is wholly unconnected with anything that the manufacturer may have done, the claimant will fail (*Evans v Triplex Safety Glass Co* (HC, 1936)).

EVANS V TRIPLEX SAFETY GLASS CO LTD (1936)

The claimant bought a Vauxhall car fitted with a windscreen made of "Triplex Toughened Safety Glass". A year later when he was driving the car, with his wife and son as passengers, the windscreen suddenly and for no apparent reason cracked and disintegrated. The occupants of the car were injured and brought an action against the manufacturers of the windscreen.

Held: (HC) The defendants were not liable. To establish liability there must be sufficient evidence that the defect existed in the product when it left the manufacturer. Here, the windscreen might have been interfered with and the defect introduced by any one of a range of alternative causes other than a defect in manufacture. Relevant factors were the lapse of time between the purchase of the windscreen and the accident and the possibility that the glass may have been strained when screwed into its frame.

What is the position where the defect is in the design of the product (as distinct from a manufacturing fault)?

Where the alleged defect is in relation to the design of the product, the claimant may face greater difficulty in that the issue of negligence is to be judged in the light of current knowledge which must be proved to have been such as to render the damage foreseeable (cf. the "state of the art" defence under s.4(1)(e) of the Consumer Protection Act 1987 where it is for the defendant to prove that such knowledge did not exist).

As far as damage is concerned, liability exists only in respect of personal injury or damage to other property, though consequential financial loss is also recoverable. Pure economic loss is, however, irrecoverable (*Muirhead v Industrial Tank Specialities Ltd* (CA, 1985)), and it is clear from *Murphy v Brentwood DC* (HL, 1990) that both damage to the product itself and "preventive damage" represented by the cost of avoiding apprehended physical damage to persons or property (e.g. by repairing or discarding the product) is regarded as pure economic loss (see further Ch.2). The difficulty remains of determining the circumstances in which a defective product can be said to have caused damage to "other" property.

When can a defective product be said to have caused damage to "other" property?

In *Aswan Engineering Establishment Co v Lupdine Ltd* (CA, 1987) the claimants lost a quantity of waterproofing material when the plastic buckets in which it was contained collapsed as a result of exposure to high temperatures. In an action against the manufacturers of the buckets Lloyd L.J. thought that the contents could be regarded as property distinct from their container, thus bringing the case within *Donoghue v Stevenson* principles (though the claim failed on other grounds). If this analysis is correct, the claimant would seem to be in a better position at common law than under the 1987 Act (see s.5(2)).

REVISION CHECKLIST

You should now understand:

☐ English law on product liability has been developed both through the common law and the wider European Community context.

☐ The justifications for the imposition of strict liability on manufacturers and producers for defective products which cause harm.

☐ The Consumer Protection Act 1987 sets down a strict liability regime for defective products on a wide range of potential defendants.

☐ The limits on the scope of the Act such as cases where the loss concerns damage to property not intended for private use and where the 10-year "cut-off" limitation period applies; these restrictions do not apply in common law negligence.

QUESTION AND ANSWER

QUESTION

The most notable feature of the Consumer Protection Act 1987 is that it removes the need for a claimant who has been harmed by a defective product to establish fault on the part of the defendant but there are limitations on its scope. To what extent does the Act improve on the law of common law negligence in respect of product liability?

This question requires an analysis of the provisions of the Consumer Protection Act 1987 with discussion of its limitations.

Outline the regime of strict liability under the Act which is not dependent upon proof of negligence. This eliminates the uncertainty as to what standard will be demanded in the particular case: *Grant v Australian Knitting Mills* (1935), *Daniels v White* (1938) and *Hill v J. Crowe (Cases) Ltd* (1978) illustrate the possibility of inconsistency or uncertainty here.

Explain the meaning of "product" and the range of potential defendants who can be liable under the Act. Primary liability rests on the producer, but an importer or "own-brander" may also be liable for policy reasons, as may a supplier. The idea is that a defendant can always be identified.

Discuss the meaning of "defect" and the factors taken into account in determining what persons generally are 'entitled to expect'. It must be safety related. It can apply to the packaging, labelling or instructions, but the level of safety is "what persons generally are entitled to expect", so it is strict, but not absolute liability.

Evaluate the defences available under the Act.

Consider the interpretation of the Act in cases such as *A v National Blood Authority* (2001) and *Ide v ATB Sales Ltd* (2008) which suggest that liability under the statute is considerably stricter than the common law, in particular that the standard of safety is based on objective standards, not what is practicable, and that the claimant does not have to show exactly how the defect caused the harm. It should be noted that claims for damage are limited in several important respects under the Act and there is no liability for damage to business property or where its value does not exceed £275 so that a claimant must rely on common law negligence for recovery of such losses.

Employers' Liability at Common Law

INTRODUCTION

This Chapter is concerned with an employer's personal liability for common law negligence *to* its employees in respect of harm suffered at work. The incidence of an employer's vicarious liability for the torts committed *by* its employees is dealt with in Ch.10. In addition to this common law duty there is a large body of statutory obligations cast upon the employer for the protection of its workmen, and it is not uncommon for an employee to sue both in negligence and for breach of statutory duty (see Ch.9). Indeed, in recent times, the scope and content of the statutory duty has meant that it is the primary cause of action. This is however likely to change following the restriction of actions for breach of statutory duty for cases arising after 1 October 2013, with the common law duty assuming much greater importance.

The employer is under an obligation to have liability insurance to cover claims: section 1 of the Employers' Liability (Compulsory Insurance) Act 1969. Ironically no civil action will lie for breach by an employer of this statutory duty: *Richardson v Pitt-Stanley* (CA, 1995).

Since 1897 there has also been statutory compensation for employment related injuries which was not based on fault, but it initially had limited coverage; see the Workmens Compensation Act 1897 as amended. Since 1948 this scheme, which placed the liability to pay on the employer, has been replaced by a national insurance system providing benefits to the victims of industrial accidents and to those who contract certain prescribed industrial diseases. Although the statutory scheme is not dependent upon proof of fault, it has not led to any diminution in the number of actions brought by employees against their employers.

In any given situation, an injured employee may be able to rely on a number of causes of action:

- Breach of statutory duty.
- Breach of the specific common law duty we are about to consider.
- Vicarious liability for the negligence or other tort of a fellow worker.
- Breach of some other duty—e.g. the common duty of care under the Occupiers Liability Act 1957.

Any or all of these can be alleged, and any or all may succeed, but of course damages can only be recovered once.

A claim may also be joined to a claim against a third party, for example the supplier of a product which has injured the employee.

Example

Javaid worked in a bakery. His job was to clean the bread tins in an industrial scale dishwasher, using a strong cleaning fluid. It came in a partly dilute form; if it spilt onto skin it needed to be cleaned off at once, but if it spilt onto clothing, even though Javaid did not wear special safety boots or clothing, it was not dangerous.

One day Javaid's manager, Kate, called him to a meeting. A stranger, Lee, was there. He was the representative of a cleaning fluid supplier. Kate told Javaid that the bakery was changing from the cleaning fluid they had been using to a new one. Javaid asked Lee whether he should use the new fluid in the same way and take the same precautions. Lee said that he should.

A few days later Javaid spilled some of the new fluid on his foot. He ignored it, but later found that the fluid had eaten through his shoe and sock and caused a serious chemical burn to his foot.

It now appears that the new fluid only comes in a concentrated form, which must be handled only when wearing special safety clothing and boots, and decontamination must be undertaken immediately if there is a spillage. There are regulations covering this. The original fluid came in this concentrated form, but also in the dilute form Javaid was used to. Lee was only aware that it came in the concentrated form.

There is no evidence that any risk assessment of the use of the new fluid was undertaken. Kate admits she did not compare the two fluids or ask any questions about the safety precautions to be taken with the new one.

Here Javaid can bring a claim under the regulations (if the accident was before 1 October 2013) a common law claim (specifically for failing to establish or operate a safe system of work—as we will see shortly), a claim alleging that Kate was negligent in relation to the introduction of the new fluid, and the bakery is vicariously liable, and also a claim that Lee was negligent in his advice about the use of the new fluid, for which *his* employer is vicariously liable. If he only sued the bakery, it could bring a claim for contribution against the cleaning fluid supplier.

TORT

THE NATURE OF THE DUTY

KEY CASE

WILSONS & CLYDE COAL CO LTD V ENGLISH (1938)
The claimant miner was injured at the defendant's coal mine. He was travelling through the pit at the end of a day shift and was crushed when the haulage plant was set in motion. The haulage equipment should have been stopped during travelling time. The defendant employers claimed that they had discharged their duty of providing a safe system of work by appointing a competent and qualified manager.

Held: (HL) The employers were liable. The obligation for the employee's safety is fulfilled by due care and skill but it is not fulfilled by delegation to employees, even though selected with due care and skill. The employers could not avoid their duty to provide a reasonably safe system of working by delegation to a competent employee.

Traditionally, the duty is said to be threefold, as explained in *Wilsons and Clyde Coal Co Ltd v English*:
- the provision of a competent staff of men;
- adequate premises, plant and equipment;
- a proper system and effective supervision.

This wording is now somewhat dated, and most of the significant aspects of the duty today centre around risk assessment and management, planning activities and ensuring that premises and equipment are suitable and in good condition. In other words they largely relate to a safe system of work. The duty is not absolute but is discharged by the exercise of reasonable care and is thus typical of the duty of care in the tort of negligence generally. Indeed employer and employee is one of the classic duty situations traditionally recognised in negligence. It is important to recognise that although we talk about "the employer's duty of care", it is in reality "this employer's duty of care to this employee (or group of employees)". This is because there are so many types of employment, and they arise in very different circumstances and conditions. What is relevant in a steel mill is not what is relevant on a construction site, or in an office. Also some employees are regularly asked to work at customers' premises, or elsewhere "off-site".

The employer's non-delegable duty is owed to each employee individually, so it will be affected by knowledge of particular circumstances. In *Paris v Stepney BC* (HL, 1951), it was held that, where a garage worker known by his employer to be one-eyed was engaged on work involving a risk of injury to his remaining eye, the employer was under a duty to provide him with goggles, even though as the law then was, there was no such duty generally (there is today). This was because the consequences of the loss of the second eye were such that the employer should have taken special measures.

Although most of the cases concern work accidents, the duty clearly extends to guarding against disease and gradual deterioration in health as a result of adverse working conditions: *Thompson v Smith's Shiprepairers (North Shields) Ltd* (HC, 1984). An employer's liability to safeguard employees against these particular types of harm has expanded as the result of advances in medical and scientific knowledge about the effects of materials such as asbestos and conditions such as repetitive strain injury and industrial deafness.

COMPETENT STAFF

At one time there was an implied term in a contract of service that employees accepted certain risks incidental to their employment. One of those risks was that they might be injured by the negligence of a fellow employee for whom the employer was not, therefore, vicariously liable. This was the doctrine of common employment. This meant that where the immediate cause of the accident was the carelessness of a fellow employee, the employer was not liable. The doctrine did not in principle apply to the negligence of managers and supervisors, but this was often hotly disputed.

As means were sought to mitigate the harshness of the doctrine, the courts started to hold the employer liable for negligence in the selection and deployment of workers. This was part of the employer's own, non-delegable, responsibility. Although the doctrine of common employment was abolished in 1948, and therefore there is today no obstacle to an action based on vicarious liability, its ghost continues to influence the content of the employer's personal duty in this area, which survives and co-exists with his vicarious liability.

The abolition of the doctrine of common employment has of course drastically reduced the significance of this particular aspect of the duty, since employees will usually be able to sue their employer vicariously for the wrongdoings of a colleague. This is even more likely since the expansion of vicarious liability in *Lister v Hesley Hall* (HL, 2001). The personal duty may still be relevant, however, where the wrongful act, such as an assault or violent horseplay, takes place outside the course of employment. In this case the employer may be liable for breach of its personal duty if he or she knew or ought to have known of his employee's vicious or playful tendencies: *Hudson v Ridge Manufacturing Co Ltd* (HC, 1957). So, too, if an employee is instructed to perform a task for which he or she has not been properly trained and thereby injures a workmate, the employer may be liable, even though there might be difficulty in establishing negligence by the employee for the purposes of vicarious liability, although this is in truth more an aspect of the organisation of the work.

KEY CASE

GENERAL CLEANING CONTRACTORS V CHRISTMAS (1953)
A window cleaner was sent to clean the windows of a club. He was instructed by his supervisors in the sill method of cleaning windows and, while he was holding on to a window-sash for support, the window came down on his fingers causing him to fall to the ground.

Held: (HL) The employers were liable. The employer owes a duty to employees to select competent employees and to give proper instructions and supervision; the claimant should have been given proper instruction and told to test the sashes.

Comment
This duty to select competent employees is of little importance since the abolition of the doctrine of common employment because the employer will be vicariously liable for the tort of one employee against another. However, it can be relevant. The duty to plan, risk manage, train and supervise is, however, much more important.

SAFE PLANT AND EQUIPMENT

The duty here is to take reasonable care to provide proper plant and equipment and to maintain them as such. This includes the provision of protective devices and clothing, and, in appropriate cases, a warning or exhortation from the employer to make use of such equipment: *Pape v Cumbria CC* (HC, 1992).

Although compliance with a statutory obligation is evidence of a discharge of the common law duty, it is not conclusive.

In *Bux v Slough Metals Ltd* (CA, 1973), the claimant foundry worker lost the sight of one eye when splashed with molten metal. Although the employer had, in compliance with statutory regulations binding upon him, provided protective goggles, he was held liable for breach of his common law duty, which here extended to persuading and even insisting upon the use of protective equipment. This case also demonstrates that compliance with a statutory obligation, whilst evidence of a discharge of the common law duty, is not conclusive of the matter. Most employees will now be protected (for pre-October 2013 cases) by the Personal Protective Equipment at Work Regulations 1992, which impose a statutory duty to take all reasonable steps to see that protective equipment is properly used, though it is also the employee's duty to use it.

With regard to injury caused by defective equipment, it was held in *Davie v New Merton Board Mills Ltd* (HL, 1959) that the duty to provide proper tools was satisfied by purchase from a reputable supplier. The decision has now been reversed, however, by the Employers' Liability (Defective Equipment) Act 1969, which renders an employer personally liable in negligence if two conditions are met: first, that the employee is injured in the course of his employment by a defect in equipment issued by the employer for the purposes of the employer's business; and, secondly, that the defect is attributable wholly or partly to the fault of a third party (whether identifiable or not). Strict liability is thus imposed upon the employer if his employee can prove that some third party, such as the manufacturer, was at fault, though contributory negligence is a defence. The manufacturer may now, of course, be strictly liable under the **Consumer Protection Act 1987** (see Ch.7), but this does not in any way affect the employer's position under the 1969 Act.

Equipment is defined as "any plant and machinery, vehicle, aircraft or clothing". In *Coltman v Bibby Tankers Ltd* (HL, 1988) "equipment" for the purposes of the Act was widely defined to include a ship on which the claimant was employed.

KEY CASE

COLTMAN V BIBBY TANKERS (1988)

This case arose out of the sinking of *The Derbyshire* with the loss of all hands off the coast of Japan in 1980. The claimants, personal representatives of a crew member, alleged that, due to the manufacturer's negligence, the ship was defectively constructed. They claimed that these were defects in equipment and argued that the ship was "equipment" within s.1 of the Employers' Liability (Defective Equipment) Act 1969.

Held: (HL) For the purposes of the Act the meaning of the word "equipment" can include ships or vessels. It was what the crew were working with, as well as being the workplace. The Act should, as protective legislation, be broadly interpreted.

Comment

Equipment is given a broad interpretation. In *Knowles v Liverpool City Council* (HL, 1993) the word embraced any material furnished by the employer for the purposes of his business and was not confined to

such things as tools and machinery, and their Lordships also considered that the Act would apply even though the employee was neither required to use, nor had in fact used, the equipment in question,
as long as it harmed him. Here it was held to include a flagstone being
laid by a council workman. This was what he was working on, not what
he was working with, but the distinction is immaterial.

Apart from the 1969 Act the employee may be able to rely (for pre-October
2013 claims) on the **Provision and Use of Work Equipment Regulations 1992**
which provide, inter alia, that employers must ensure that work equipment is
so constructed or adapted as to be suitable for the purpose for which it is
used or provided, and that such equipment is maintained in an efficient
state, in efficient working order and in good repair. The definition of "work
equipment", however, is not as wide as under the 1969 Act. In one case a
mechanic was injured due to a defect in the van he was working on. It was
held that the van was not equipment issued to him to enable him to do his
job so was not his work equipment. The van driver might have had a claim if
injured in the same way.

SAFE PREMISES

As far as "premises", or "place of work" is concerned, the employer is
expected to make the place, and the access to that place, as safe as reasonable care and skill will allow. In *Latimer* v *A.E.C. Ltd* (HL, 1953) the claimant slipped on the factory floor. The floor had been flooded as the result of
a very heavy thunderstorm, and when the flood subsided it left a slippery oily
film on the surface. The House of Lords held that it was not unreasonable for
the defendants to work the night-shift rather than close the factory until the
oily surface had been made completely safe. In the circumstances there was
insufficient evidence of want of reasonable care. So danger caused by some
fleeting, or temporary, or exceptional condition might not invoke liability; but
each case must always be considered on its facts. Again, attitudes to health
and safety at work have developed in the past half century, and there is today
more emphasis on risk assessment and management. Note also that this
claim could have been brought under the **Occupiers Liability Act 1957**, but
there is a tendency, here and elsewhere, to treat employment cases as part of
a closed system.

In *Mitchell v United Co-operatives Ltd* (CA, 2012) the extent of an
employer's duty to provide a safe place of work for assistants working in a
shop located in an area at high risk of robberies was considered. The Court of

Appeal held that the employer was not, in all the circumstances of the case required to provide full-time guards to deter the criminals nor expected to prevent the robberies taking place. This followed a full analysis of the cost and likely effectiveness of the provision of guards or other measures, such as security screens. On the facts, none of the suggested measures represented sufficiently good "value".

The duty to provide a safe place of work has been held to apply equally in relation to premises in the occupation or control of a third party when the employee is working away from the employer's premises: *Wilson v Tyneside Window Cleaning Co* (CA, 1958). In appropriate circumstances an employer may therefore be expected to go and inspect the premises to see that they are reasonably safe for the work to be done upon them; but the fact that the employer does not have control of the premises is important in determining whether he has been negligent.

SAFE SYSTEM OF WORK

This is the expression used to describe such matters as the organisation of the work, the manner in which it is to be carried out, the number of men required for a particular task and the part that each is to play, the taking of safety precautions, and the giving of special instructions, particularly to inexperienced workers: *Speed v Thomas Swift & Co Ltd* (CA, 1943). There are three principal aspects, namely the evaluation of the situation—often called the "risk assessment", the design and putting in place of a system covering all relevant aspects, and finally ensuring the continuing effective operation of the system. In *Wilsons and Clyde Coal Co* (HL, 1938) it was said that there is no responsibility on the employer for "isolated or day-to-day acts of the [employee] of which the [employer] is not presumed to be aware and which he cannot guard against". He is responsible for "the practice and method adopted in carrying on the [employer's] business of which the [employer] is presumed to be aware and the insufficiency of which he can guard against". In this case the employer had placed dangerous cutting machinery in a narrow mine passage, despite being aware that employees used this passage on a frequent basis. It was held that this amounted to an unsafe system of work. In many instances employees do not follow approved schemes of work, ignoring measures established for their own safety. The reasons for this state of affairs cover a wide spectrum, ranging from wilful disregard, through inexperience, mere inattention, annoyance, to the safety measure getting in the way of work. This is something the employer must recognise and put measures in place to guard against. It is the common law equivalent of the requirement under Article 6.1 of Directive 89/391 that the employer:

"shall take the measures necessary for the safety and health protection of workers, including prevention of occupational risks and provision of information and training, as well as provision of the necessary organisation and means".

SPEED V THOMAS SWIFT AND CO LTD (1943)

The claimant was loading a ship from a barge, an operation which was normally carried out while the ship's rails were left in position. Sections of the rail had been damaged and the resulting circumstances made it unsafe on the occasion in question to load the ship. As a result the claimant was injured.

Held: (CA) The employers were liable because in the circumstances they had not laid out a safe system of work.

Comment

(1) The general practice of a particular trade will be relevant in deciding whether or not the duty has been breached, but in *General Cleaning Contractors v Christmas* (HL, 1953) the House of Lords said that where a practice of ignoring an obvious danger has evolved it is not reasonable to expect an individual workman to devise precautions. In this case the claimant was cleaning outside windows. He opened a window slightly, and held on to the ledge to balance. As he did so, the bottom sash moved; he fell and was injured. It was held by the House of Lords that it is not up to workmen to devise and take safety precautions. It is the duty of the employer to consider the situation, devise a suitable system, instruct the men what they must do and supply any necessary equipment, for example, window wedges in this case. Lord Oaksey said:

> "An employer must take into account that workmen may have disregard for their own safety. This means they must minimise the danger of a workman's own carelessness and take reasonable care to ensure that employees comply with necessary safety precautions."

Here, of course, the workman was working on the customer's premises, so the employer was not directly responsible for them, but this did not affect the requirement for a proper system.

(2) What is reasonable depends on the circumstances. In *Hopps v Mott MacDonald Ltd* (CA, 2009) a consultant electrical engineer was injured by an explosive device as he was working in and around Basrah. He

claimed that his employer should have carried out a risk assessment to assess the suitability of the proposed transport arrangements and should only have allowed him to travel in an armoured vehicle. In determining whether particular steps, such as confinement to the airport until armoured vehicles were available for transport, should have been taken, the court took account of the risks to which the claimant and others were exposed. It was held that the risks the claimant faced could not, if he was to carry out his job, be eliminated and it was not unreasonable for the claimant to have been carried around Basrah in an unarmoured vehicle. In this case the Compensation Act 2006 (section 1) applied on the ground that a finding of liability on the employer would prevent the desirable activity of reconstructing the infrastructure of Iraq being undertaken.

The employer is always under a duty to take reasonable precautions for his employee's safety, but he is not an insurer of safety, nor is his relationship to his employee similar to that of a schoolteacher to his pupil. In appropriate circumstances, no doubt, an employer can rely on the good sense of a skilled worker to avoid danger of which he has been warned. In general, however, an employer cannot expect his employees to lay down and operate a system for themselves.

The employer does not discharge his duty merely by providing a safe system unless reasonable steps are also taken to see that it is put into operation, and the employer must be mindful of the fact that workers are often careless of their own safety. On the other hand, it may not be necessary to warn or advise an experienced worker of the risks with which he should be familiar: *Baker v T. Clarke (Leeds) Ltd* (CA, 1992). See also *McDermid v Nash Dredging and Reclamation Co Ltd* (HL, 1987)—even though the employer has devised a safe system, it will be liable upon proof of a negligent failure to put it into practice.

In *Johnstone v Bloomsbury Health Authority* (CA, 1991) it was held that requiring the claimant to work such long hours as might foreseeably injure his health could constitute a breach of duty, although a majority expressed the view that the implied contractual duty to take reasonable care for an employee's safety is subject to any express term imposing an absolute duty to work certain specified hours.

However, an employer's liability does not extend to the prevention of economic loss by, for example, advising the employee to take out insurance: *Reid v Rush & Tomkins Group Plc* (CA, 1989), nor to the prevention of injury to health caused by self-induced intoxication: *Barrett v Ministry of Defence* (CA, 1995).

PSYCHIATRIC INJURY CAUSED BY "STRESS AT WORK"

An employer's liability for psychiatric harm as the result of occupational stress is a developing area of liability.

An employer who becomes aware that stress at work is having an adverse effect on the mental health of an employee is under a duty to take positive steps to prevent the harm.

Walker v Northumberland CC (HC, 1995) held that a safe system of work extends to a duty to take extra steps to protect an employee against the risk of foreseeable psychiatric harm. The special control mechanisms for psychiatric harm claims arising from accidents (as laid down in *Alcock v Chief Constable of South Yorkshire* (1992)) do not apply to claims for psychiatric injury arising from occupational stress, which are a quite different type of case. The question is simply whether the employer has breached his duty not to injure the health of his employees.

KEY CASE

WALKER V NORTHUMBERLAND COUNTY COUNCIL (1995)
The claimant, an area social services officer, having suffered two mental breakdowns was dismissed on grounds of ill health. He alleged that his ill health was caused by the stress of his work and claimed damages from his employers.

Held: (HC) The first nervous breakdown was unforeseeable. However, when the claimant returned to work after this nervous breakdown the risk to his mental health was reasonably foreseeable. The employer was liable for failing to take extra steps to protect him against the risk of foreseeable psychiatric harm.

Comment
The concept of a safe system of work includes an employer's duty to protect against psychiatric harm in circumstances where such harm is foreseeable as the result of occupational stress.

Sutherland v Hatton (2002)

Here, four conjoined appeals were made against the trial judges' findings that the employers concerned were liable for psychiatric injury as the result of stress at work (three of the cases involved public sector employers).

Held: (CA) Three of four appeals were allowed. The Court of Appeal stressed that the ordinary principles of employers' liability applied; an employer will only be liable if he had reason to believe that the damaging stress was foreseeable and had failed to take reasonable steps to prevent it. There are no special control mechanisms (as per *Alcock*) applying to claims for psychiatric injury arising from the stress of the work; the issue is simply whether the employer has breached his duty not to injure the health of his employees. The House of Lords affirmed this.

Comment

(1) There are no intrinsically stressful occupations (in the sense that an employer ought to anticipate stress issues "on general principles") and unless an employer knows of some particular problem or vulnerability of an employee he is entitled to assume that employees can withstand the normal pressures of a job. The indications of the employee's vulnerability to psychiatric injury caused by occupational stress must be plain enough for any reasonable employer to realise that steps should be taken to assist the employee. According to Hale L.J.:

> "His duty is to take reasonable care. What is reasonable depends, as we all know, upon the foreseeability of harm, the magnitude of the risk of that harm occurring, the gravity of the harm which may take place, the cost and practicability of preventing it, and the justifications for running the risk ... ".

(2) Hale LJ stressed that in every case it is necessary to ask not only what the employer could but what the employer should have done. Also, whether the claim involves a public or a private sector employer, its resources and the size and scope of the employer's operation will be relevant to this question.

Unless an employer knows of some particular problem or vulnerability of an employee he is entitled to assume that employees can withstand the normal pressures of a job. An employer's duty of care in respect of psychiatric harm is owed to workers as individuals and, since vulnerability to stress varies between employees, an employer must heed warnings from those who are less able to cope, and take reasonable notice of what is going on in relation to its employees. The test for liability takes account of the conduct of the reasonable and prudent employer, taking positive thought for the safety of his employees in the light of what he knew or ought to have known: *Barber v Somerset CC* (HL, 2004), which approved the dicta in *Sutherland* referred to above. An employer was not fixed with knowledge of the vulnerability to stress where it was provided in a confidential medical questionnaire submitted to the occupational health department: *Hartman v South Essex Mental Health and Community Care NHS Trust* (CA, 2005).

KEY CASE

BARBER V SOMERSET CC (2004)

Barber, a conscientious school teacher and one of the unsuccessful claimants in *Hatton*, appealed to the House of Lords. He had spoken about his work overload with one of the senior management team and was subsequently on certified sickness absence suffering from stress and depression. On his return to work he told his managers that he was not coping with his workload. No steps were taken to assist him and as a consequence of the pressure he developed a psychiatric illness and had to stop working.

Held: (HL) Barber's appeal against the Court of Appeal's finding, that it was not foreseeable that if he continued with his existing workload he was liable to develop a psychiatric illness, was allowed. The House of Lords unanimously approved of the general guidance in respect of psychiatric harm caused by stress at work set out in *Hatton v Sutherland*.

Comment

(1) In terms of the steps the employer should take to prevent harm their Lordships approved the 16 guiding propositions and statement by Hale L.J. in *Hatton*.

(2) In *Daw v Intel Corporation* (UK) Ltd (CA, 2007) the Court of Appeal held that in reference to counselling services in *Barber* did not make such services a panacea by which employers could discharge their duty of care in all cases. Here the employee repeatedly told her managers that she had to work excessive hours to complete her work and it was held that the only way of dealing with her problems would have been for management to reduce her workload. The consequences of these management failings were not avoided by the provision of counsellors.

Serving forces personnel who allege breach of their employer's duty of care may be met by an argument of combat immunity. This was first articulated in England in *Mulcahy v Ministry of Defence* (CA, 1996) where it was held that there were policy reasons for denying the existence of a duty of care to a serviceman who, at the time of the accident, was engaging the enemy in hostilities. This immunity was initially extremely broad, although it never covered actions simply because they occurred during military or naval operations: *Shaw Savill v Commonwealth* (HC Australia, 1940). The scope of the immunity was considered by the Supreme Court in *Smith v MoD* (SC, 2013). It applies to activities and decisions which take place during actual combat operations, and may extend to tactical decisions closely associated with combat. However it will not extend to decisions on matters such as training and the selection and provision of equipment which have been taken remotely from the "heat of battle". In one of the cases considered in *Smith* the troops directly responsible for "friendly fire" casualties were covered by combat immunity, but issues relating to whether the tanks fired on should have been fitted with electronic identification were not. The Supreme Court expressly rejected a broad policy argument that the whole conduct of the armed forces as such should be excluded from a duty of care.

One clear instance where combat immunity will not apply is where the activity is merely training. There are many examples. *Jebson v Ministry of Defence* (CA, 2000) is a case where the defendant employers were liable when the claimant, one of a group of soldiers returning in a drunken state from a night out, fell when he tried to climb onto the roof of the army truck. The trip had been organised by the employer, and, although the claimant was not on duty as such, the trip was subject to military regulations. He claimed that in failing to have someone in the back of the truck to supervise him and his fellow soldiers the employers had breached their duty of care. It was held that:

- the defendant owed a duty to supervise;
- the defendant was in breach of a duty to supervise the soldiers;
- the damage was not too remote because it was not specifically fore-seeable that the soldier would have tried to climb onto the roof, under the circumstances rowdy behaviour was foreseeable and the damage was within that risk.

Of course in such cases all the usual elements must be established.

THE SCOPE OF THE DUTY

The duty arises only where the employer-employee relationship exists so that it will not, for example, avail an independent contractor. However, the defendant may owe other duties to an independent contractor, e.g. under the **Occupiers Liability Act 1957** although it can expect the contractor to guard against the risks of his own trade: *Roles v Nathan* (CA, 1963) applying section 2 (3) (b) of the Act "an occupier may expect that a person, in the exercise of his calling, will appreciate and guard against any special risks ordinarily incident to it, so far as the occupier leaves him free to do so."

It extends to those acts which are reasonably incidental to the employment and is owed to each employee individually, the consequence of which is that the personal circumstances of the employee must be taken into account, in so far as the employer knew or ought to have known of them.

Finally, although the duty is frequently dealt with under its various sub-headings, it is to be remembered that there is in effect but a single duty to take reasonable care in the conduct of operations so as not to subject employees to unnecessary risks.

DELEGATION

Since the duty is personal it is said to be non-delegable, so that the employer does not discharge its obligation by entrusting its performance to another, whether that other be an employee or independent contractor (*Wilsons and Clyde Coal Co Ltd v English* (HL, 1938)). Although, as far as the employment of contractors is concerned, some doubt was cast upon this proposition by *Davie v New Merton Board Mills Ltd* (HL, 1959), the effect of that decision was reversed by the **Employers' Liability (Defective Equipment) Act 1969,** and the widely accepted view is that an employer who entrusts performance of his duty to a person other than an employee remains responsible for the defaults of that person: *McDermid v Nash Dredging & Reclamation Co Ltd* (HL, 1987).

REVISION CHECKLIST

You should now understand:

☐ **The distinction between an employer's liability for harm caused *by* his employees (vicarious liability) and liability for harm caused *to* his employees (personal liability).**

☐ **The personal and non-delegable nature of the employer's responsibility for the safety of his employees.**

☐ An employer's liability arises not only for failure to adopt a safe system of working but also when a safe system is operated negligently.

☐ Occupational stress is a developing area of liability; an employer who becomes aware that work-related stress is having an adverse effect on the mental health of an employee is under a duty to take positive steps to prevent the harm.

QUESTION AND ANSWER

QUESTION

Hendrick had been struggling to meet the demands of his creative job at Rexcel Designs which, because of cost cutting measures introduced by Rexcel, had increased significantly over the past two years. Hendrick did not complain to his manager about his workload because he was keen to be promoted and was concerned that he would be disadvantaged if he complained. However, for months all Hendrick's colleagues could see that Hendrick was exhibiting signs of stress and anxiety. Gill, who has a reputation as the workplace practical joker, emailed Hendrick with a message pretending to have come from the Managing Director of Rexcel Designs containing the statement: "Hendrick is really hopeless, he has no new creative ideas and the work he produces is dull and boring." Upon receiving the email Hendrick suffered a severe mental breakdown and is now unable to work.

Advise Rexcel Designs as to its liability for Hendrick's nervous breakdown

ANSWER

There are two distinct issues. Employers are under a duty to take reasonable care for the health, including mental health, of employees: *Walker v Northumberland* (1995), but the question of whether Hendrick's stress was foreseeable will need to be explored. Employers are under a duty to employ competent and suitable staff and the extent to which Gill's practical joke caused the harm and, if so, whether Rexcel Design is liable for her act, either under this principle: *Hudson v Ridge Manufacturing Co Ltd* (1957), or vicariously, if the act is in the course of Gill's employment.

As to the first issue, the crucial point is, did Rexcel know or should they, through the management, have known that Hendrick was susceptible to psychiatric injury as a result of stress at work? If yes, then Rexcel is under a duty to take extra care to avoid such harm. However, an employer is entitled to assume that an employee can withstand normal pressures of job unless he knows of some vulnerability: *Hatton v Sutherland* (2002) approved in *Barber v Somerset* (2004).

The key proposition set out by Hale L.J. in *Hatton v Sutherland* will need to be considered: "The threshold question is whether this kind of harm to this particular employee was reasonably foreseeable."

What was reasonable foreseeable here depends on what Rexcel knows or ought reasonably to know about Hendrick's stress. In Hale L.J.'s 16 guiding propositions foreseeability of stress is identified as the key determinant in any claim. The employer must have prior knowledge of the problem in order for a claim to succeed whether the employee has a duty to inform the employer of their condition or not. In *Walker v Northumberland CC* the claimant's first nervous breakdown was unforeseeable but when he returned to work the risk to his mental health was reasonably foreseeable and the employer was liable.

In *Hartman v South Essex NHS Trust* (2005), applying the *Hatton* principles, the Court of Appeal held that the employer could not be fixed with knowledge of the employee's vulnerability. It was not reasonably foreseeable to her employers that she would suffer psychiatric injury and, accordingly, they were not in breach of their duty to her. In Hendrick's case we are told that he has not informed his manager of his stress but we are also told that it is apparent to all his colleagues that Hendrick is stressed and anxious. In these circumstances Hendrick may argue that Rexcel, through the manager, ought reasonably to have known about his work-related stress.

Rexcel is vicariously liable for the tort of one employee against another but the position in respect of liability where one employee is injured by an attack or horseplay by another is less straightforward. As well as vicarious liability, as an employer Rexcel owes a duty to employees to select competent employees and to give proper instructions and supervision. In *Hudson v Ridge Manufacturing Co Ltd* (1957) an employee was injured by a known, persistent practical joker. The employer was liable for breach of his personal duty because he should have dealt with this. Gill has a reputation as a practical joker, so Rexcel may similarly be liable for the harm caused by her email to Hendrick.

Until recently Gill's actions would definitely be seen as outside the course of employment—it was entirely separate from work; in Ch. 10 you will see that the scope of vicarious liability now extends to acts 'closely connected to the employment', but even this is unlikely to apply to what seems to be a purely private piece of malicious harassment.

Breach of Statutory Duty

INTRODUCTION

Breach by the defendant of an obligation cast upon him by statute (other than one which expressly seeks to impose liability in tort) may, apart from giving rise to any criminal sanction laid down in the Act, also enable a person injured by the breach to bring a civil action for damages for breach of statutory duty. This is a tort in its own right independent of any other form of tortious liability. Whether a claimant can sue depends on whether the statute, upon its proper construction, confers a right of civil action upon her. This may be explicitly stated, but if not, it will be necessary to determine whether Parliament implicitly intended to confer such a right.

In many cases, particularly in more recent legislation, there is an explicit provision: s.47 of the Health and Safety at Work Act 1974 provided until October 2013 that breach of the duties set out in sections 2-7 of the Act does not give rise to a civil action, but breach of a duty imposed by health and safety regulations does, provided it causes damage. This is enormously important. Regulations such as the Provision and Use of Work Equipment Regulations 1998, Lifting Operations and Lifting Equipment Regulations 1998, Manual Handling Operations Regulations 1992, Control of Substances Hazardous to Health Regulations 1992 and many others are routinely relied on in personal injury claims. In general, in relation to health and safety at work, breach of statutory duty is an available cause of action. It should be noted that these regulations ultimately derive from EU law. Art 153 of the Treaty on European Union gives power to the Council and Parliament to harmonise the law on health and safety through Directives, including the "umbrella" Directive 89/391 and specific directives underpinning the UK regulations referred to above. The key requirement is set out in Article 6.1 of the Directive; the employer:

> "shall take the measures necessary for the safety and health protection of workers, including prevention of occupational risks and provision of information and training, as well as provision of the necessary organisation and means".

However, following amendment as a result of s.69 of the Enterprise and Regulatory Reform Act 2013, s.47 now provides that there will be an action for breach of health and safety regulations under s.15 of the **Health and Safety at Work Act 1974** only where further regulations so provide. The stated intention of the Government was that employer's liability should be based on negligence, but it is not clear whether reliance on statutory duty is to be excluded, or whether the existing regulations are to be actionable if the breach is negligent. However, as the previous law still applies to all claims arising prior to 1 October 2013 it will be relevant and important for many years in practice.

Similarly the **Consumer Protection Act 1987** confers a right of action under Part I in relation to product liability, and for breach of safety regulations, but not otherwise: section 41. Some statutes expressly negate civil liability, e.g. section 13 of the Safety of Sports Grounds Act 1975.

Unfortunately, prior to the 1970s, statutes were often silent as to whether a civil action was available. As a result, the courts had to develop an elaborate, and somewhat artificial, set of criteria for determining whether an action was available.

WAS A RIGHT OF ACTION INTENDED?

The claimant must prove that the legislature intended to create a right to sue. It should be said at the outset, however, that there is considerable inconsistency in judicial approach to the problem, because, as Lord Browne-Wilkinson observed in *X v Bedfordshire CC* (HL, 1995), although the general principles applicable in determining whether an action lies are well established, the application of those principles in any particular case remains difficult. His Lordship said that the basic proposition is that a breach of statutory duty does not, by itself, give rise to a private law action. Such an action will arise, however, if it can be shown that, on the proper construction of the statute, the duty was imposed for the protection of a limited class of the public and that Parliament intended to confer upon members of that class a right to sue for breach. There is no general rule for determining whether the Act does create such a right, but if no other remedy is provided for its breach that is an indicator in the claimant's favour (though by no means conclusive, see *O'Rourke v Camden London BC* (HL, 1997)).

If the Act does contain other provisions for enforcing the duty that is an indication of an intention that it was to be enforced by those means alone and not by private law action: *Cutler v Wandsworth Stadium Ltd* (HL, 1949); *Lonrho Ltd v Shell Petroleum Co Ltd (No.2)* (HL, 1982).

Similarly in *Cullen v Chief Constable of the Royal Ulster Constabulary* (HL, 2003), the House of Lords held that the claimant could not rely on the tort of breach of statutory duty for the failure of the police to give him reasons for delaying his access to a solicitor, on the ground that the duty concerned could be enforced through judicial review. This confirms the point about alternative remedies.

However, the mere existence of some other statutory remedy is not decisive, since it is still possible to show that the protected class was intended to have a private remedy. A classic example is that a civil action lay for breach of industrial safety regulations imposed upon employers, despite the imposition of criminal penalties (*Groves v Lord Wimborne* (CA, 1898)). This common law principle underlies the pre-2013 approach to breach of statutory duty in relation to health and safety at work, which may extend beyond the employer-employee context.

In *X v Bedfordshire CC*, two sets of appeals came before the House of Lords relating in the one set to alleged breaches of a local authority's statutory duties in respect of child welfare, and in the other of the duties of other authorities' duties with regard to the provision of education for children with special needs. It was held that, as in the case of legislation regulating the conduct of prisons (see *Hague v Deputy Governor of Parkhurst Prison* (HL, 1991)), no civil action lay on the grounds, inter alia, that although the legislation did in fact protect individuals adversely affected by the local authorities' activities, it was intended not for the benefit of those individuals but that of society as a whole. Lord Browne-Wilkinson said that the cases where a right of action has been held to arise are all cases in which the duty has been very limited and specific as opposed to general administrative functions imposed on public bodies, involving the exercise of administrative discretion. One good example is the duty to maintain highways in a safe condition imposed by section 41 of the Highways Act 1980, which now extends also to clearing away or treating snow and ice. This duty does give rise to an action if the highway is dangerous and the highway authority has not used reasonable care. In *Stovin v Wise* (HL, 1996) it was accepted that the other functions of the highway authority under the Act created powers rather than duties, and these entailed decisions on resources allocation etc. By a bare majority the House also held that there was no common law duty to deal with issues other than the dangerous condition of the highway itself.

KEY CASE

STOVIN V WISE (1996)

A road junction at which a bank of earth obstructed drivers' views had been the location for several accidents. Norfolk County Council, which was aware of the problem, had a power (under the Highways Act 1980) to improve the road junction by removing the bank of earth which obstructed visibility. A decision to take action to remove the hazard was taken but the authority then failed to follow through to execute the decision. Wise negligently drove out from a side road and collided with Stovin. To reduce her liability to the claimant she alleged that the dangerous junction had significantly contributed to the accident.

Held: (HL) The House of Lords (by a bare majority) held that the local authority owed no duty of care to road users for failure to exercise its powers: there was a statutory power to improve the dangerous road junction but the local authority was not under a duty to do so. This case was complicated by the fact that it involved an *omission* to act and in finding the local authority not liable for its *omission* to act, the court applied the principle that there is no liability where a breach consists of a pure omission and the defendant has not created the harm suffered.

Comment (1) The significant factor in this case was that Parliament had chosen to give the council a *power* rather than a *duty* in respect of the removal of obstructions. According to Lord Hoffmann:

" ... the fact that Parliament has conferred a discretion must be some indication that the policy of the act conferring the power was not to create a right to compensation."

(2) In *Gorringe v Calderdale MBC* (2004) the House of Lords applied *Stovin v Wise* and found that a highway authority's failure to place a marking or to install a road sign warning motorists that they were approaching a dangerous part of the road did not constitute a breach of statutory duty. The provision of road signs or markings was quite different from keeping the highway in repair and the existence of statutory powers and duties to promote and improve road safety under the Road Traffic Act 1988 did not create a parallel common law duty.

In *Clunis v Camden & Islington Health Authority* (CA, 1998) the Court of Appeal held that breach of duty under the **Mental Health Act 1983** did not give rise to an action for damages. The claimant, who had a long history of mental illness, was convicted of manslaughter and claimed that he would have been prevented from committing the stabbing if the after-care services specified under the Act had been effectively provided by the defendant.

In conclusion, in determining whether, in any particular case, a civil action for breach of statutory duty will lie, the starting point is to look to precedent or for a clearly stated Parliamentary intention. In the absence of either, the above principles may assist, but it is in all cases a question of ascertaining the fundamental purpose the legislation intended to achieve, and that can only be done by a consideration of the enactment as a whole.

THE ELEMENTS OF THE TORT

Duty owed to the claimant

In establishing that breach of the particular duty will in principle found a right of action the claimant will in most, if not all, cases have established that the obligation was imposed for the benefit of a limited class. He must then prove that, on the proper construction of the statutory provision, he is a member of that class.

In *Hartley v Mayoh & Co* (CA, 1954), the widow of a fireman electrocuted while fighting a fire at the defendants' factory had no cause of action because the regulations existed for the benefit of "persons employed" at the factory, and her husband was not such a person.

Similarly the expression "person employed or working on the premises", was held in *Napieralski v Curtis (Contractors) Ltd* (HC, 1959) not to include a person working for his own private purposes and after normal working hours. In contrast, the same expression has been held to cover a worker who was not acting within the course of his employment but was on a frolic of his own (*Uddin v Associated Portland Cement Manufacturers Ltd* (CA, 1965), approved in *Westwood v Post Office* (HL, 1974), where the claimant was a trespasser on that part of the premises to which the action related).

Defendant in breach of duty

The claimant must prove that the defendant was in breach, and this can only be ascertained by having regard to the precise wording of the legislation to determine the nature of the obligation. Some obligations are absolute, such as that formerly contained in s.14(1) of the Factories Act 1961 requiring that "every dangerous part of any machinery shall be securely fenced", so that whether reasonable care was taken is irrelevant, see *John Summers & Sons Ltd v Frost* (HL, 1955), where compliance with the regulation would have rendered the machine unusable. Other safety provisions require measures to be taken "so far as is reasonably practicable", which is similar to the ordinary common law negligence formula with the important proviso that the burden is upon the defendant to prove that compliance was not reasonably practicable: *Nimmo v Alexander Cowan & Sons Ltd* (HL, 1967); *Larner v British Steel Plc* (CA, 1993)). Effectively it is the same standard with the burden of proof reversed.

The provisions of the Factories Acts and other early work safety legislation have been replaced, as we have seen, by a coordinated series of regulations pertaining to particular aspects of work, and based on a harmonised EU standard. As with the old legislation some of the duties contained in the current regulations impose an absolute obligation, while others are qualified in some way, so similar problems of interpretation are likely to arise.

Damage of the contemplated type

For the claimant to succeed, the harm suffered must be of a type which the Act was designed to prevent. In *Gorris v Scott* (Ex., 1874), the claimant's sheep were swept overboard from the defendant's vessel during a storm. The sheep were not penned, contrary to statutory regulations, but the claimant nevertheless failed in his action because the object of the regulations was to prevent the spread of disease, not to afford protection from the perils of the sea. So, too, it has been held that the aim of the fencing provisions of the Factories Acts is to prevent the operator from coming into contact with the machine and not to stop parts of the machine, or the materials on which it is working, from flying out and striking the operator: *Close v Steel Co of Wales* (HL, 1962); *Nicholls v F. Austin (Leyton) Ltd* (HL, 1946). There has been a tendency in more recent times, however, to adopt a more flexible approach, with a slightly different test.

Harm of a type which the Act was designed to prevent

In *Grant v National Coal Board* (HL, 1956) the Coal Mines Act 1911 provided that "the roof and sides of every travelling road ... shall be made secure". The accident occurred because a bogie on which the claimant was travelling was derailed as a result of a fall of stone from the roof. It was held that the protection of the statute was not limited to direct falls from the roof but covered accidents caused indirectly by such falls.

DONAGHEY V BOULTON & PAUL LTD (1968)
The claimant slipped and fell through an open space in an asbestos roof on which he was working. In breach of their duty the defendants had failed to provide him with adequate crawling boards, but argued that the object of the regulations was to prevent workers from falling through fragile roofing materials, not through holes in the roof.

Held: (HL) The House of Lords rejected such a narrow interpretation and held the defendants liable. Lord Reid said that if the damage is of a kind which the regulation seeks to prevent, it matters not that it happens in a manner not contemplated by the enactment, though this is not easy to reconcile with the decisions on fencing provisions cited above.

However, the harm must be within the scope of the regulation—there can be no liability by analogy. In *Chipchase v British Titan Products* (CA, 1956) regulations provided that every platform from which a workman could fall more than six feet six inches must be at least 34 inches wide. The claimant fell from a platform which was six feet from the ground and only nine inches wide. It was held that there was no breach of the statutory duty, which simply did not apply to the platform in question.

Causation

The burden rests upon the claimant to prove on a balance of probabilities that the breach of statutory duty caused or materially contributed to the damage: *Bonnington Castings Ltd v Wardlaw* (HL, 1956). This case concerned the inhalation of dust, which caused a cumulative and progressive lung disease. Some, but not all, of the dust was being emitted in breach of regulations, and this made a significant contribution to the total. This was held to be a material contribution. In this respect there is no distinction between this tort and a common law negligence action, so that the claimant must show that he would not have sustained injury but for the defendant's breach. A variant on this theme is where the claimant is successively exposed to dust or noise in breach of duty in two or more successive employments, and develops a cumulative disease of disability. Each employer is liable in proportion to the degree of exposure: *Holtby v Brigham & Cowan* (CA, 2000) (a deafness case).

Where industrial disease is not cumulative in the above sense, an alternative analysis is possible. *McGhee v National Coal Board* (HL, 1973) was a case where the claimant developed dermatitis as the result of exposure to brick dust. Again, some, but not all of the exposure in point of time was in breach of regulations. The medical evidence was that dermatitis was not a cumulative disease; some experts thought it arose from a single contact of an irritant with a weak or compromised area of skin, others than some period of exposure was needed, but no-one could say that the wrongful exposure had caused or contributed to the disease, merely that the extra exposure increased the overall risk. That was, however, according to the House of Lords, a legally sufficient alternative basis of causation. This was developed in the mesothelioma case of *Fairchild v Glenhaven* (HL, 2002), where a series of employers had exposed the claimant to asbestos in breach of regulations. Mesothelioma is caused by asbestos, but is not cumulative—it results from a single contact between a fibre and a pre-cancerous cell. Again, while it was not possible to identify the source of the fatal fibre, each period of exposure increased the risk that such a contact would take place.

In *McWilliams v Sir William Arrol & Co Ltd* (HL, 1962), an experienced workman fell to his death because he was not wearing a safety harness. Although the employer was in breach of duty for failing to provide a harness he was held not liable since, on the evidence, the deceased would probably not have worn the harness anyway and the accident would still have occurred. In other words, basic but-for causation was not made out once all the facts were considered. Note that the duties in respect of this class of work (steel erection) are now much more extensive; it is not merely a duty to provide equipment, but to ensure that it is used.

The claimant must also show that the damage is not too remote and the usual test of reasonable foresight applies. As in an action for negligence at common law, the precise way in which the damage is caused need not be foreseeable, provided that the other elements of the tort are satisfied: *Millard v Serck Tubes Ltd* (CA, 1969).

One problematic area is where there are regulations, which apply to both the employer and the worker, such that if the worker breaches his duty, by, for instance not using safety equipment, he puts the employer in breach of a strict duty to ensure that it is used. The incidence of liability will then depend on where responsibility is found to lie. In *Ginty v Belmont Building Supplies Ltd* (HC, 1959), a regulation binding upon both parties required the use of crawling boards on fragile roofs. The defendant had provided the boards and given full instructions as to their use to the claimant who, although an experienced workman, neglected to use them and fell through a roof. Both parties were clearly in breach of their statutory obligation but it was held that the claimant was the sole author of his injury and his action failed. It is of course the responsibility of the employer to adduce evidence, as explained by Lord Reid in *Boyle v Kodak Ltd* (HL, 1969) in the following terms:

"... once the claimant has established that there was a breach of an enactment which made the employer absolutely liable, and that that breach caused the accident, he need do no more. But it is then open to the employer to set up a defence that in fact he was not in any way in fault but that the claimant employee was alone to blame".

In *Boyle,* the House of Lords concluded that the employer was partly at fault—the worker had not been adequately supervised, and liability was apportioned 50:50. In *Ross v Associated Portland Cement Manufacturers Ltd.* (HL, 1964) the employers had failed to provide necessary equipment, and the workers decided to carry on with what was to hand; in this case liability was apportioned 2:1 against the employers. As long as it is understood that the word "defence" used by Lord Reid is not a reference to a complete defence in law, but a rather oblique reference to contributory negligence, his dictum is correct.

Even if the claimant is not in breach of his statutory duty he will, for similar reasons, fail in his action if it is his own deliberate act of folly which puts the defendant in breach: *Horne v Lec Refrigeration Ltd* (HC, 1965). The operation of this principle is, however, confined within narrow limits and it will not avail a defendant who is in some way personally at fault. The employer who, for example, fails to provide adequate instructions or supervision or who acquiesces in the breach will still be liable, though there may be a reduction for contributory negligence (see *Boyle v Kodak Ltd* (above)).

DEFENCES

Volenti non fit injuria

As a matter of public policy this defence is not available to an employer who is sued for a breach of her own statutory duty. In *Imperial Chemical Industries Ltd v Shatwell* (HL, 1965), it was held that the defence is available where the claimant sues his employer vicariously for the default of a fellow worker, provided that the claimant is not of lower rank to, or in the habit of taking orders from, his colleague. In cases other than employer and employee there seems no reason why, in principle, the defence should not be available (see Ch.5). Note however that *Shatwell* is a very extreme case. ICI operated minerals quarries and were known for their exemplary approach to health and safety; indeed their internal regulations were adopted as a statutory code. Primary responsibility for carrying out blasting operations was placed on the shotfirers, who were highly trained and certificated safety officials, operating with no direct supervision. Two brothers, both shotfirers, conspired to disregard the regulations and adopt their own unsafe practices, which they knew the company did not tolerate. One of them caused an explosion which injured both of them. The combination of circumstances here warranted a finding of volenti.

Contributory negligence

This is clearly available as we have already seen (and see Ch.5) but, as far as workmen are concerned, the House of Lords in *Caswell v Powell Duffryn Associated Collieries Ltd* (HL, 1940) said that regard must be had to the conditions in which they work, bearing in mind the noise, fatigue and repetitive nature of the job. All the same, whilst momentary lapses of concentration may not be too harshly penalised, a finding of contributory negligence is by no means uncommon in this type of case. It is to be noted that whilst a breach by the claimant of a statutory duty imposed upon her may well amount to contributory negligence, she is not (other perhaps than in very exceptional circumstances) defeated by the ex turpi principle: *National Coal Board v England* (HL, 1954) (and see Ch.5).

Delegation

The general rule is that where a statutory duty is imposed upon the defendant it is a non-delegable duty, in the sense that, although the performance of the duty may be delegated, the defendant remains liable. Where, however, the alleged delegation is to the claimant herself, this is a relevant factor in deciding the issue of causation. In other words it is not so much a question of whether there has been a delegation, but rather whose fault it was that the damage occurred (Pearson J. in *Ginty*).

REVISION CHECKLIST

You should now understand:

☐ **Breach of statutory duty is a tort in its own right independent of any other form of tortious liability.**

☐ **Whether a claimant can sue depends on whether the statute, upon its proper construction, confers a right of civil action.**

☐ **Where the statute is silent on the issue, it is then for the courts to interpret the statute and give effect to the intention of Parliament.**

☐ **There is considerable inconsistency in judicial approach to interpretation, because, as Lord Browne-Wilkinson observed in *X v Bedfordshire CC* (HL, 1995), although the general principles applicable in determining whether an action lies are well established, the application of those principles in any particular case remains difficult.**

QUESTION AND ANSWER

QUESTION

Outline the factors taken into account by the courts in determining whether a claim for breach of statutory duty should be treated at giving rise to a civil claim.

APPROACH TO THE ANSWER

The courts would firstly refer to the wording of the statute in question to determine the intention of Parliament as to whether a claim will lie in tort for breach of the duty imposed: *Lonrho Ltd v Shell Petroleum Co Ltd (No.2)* (HL, 1982). If the statute is silent on the matter, indicators of what Parliament intended are found by looking at whether the statute:

(a) was designed to protect a limited class of the persons and intended to confer upon members of that class a right to sue for breach;

(b) provides an alternative method of enforcement—if the Act does contain other provision for enforcing the duty that is a non-conclusive indication of an intention that it was to be enforced by those means alone and not by a civil law action: *Cutler v Wandsworth Stadium Ltd* (1949) but compare *Groves v Lord Wimborne* (1898).

The claimant must then prove that, on the proper construction of the statutory provision, he is a member of that class (see *Hartley v Mayoh & Co* (1954)).

The claimant must then prove that the defendant was in breach of this duty and this can only be ascertained by having regard to the precise wording of the Act to determine the nature of the obligation. There can be no liability by analogy: *Chipchase v British Titan* (1956). Some obligations are absolute so that whether reasonable care was taken is irrelevant whereas other safety provisions require measures to be taken "so far as is reasonably practicable", which is similar to the ordinary common law negligence formula. However, the burden is upon the defendant to prove that compliance with the statute was not reasonably practicable.

For the claimant to succeed the harm suffered must be of a type which the Act was designed to prevent: *Gorris v Scott* (1874), *Close v Steel Company of Wales* (1962) and, on a balance of probabilities, it must be established that the breach of statutory duty caused or materially contributed to the damage (see *Bonnington Castings Ltd v Wardlaw* (1956)).

Vicarious Liability and Non-Delegable Duties

INTRODUCTION

The general rule is that tortious liability attaches to the person actually responsible. It may also attach to someone who expressly authorises or ratifies a tort. That person is personally liable, but there are circumstances in which a person is liable for the torts of another even in the absence of such authorisation or ratification. The liability which thus arises is known as vicarious liability and the most common example of it is the liability of an employer for the torts of its employees committed in the course of their employment. There is no clear single rationale for the imposition of vicarious liability. However the generally accepted rationale is that the employee's work ordinarily benefits the employer and is done within the general supervision of the employer, so the employer should take the consequences. It is also relevant that the employer is more likely to have "deep pockets" to pay damages; see *JGE v The Trustees of the Portsmouth Roman Catholic Diocesan Trust* (CA, 2012). It is also said to act as an inducement to the employer to promote high standards of safety within his organisation. We will also consider some of the other areas where vicarious liability can exist. In addition, there is a second principle—that of the non-delegable duty. This also fixes liability with the "responsible organisation", but by a very different conceptual process.

VICARIOUS LIABILITY

Employer and employee

It is not necessary, for the purposes of the doctrine, that the employer be in breach of any duty owed to the injured party (who may himself be either a fellow-employee or a stranger). What is required is that the wrongdoer be an employee and the wrong be done in connection with what he is employed to do. There must be a tort committed by an employee in the course of employment. The concepts of "employee" and "course of employment" have generated much case law, and have both developed over time.

The meaning of employee

An employee is employed under a contract of service, an independent contractor under a contract for services, but this does not explain the essential distinction between the two types of contract. We used to talk about "master and servant", but this is now archaic.

No single factor or group of factors has yet been devised which is or are capable of application in all cases to determine whether there is employment under a contract of service in any given case. Even the express declaration of the parties as to the nature of their contract is simply one factor to be taken into account (*Ferguson v John Dawson & Partners (Contractors) Ltd* (CA, 1976)). Originally much weight was placed on the extent to which the employee was under the control of the employer as to how he did his work. If the employer controls not only the type of work to be done but also the manner in which it is to be done, that points to a contract of service; but this so-called "control" test has, where the task to be performed requires a high degree of skill or expertise, proved inadequate as an all-purpose test, for the employee will in practice frequently be left to decide for himself how best to carry out the job. Attention then moved to the extent to which the employee's activities were integrated into the business. In *Stevenson, Jordan and Harrison Ltd v Macdonald and Evans* (CA, 1952), Denning L.J. suggested that, under a contract of service, the employee's work is done as an integral part of the business, whereas under a contract for services his work is not integrated into the business but is merely accessory to it. Again, while helpful in some cases, this proved inadequate as a general test.

In *Ready Mixed Concrete (South East) Ltd v Minister of Pensions and National Insurance* (HC, 1968), it was held that three conditions must be fulfilled for a contract of service to exist. First, the servant agrees, in consideration of a wage or other remuneration, to provide his own work and skill in the performance of some service for his master; secondly, he agrees to be subject to the other's control to such degree as to make that other the master; thirdly, the other provisions of the contract are consistent with its being a contract of service. A slightly different approach was adopted in *Market Investigations Ltd v Minister of Social Security* (HC, 1969), where it was suggested that the basic test is whether the worker is performing the service as a person in business on his own account. In answering this question it is relevant to consider whether the person uses his own premises and equipment, whether he hires his own helpers, the degree of financial risk he takes and the degree of responsibility, if any, which he has for investment and management. Although this approach has been followed in later cases, judicial warnings have been given that the test is not of itself to be regarded as conclusive of the question. All that can be said is that there is no exhaustive category of matters relevant in deciding the issue, and what is regarded as the crucial factor in one case may well be outweighed by different considerations in another.

KEY CASE

FERGUSON V JOHN DAWSON & PARTNERS (CONTRACTORS) LTD (1976)
The claimant, a building worker, was injured when he fell off a roof at the defendant's construction site. Contrary to regulations there was no guard rail on the roof. If he was an independent contractor he would be responsible for his own safety and unable to sue the company. At the time of hiring the claimant was expressed to be a "labour only sub-contractor" although he was an unskilled labourer and subject to the control of the site agent.

Held (CA) The employers were liable. Despite the label that the parties had given to the relationship, in all other respects the claimant was treated as an employee working under a contract of service. That was the relevant consideration.

Comment
The express intention of the parties as to the classification of their working relationship is an important factor, but it is not conclusive.

1) In *Ready Mixed Concrete (SE) Ltd* it was held that where the parties have specified that a person will be self-employed, and the other terms of the contract do not show otherwise, the contract will be regarded as a contract for services. The expressed intention is therefore significant, as long as it is consistent with the other circumstances.

2) In *Stevenson, Jordan & Harrison Ltd v Macdonald & Evans* (1952) the "integration test" was proposed by Lord Denning: an employee is someone whose work is an integral part of the business; an independent contractor is someone who would work for the business, but as an accessory rather than an integral part of it. This test has been applied in some situations but it has failed as a universal test and the courts have now moved to a multiple approach.

3) In *Ready Mixed Concrete (SE) Ltd* one of relevant factors in determining the nature of the employment relationship was held to be the allocation of financial risk. This particular question should be addressed by asking: is the person in business on his or her own behalf?

A further complicating factor is that it may be necessary to establish the status of a worker for other reasons, such as liability for income tax and national insurance, and in relation to claims for unfair or wrongful dismissal. *Ferguson v John Dawson & Partners (Contractors) Ltd* (above) was a case where Ferguson was happy enough to be self-employed when it came to not paying tax under PAYE and Class 1 NIC, but wanted to be an employee when he was injured. People working as "regular casual" waiters may not have a single long term contract of employment, but will be under at least a short term contract while actually at work, so the employer will be vicariously liable for their actions.

CHECKPOINT

Establishing criteria for whether a person is an employee has proved difficult. Today the court will examine all the circumstances. Control, integration and the "label" attached by the parties will be important, but the court must balance all factors.

Lending an employee

A particular problem is that of lending an employee, even if he clearly is under a contract of service, for the difficulty then arises as to who is the employer for the purposes of vicarious liability. In *Mersey Docks and Harbour Board v Coggins and Griffith (Liverpool) Ltd* (HL, 1947), the Board hired a crane driver, together with his crane, to X, under a contract which provided that the driver was to be the servant of X.

KEY CASE

MERSEY DOCKS AND HARBOUR BOARD V COGGINS AND GRIFFITH (LIVERPOOL) LTD (1947)

A mobile crane and a driver had been hired out to a firm of stevedores under a contract which stipulated that the driver was to be the employee of the stevedores. In spite of this term his original employer, the Board, paid his wages and retained the right to dismiss him. He was also responsible to them for keeping the crane in good order, and they trained him in the operation of the crane. The hirer directed the tasks which were to be performed by the driver but not how he was to operate the crane. In the course of working the crane the driver negligently injured a third party. Although X had, at the time, the immediate direction and control of what was to be done, they had no power to direct how the crane should be worked. Furthermore, the driver continued to be paid by the Board, which alone had the right to dismiss him. It was held that, notwithstanding the terms of the hire contract, the Board had failed to discharge the burden of proof to shift responsibility for the driver's negligence onto X. It was said in this case and repeatedly since that this is a heavy burden. The question to be determined was whether the stevedores or the Board were vicariously liable.

Held (HL) Several factors have to be considered but the decisive question to be asked was who had the ultimate control over the manner in which the work was performed. On the facts of the case the Board remained liable.

Comment

Where an employee is lent out to another employer on a temporary basis the presumption is that the general (or original) employer remains vicariously liable. It was said in this case and repeatedly since that this is a heavy burden. This case establishes no universal test but Lord Porter said that factors for consideration are: who is paymaster, who can dismiss, how long the alternative service lasts and what machinery is employed. It was also held that an express term in the contract of hire stating that the workman is the employee of the hirer is not to be treated as conclusive.

A more recent case, which went the other way, is *Hawley v Luminar Leisure* (CA, 2006) where a nightclub obtained the services of a door supervisor from a security company. Although the security company selected, trained and paid the door supervisor, the nightclub manager controlled his actual activity. In all the circumstances, the nightclub owner alone was vicariously liable.

CHECKPOINT

Where an employee was lent by one employer to another

Mersey Docks shows that the degree of control exercised by the respective employers is clearly important and that the right to control is more readily transferred in the case of an unskilled servant. In *Via-systems Ltd v Thermal Transfer Ltd* (2005), however, where both employers were vicariously liable, the Court of Appeal held that entire and absolute control of the employee was not a precondition of vicarious liability. It had previously been assumed that where an employee was lent by one employer to another, vicarious liability for the employee's negligence had to rest with one employer or the other, but not both.

The course of employment

For the employer to be liable, the wrong must be committed in the course of the employee's employment. For many years the standard test for this was the "Salmond Test", first articulated by a leading academic lawyer. An act will be in the course of employment under the test if it is "(a) a wrongful act authorised by the [employer], or (b) a wrongful and unauthorised mode of doing some act authorised by the [employer]". However, since the decision in *Lister v Hesley Hall Ltd* (HL, 2001), a different test has been applied. the House of Lords said the proper approach to the course of employment is no longer to ask the question whether the acts were modes of doing authorised acts in the course of employment. A broad assessment should be adopted and the relevant question is whether the tort was so closely connected with the employment that it would be fair and just to hold the employer liable. Note that any act which would be within the course of employment under the old test will continue to be, since both specifically authorised acts and careless performance of ones duties are clearly "closely connected". It may be, however, that some of the situations which were held to fall outside the course of employment under the old test will fall within the new one. So far the focus has been on wrongful and unauthorised acts, and the courts have not really been called on to consider some of the other problem areas. All pre-2001 decisions denying that the employee was in the course of employment are liable to be reconsidered, and should not be treated as clear authority.

The most straightforward cases are those where the employee performs negligently—e.g. a lorry driver causing a collision by lack of attention. Generally even quite serious dereliction of duty will count. Thus, a tanker driver who, whilst delivering petrol, lit a cigarette and carelessly discarded a match causing a fire, was held to be acting within the course of his employment. It was said that the act of lighting the cigarette, whilst not in itself connected with his job, could not be looked at in isolation from the surrounding circumstances (*Century Insurance Co Ltd v Northern Ireland Road Transport Board* (HL, 1942)).

CHECKPOINT

Where the employee's act is wholly unconnected to the job for which he is employed, he is said to be "on a frolic of his own" and the employer is not liable. In *Beard v London General OmnibusCo* (CA, 1900), the employer of a bus conductor who, in the absence of the driver, negligently drove the bus himself was held not liable. This may be contrasted with *Kay v ITW Ltd* (CA, 1968) where the employee attempted to move a lorry belonging to another firm because it was blocking the entrance to his employer's warehouse to which he had been instructed to return a fork-lift truck. It was held that, since the attempted removal of the obstruction was done in order that the servant could complete his own task, the employer was vicariously liable. However, as the employee in *Beard* was driving the bus to put it in position for its next journey, under the new "close connection" test a different view might be taken.

It was held in *General Engineering Services Ltd v Kingston and St Andrew Corp* (PC, 1988) that firemen operating a "go-slow" policy who took five times as long as they normally would have done to drive to the scene of a fire (with the result that the plaintiff's premises were destroyed) were not within the course of employment. The Privy Council indicated that it was as though they had simply ignored the call which would not be a mode of performing their duties. This is however a case which founds itself firmly on the Salmond test and holds that a wrongful and unauthorised act is outside the course of employment. This is no longer the case, and this is a case which might well have been decided differently under the current test.

The courts have been faced with problems where the employee's act has been expressly prohibited. In principle, if the prohibition amounts to a restriction on the class of acts which the employee is employed to do, the employer is not liable; but he is liable if the prohibition relates merely to a mode of performing the employment. So an employee who, contrary to written instructions, raced his employer's bus with that of a rival company was held to be within the course of his employment (*Limpus v London General Omnibus Co* (HC, 1862)).

KEY CASE

LIMPUS V LONDON GENERAL OMNIBUS CO (1862)
A bus driver was instructed not to race with or obstruct the buses of rival companies. He disobeyed this instruction and caused an accident in which the claimant's horses were injured.

Held Despite the prohibition the employers were liable since this was simply an improper method adopted by the employee in performing his duties.

Comment
It is outside the course of employment for an employee to do something which is not connected with what he is employed to do. In *Beard v London General Omnibus Co* (above) a bus conductor, in the driver's absence, decided to turn the bus around for the return journey. As a conductor, it was not his job to drive the bus and he was therefore acting outside the course of his employment.

Cases which have dealt with the problem of the giving of lifts to unauthorised passengers

- In *Twine v Bean's Express Ltd* (CA, 1946), it was held that such an act was outside the course of employment, though the view was expressed that, in so far as injury to persons other than the passenger was concerned, the driver would be within the course of his employment.
- Where a driver's foreman consented to the passenger's presence in the vehicle, however, the employer was held liable because the foreman, of whose lack of actual authority the passenger was unaware, was nonetheless acting within the scope of his apparent authority (*Young v Edward Box & Co Ltd* (CA, 1951)).
- The decision in *Twine's* case is not easy to reconcile with *Rose v Plenty* (CA, 1976) where a milkman, in allowing a young boy onto his float to help him with his milk round in contravention of his employer's instructions, was held to be within the course of his employment when the boy fell off and was injured. The majority of the court distinguished the earlier case on the ground that the engagement of the boy was done in furtherance of the master's business.

There are cases where the employee's act, although not part of his regular employment as such, is necessarily incidental to it. In *Staton v National Coal Board* (HC, 1957), for example, an employee cycling to the pay office on his employer's land to collect his pay after work had finished was held to be within the course of his employment. But whilst employment may start as soon as the employee enters his employer's premises, those travelling to or from work are not usually considered to be in the course of employment, unless, of course, they are travelling specifically on the employer's business or on some errand which is incidental to it. In *Smith v Stages* (HL, 1989), a worker travelling between home and a temporary workplace, and who was paid wages during that time, was held to be within the course of employment, notwithstanding that he might have a discretion as to the mode and time of travel.

KEY CASE

SMITH V STAGES (1989)
A peripatetic lagger was working at a power station in the Midlands when his employer sent him and another employee to perform an urgent job in Wales. In addition to their hourly rate they were paid

travelling expenses for the journeys there and back. They were using a private vehicle and had discretion as to how and when they would travel. Having worked without sleep they finished the job two days early and decided to drive straight home. As they were travelling back together in the car they were both injured when the employee driving the car crashed into a wall. The driver was uninsured and the claimant sued the employer on the basis of vicarious liability.

Held: (HL) The employers were liable. An employee travelling between home and work will not generally be in the course of employment. But an employee travelling in the employer's time from home to a workplace other than the regular workplace or between workplaces will be within the course of employment. Lord Goff said the fact that the men were travelling back early was immaterial since they were still being paid wages to travel there and back. Lord Lowry thought the crucial point was that the employees were "on duty" at the time of the accident.

In principle, if an employee chooses to make a journey to take a meal-break, that is a matter for him. However the cases in this area are very inconsistent. In *Hilton v Burton (Rhodes) Ltd* (HC 1961) a journey from a demolition site to a café was held not to be within the course of employment. However, in *Harvey v O'Dell* (HC 1958) a very similar journey from a temporary workplace to a café was held to be within the course of employment. *Hilton* is in principle the preferable decision, because it is the worker's lunch break and the decision to make the journey (rather, say, than bringing a packed lunch) is for his own convenience. These cases do relate to a period when compulsory motor insurance was not as comprehensive as it is today and there was therefore some practical justification for finding the employer liable.

An employee who uses force in the mistaken but honest belief that he is protecting his employer's property or premises does an act incidental to his employment rendering the employer liable (*Poland v John Parr & Sons* (CA, 1927)). Clearly, though, violence inflicted as part of a private disagreement is not normally within the course of employment (*Warren v Henlys Ltd* (HC, 1948); however, depending on the precise facts it may meet the close connection test (*Mattis v Pollock* (CA 2003).

The "close connection" test was developed to deal with cases where it was alleged that there had been intentional wrongdoing, typically physical or sexual abuse by teachers or care workers. Some forms of wrongdoing, such as dishonesty, had been treated as falling within the Salmond test, rather awkwardly. These include *Lloyd v Grace, Smith & Co* (HL 1912) (fraud by a solicitor's clerk) and *Morris v Martin* (CA, 1966) (theft of customer's property from a cleaner). In *Brinks Global Services v Igrox* (CA, 2010) a similar case of theft was held to be in the course of employment under the close connection test. This seems a sounder basis of liability.

In *Lister v Hesley Hall Ltd* (above) a long line of cases in which liability had been denied on the basis that this was not a mode of performing the duties of the employment was overturned. The courts now adopt a broad assessment to determine whether the acts were so closely connected with the employment that it would be fair and just to hold the employers liable.

Lister v Hesley Hall Ltd concerned a warden at the defendants' school for boys with emotional and behavioural difficulties who had subjected the claimants to systematic sexual abuse. It was held that the defendants had entrusted the care of the children to the warden and his torts had been so closely connected with his employment that it would be fair just to hold the defendants vicariously liable. An earlier case, *Trotman v North Yorkshire CC* (CA 1999), where an employer was found not to be vicariously liable for a teacher who used school trips to commit sexual assault on the ground he was not acting in the course of employment, was declared to be wrongly decided.

LISTER V HESLEY HALL LTD (2001)
The defendants ran a school for boys with emotional and behavioural difficulties. The school, which had a boarding annex, had been managed by the defendants as a commercial enterprise. They had employed Grain and his wife as warden and housekeeper to take care of the boys. The claimants attended the school and boarded in the annex where they were subjected to systematic acts of sexual abuse by Grain.

Held (HL) The test for the course of employment was restated by the House of Lords and directed to the connection between the employee's duties and his wrongdoing. The proper approach to the nature of employment is not to ask the simplistic question of whether the acts were modes of doing authorised acts but to adopt a broad assessment and to consider whether the torts committed were so *closely connected* with the employee's duties that it would be fair and just to hold the employers liable. The fact that the employment provided a warden with the opportunity to commit the abuse was not enough to make the employer vicariously liable. The central question was whether the acts of abuse constituted a particular risk that was inextricably linked to and inherent in the performance of the warden's duties. The defendants had entrusted the care of the children to the warden and the acts of abuse committed by him had been inextricably interwoven with the carrying out of his duties. His torts had been so closely connected with his employment that it would be fair and just to hold the defendants vicariously liable.

Comment

In *Dubai Aluminium v Salaam* [(2002) the House of Lords widened the principle in *Lister v Hesley Hall* to include, not just intentional torts, but also breaches of equitable duty which were so closely connected with the acts that the employee was authorised to do while acting in the course of the firm's business.

The broader approach in *Lister v Hesley Hall* was applied by the Court of Appeal in *Mattis v Pollock* (CA, 2003) where the owner of a nightclub was held vicariously liable to the claimant who suffered paraplegia following a stabbing by a doorman employed by the nightclub. The doorman, who had started a fight in the nightclub, went home to arm himself with a knife and returned to the vicinity of the club where he stabbed the claimant. The stabbing was found to be directly linked to the incident which had gone before and was so closely connected with what the doorman was expected to do that it fell within the scope of his employment.

CHECKPOINT

The intense focus on the connection between the nature of employment and the tort committed was further emphasised in the following cases:

- In *Gravil v Carroll* (2008), where the wrongful act of a rugby player during a match was so "closely connected" with his employment that his club was vicariously liable.
- In *Ministry of Defence v Radclyffe* (2009), the *Ministry of Defence* was vicariously liable for the negligence of an officer who urged Radclyffe to jump from a bridge in a recreation break during an adventure training exercise in Germany. The connection between the nature of his employment as an officer in the army and his breach of duty was held to be well within the *Lister* test.

Religious organisations: vicarious liability for clerical sexual abuse

The finding of vicarious liability in *Lister* has widened the scope of vicarious liability for sexual abuse of children. The application of the "close connection" test in *Maga v The Trustees of the Birmingham Archdiocese of the Roman Catholic Church* (below) in a case of a a Catholic priest's sexual abuse of the claimant concluded that it would be fair and just to hold the Archdiocese which had employed him vicariously liable.

MAGA V THE TRUSTEES OF THE BIRMINGHAM ARCHDIOCESE OF THE ROMAN CATHOLIC CHURCH (2010)

The claimant (a non-Catholic boy who at no time had anything to do with the Church itself) claimed that the Archdiocese was vicariously liable for a Catholic priest purporting to carry out his work as a priest when his true motive was to abuse the claimant. The trial judge had found the Catholic Church was not vicariously liable for the actions of the priest on the ground that he did not meet the claimant as part of his priestly duties and had not involved him in the activities of the church itself.

Held: (CA) The Court of Appeal reversed the first instance decision. Lord Neuberger said that while there was no doubt that the claimant's case was weaker than that of the claimant in *Lister*, nevertheless—he concluded that the test laid down by Lord Steyn in *Lister was* satisfied.

Comment

In *JGE v Trustees of the Portsmouth Roman Catholic Diocesan Trust* (CA, 2012) the Church denied vicarious liability for acts of child sexual abuse carried out by one of its priests and claimed that priests are not employees of the church; they are merely office holders and not employees. The Court of Appeal held that the relationship between a parish priest and diocese was akin to an employment relationship. However, it was not appropriate to apply tests of employment laid down in cases dealing with unfair dismissal, or taxation, or discrimination when considering vicarious liability in respect of persons not formally employed.

VARIOUS CLAIMANTS V CATHOLIC CHILD WELFARE SOCIETY (2012)

A large number of claimants alleged vicarious liability for the physical and sexual abuse to which they were subjected at a residential institution for boys in need of care. The claims were brought against two groups of defendants and the question was whether the second defendant, the Institute, was responsible in law for the alleged acts of sexual and physical abuse committed by its members.

Held: (SC) Although the priests were bound to the Institute by their vows, rather than contract, the Institute was vicariously liable for acts of abuse. Their Lordships noted that it is possible for unincorporated associations (such as the Institute) to be vicariously liable for the wrongful acts of their members.

Comment

Lord Phillips said that the criteria to establish vicarious liability involved a synthesis of two stages. The first stage considers whether the relationship between the wrongdoer and the employer (or a relationship akin to that of employment) was one which was capable of giving rise to vicarious liability. The second stage of the test requires an examination of the connection that linked the relationship between the employer and the perpetrator, the acts of abuse and the extent to which the employment created or significantly enhanced the risk of that abuse.

There are cases which fall outside the "close connection" test. In *N v Chief Constable of Merseyside* (HC, 2006) an off duty police constable, in full uniform, lay in wait outside a nightclub and when a highly intoxicated girl was being removed, took charge of her. Although he said he would take her to the police station, he took her home and raped her. The judge held that this was not in the course of employment—the uniform merely gave the opportunity for an independent act, and did not constitute a close connection. Vicarious liability also failed in *Allen v Chief Constable of Hampshire* (CA, 2013) where the Court of Appeal held that the facts did not reveal any, let alone a close connection, between the acts alleged and a police officer's position as a police officer. It was a case involving a campaign of harassment against the claimant. The claimant was married to a police officer. The person responsible for the campaign was another police officer, who had apparently been in a relationship with the claimant's husband. It was purely personal.

The essential feature is whether it is the position in which the employer places his employee that enables him to perpetrate the wrongdoing whilst acting within the scope of the authority that he appears to have.

The House of Lords in *Dubai Aluminium v Salaam* (HL, 2003) held that the personal innocence of the other co-partners could not be taken into account when determining their vicarious liability for the dishonest partner. According to Lord Millett, the mere fact that the employee was acting dishonestly or for his own benefit is seldom likely to be sufficient to show that an employee was not acting within the course of employment.

If the claimant is unaware that the fraudulent employee is the defendant's employee he cannot claim to have relied upon the employee's apparent authority and the defendant will not be liable unless, of course, the employee was within the scope of his actual authority (*Kooragang Investments Pty Ltd v Richardson & Wrench Ltd* (PC, 1982)).

Vicarious liability is not restricted to common law claims

In *Majrowski v Guy's and St Thomas's NHS Trust* (HL, 2006), a former employee claimed that he had been bullied, intimidated and harassed by his departmental manager, acting in the course of her employment. He claimed for damages against the NHS Trust for breach of statutory duty under the Protection from Harassment Act 1997. The House of Lords dismissed the NHS Trust's appeal and held that an employer might be vicariously liable for a breach of statutory duty imposed on its employee, if in all the circumstances of the case, the test of fairness and justice was met and the connection between the employee's breach of duty and the nature of the employment was sufficient.

This means that an employer may be vicariously liable under the Act for breach of a statutory duty *imposed on the employee*, but not upon the employer directly, where it is fair and just to impose a duty and where there is a close connection between the acts of harassment and the nature of the employment. *Majrowski* was applied in *Green v DB Group Services Ltd* (HC, 2006) where a former employee claimed against her employer for damages arising from her psychiatric injury as the result of a campaign of workplace bullying and intimidation by her fellow employees. The conduct in question also constituted harassment within the meaning of the Protection from Harassment Act 1997 and, since the connection between the nature of the employment of the perpetrators and their acts of harassment was so close, it was just and reasonable to hold the employer liable for it.

Joint liability

Where an employee commits a tort in the course of his employment both he and his employer are liable as joint tortfeasors. This means that if the employer satisfies the judgment he may be able to claim contribution from his employee under the Civil Liability (Contribution) Act 1978.

CHECKPOINT

An employer may (at least in theory) be able to recover from his employee under the principle in *Lister v Romford Ice and Cold Storage Co Ltd* (HL, 1957)

Here, damages equivalent to an indemnity were awarded to an employer, who, having met the plaintiff's claim, sued his negligent employee for breach of an implied term of his employment contract that he would exercise reasonable care. In practice, however, the *Lister* principle is virtually defunct in view of an undertaking by employers' liability insurers that they would not seek to recover from an individual employee except where there was evidence of collusion or wilful misconduct.

Vehicle owners

A vehicle owner who allows another to drive it in his presence makes such a person his agent and is liable for his negligent driving. So too, if a person has authority to drive on behalf of, or for the purposes of, the owner, the latter is vicariously liable for his negligence even though not himself present in the vehicle (*Ormrod v Crosville Motor Services Ltd* (CA, 1953)).

The case of *Launchbury v Morgans* (HL, 1973) establishes that the owner is not liable simply for permitting another to use the vehicle for his own purposes. It must be shown that the driver was using it for the owner's purposes under delegation of some task or duty, and the mere fact that the owner has an interest in the safety of the vehicle's occupants is not sufficient.

According to *Norwood v Navan* (CA, 1981), a wife who uses her husband's car to go on a shopping expedition is not acting for his purposes under delegation of a task or duty so as to make him vicariously liable.

Independent contractors

In general, an employer is not vicariously liable for the negligence of an independent contractor in carrying out his work. He is of course liable if he authorises or ratifies the tort, as he is if he is personally negligent, for example by selecting an incompetent contractor or failing to give proper instructions or supervision. In addition, he may be under a non-delegable duty of care which cannot be discharged merely by entrusting performance to a contractor. It is worth noting that liability in all of these instances is not vicarious but arises as a result of a breach of a primary duty owed by the employer to the plaintiff. The remainder of this section deals with these so-called non-delegable duties.

NON-DELEGABLE DUTIES

The scope and rationale of this principle was recently considered by the Supreme Court in *Woodland v Essex CC* (SC, 2013). Lord Sumption starts his judgment by stressing that the non-delegable duty is an alternative to vicarious liability. He acknowledged the recent developments in the coverage of vicarious liability, but stated that it does not apply to "genuine independent contractors".

There are some instances where the rationale for the non-delegable duty is that the activity is "ultra-hazardous", e.g. *Honeywill and Stein Ltd v Larkin Bros Ltd* (CA, 1934), where the defendants were held liable where the contractors, whom they had employed to take photographs inside a theatre, negligently caused a fire by their use of magnesium flash powder. There are others where the rationale is that the hazard affects the public in a public place, e.g. *Pickard v Smith* (1861) where the tenant of a railway refreshment room was liable to a passenger who was injured when a coal merchant negligently left a coal-hole on the platform open and unguarded. Lord Sumption suggested that the nature and scope of these classes of case needed to be reviewed. This seems correct—there are many cases, which are not always apparently consistent with these principles, nor with each other.

Another group of cases arise out of the tort of nuisance, e.g. *Rylands v Fletcher* (HL, 1868) and also *Dalton v Angus* (HL, 1881) arising from the withdrawal of support from land. See also *Alcock v Wraith* (CA, 1991) where the principle was used to impose a duty on the owner of a house who, in order to repair his own roof, necessarily had to interfere with the integrity of his neighbour's roof. See Ch.11. These are the prototype of a group of non-delegable duties, which have three key characteristics; first there is an existing relationship between the defendant and the claimant; second, the duty is a positive one to protect persons against particular risks, and not simply a duty to refrain from acting in a way that foreseeably causes injury; third, the duty is by virtue of that relationship personal to the defendant. The work required to perform such a duty may well be delegable, and usually is. But the duty itself remains the defendant's. The employer's common law duty to his employees is a classic example of this, dealt with in Ch.8.

The relationship gives rise to an assumption of responsibility. Lord Sumption treats *Hughes v Percival* (1883), a case involving a party wall, as the equivalent of this modern concept. In *Gold v Essex County Council* (CA, 1942), which was primarily concerned with vicarious liability, it was observed that the operators of a hospital had a relationship with a patient which made them personally responsible for the outcome of treatment, irrespective of who delivered it. A number of Australian cases extended this duty to the operators of schools (most recently *New South Wales v Lepore* (2003)) arguing that children, like patients, were vulnerable and it was appropriate to impose a duty to protect them. The Supreme Court endorsed this approach, and specifically applied it to an education authority. The criteria for liability are, as stated by Lord Sumption:

(1) The claimant is especially vulnerable or dependent on the protection of the defendant against the risk of injury, e.g. patients, school children, prisoners and residents in care homes.

(2) There is an antecedent relationship between the claimant and the defendant, independent of the negligent act or omission itself, (i) which places the claimant in the actual custody, charge or care of the defendant, and (ii) from which it is possible to impute to the defendant the assumption of a positive duty to protect the claimant from harm,

and not just a duty to refrain from conduct which will foreseeably damage the claimant.

(3) The claimant has no control over how the defendant chooses to perform those obligations, i.e. whether personally or through employees or through third parties.

(4) The defendant has delegated to a third party some function which is an integral part of the positive duty which he has assumed towards the claimant; and the third party is exercising, for the purpose of the function thus delegated to him, the defendant's custody or care of the claimant and the element of control that goes with it.

(5) The third party has been negligent not in some collateral respect but in the performance of the very function assumed by the defendant and delegated by the defendant to him.

In *Woodland* this meant that the Council were in principle liable for harm suffered when independent contractors engaged to provide swimming lessons failed to ensure the pupil's safety. The swimming tuition was an integral part of the educational activities provided.

Statutory duties

Where a statute imposes an obligation upon a person to do a particular thing, he cannot escape liability by delegation to an independent contractor. If the statute empowers a person to do something which would otherwise be unlawful, that person will generally be liable for the negligence of his contractor: *Hardaker v Idle DC* (CA, 1896). The precise nature of the duty depends, however, upon the construction of the Act.

Casual or collateral negligence

It is the nature of the work, and not merely the performance of it, which may cast upon the employer a non-delegable duty. He is therefore not liable for the casual or collateral negligence of his independent contractor because that does not involve him in any breach of duty. Collateral negligence is negligence purely incidental to the particular act the contractor was employed to do. Thus, in *Padbury v Holliday and Greenwood Ltd* (CA, 1912) the defendants were not liable when their sub-contractor, in fixing a casement, negligently left a tool on the window sill which the wind blew onto a passer-by below. By contrast, in *Holliday v National Telephone Co* (CA, 1899), the defendants employed a plumber to carry out work on the highway. The plumber negligently dipped his blowlamp into molten solder and the claimant was injured in the ensuing explosion. Reversing the decision of the Divisional Court, the Court of Appeal held the employer liable, though the distinction between this and the *Padbury* case is not easy to see, unless *Holliday* is really a case of public nuisance.

REVISION CHECKLIST

You should now understand:

☐ **The tests used to distinguish between an employer and an independent contractor.**

☐ **Vicarious liability imposes liability on an employer for the tort of its employee without the need to prove fault on the part of the employer.**

☐ **The *Lister* test of whether an employee is acting in the course of employment and its application in subsequent cases.**

☐ **Where an employee's acts of harassment in breach of a statutory duty imposed on the employee meets the "close connection" test, the employer could be vicariously liable (*Majrowski*).**

☐ **The nature and scope of non-delegable duties.**

QUESTION AND ANSWER

QUESTION

Mediplus Plc employs Andy as a medical sales representative and Elvira as an accountant. Although both Andy and Elvira have been repeatedly warned that Andy was not permitted to carry passengers in the company's car, he frequently gave Elvira a lift home from work. As Andy was about to leave Mediplus premises one evening, he was informed of the outbreak of a flu epidemic and instructed to deliver a supply of the anti-flu vaccine to a local hospital as a matter of urgency. He left work with the intention of delivering the anti-flu vaccine on his way home but Elvira was waiting by his car for a lift home that evening so he gave her a lift. As Andy drove at high speed through the town the car crashed into a wall. Elvira was so upset when she discovered that she had broken two of her teeth in the crash that she began to remonstrate with Andy and accused him of "reckless" driving. Andy lost his temper and struck Elvira a severe blow to the head.

Discuss the liability (if any) of Mediplus in respect of the above incidents.

Elvira will seek to claim that Mediplus is vicariously liable for: (1) her broken teeth which resulted from Andy's negligent driving and (2) her head injuries which resulted from his criminal wrongdoing. We are told that Andy is an employee of Mediplus so that the first of the conditions for vicarious liability has been met. The torts have also been committed so the next question in determining whether Mediplus will be liable is whether the wrongs were committed in the course of Andy's employment. This will be the case where the tort is so closely connected with the employment that it is appropriate to impose liability: *Lister v Hesley Hall* (2001). Cases falling within the previous "Salmond" test that the course of employment covers cases where an employee does something which is authorised by the employer, or which is an unauthorised way of doing that which he is employed to do continue to be covered, but the new test extends the course of employment further, especially in cases of wilful wrongdoing. Where the employee's act is wholly unconnected to the job for which he is employed, he is said to be "on a frolic of his own" and the employer is not liable.

Cases where the employee's act has been expressly prohibited, e.g. *Limpus v London General Omnibus Co* (1862) and *Rose v Plenty* (CA, 1976), and also cases where giving of lifts to unauthorised passengers were at issue, e.g. *Twine v Bean's Express Ltd* (1946) will need to be discussed. The question of whether any deviation from his route takes him outside the course of employment will also need to be considered (see e.g. *Harvey v R. G. O'Dell Ltd* (1958) and *Hilton v Thomas Burton (Rhodes) Ltd* (1961)). However, since insurance is now compulsory in relation to passengers, there is today less reason to force driving situations into the course of employment. Even if the driver is not covered by the employer's insurance, the Motor Insurers Bureau will meet the claim.

In the context of Andy's criminal conduct, Mediplus will seek to establish that this behaviour took him outside the scope of employment. The relevant case is *Lister v Hesley Hall Ltd* (2001). The relevant test is whether the torts were so closely connected with the employment that it would be fair and just to hold the employers liable. *Lister v Hesley Hall* was applied by the Court of Appeal in *Mattis v Pollock* (2003) where the owner of a nightclub was held vicariously liable to the claimant who suffered paraplegia following a stabbing by a doorman employed by the nightclub. The stabbing was however found to be directly linked to an incident which had gone before and was so closely connected with what the doorman was expected to do that it fell within the scope of his employment. On this basis Mediplus will argue that Andy's conduct was not connected with what he is employed to do, but a purely personal reaction and they are not therefore vicariously liable.

Nuisance and *Rylands v Fletcher*

INTRODUCTION

There are two common law torts with the word nuisance in their name. They are quite distinct and must be considered separately. The first is private nuisance, which is essentially a remedy for landowners in respect of indirect harm affecting their property. The second is public nuisance. Essentially, public nuisance is a form of criminal liability arising from a wide range of antisocial activities. Many of these have subsequently been covered by specific legislation. For example selling unfit food, and giving short weight were originally public nuisances. There is now specific statutory provision governing food hygiene and weights and measures. Civil liability in public nuisance is secondary. In addition, there are a large number of statutory provisions aimed at the control of conduct which is damaging to the environment, some of which impose civil liability in respect of certain hazards. Enforcement of these provisions is in the hands of public bodies, which means that the claimant may save a good deal of time and expense by directing his complaint to the relevant body. These are sometimes referred to as statutory nuisances. You should note that public enforcement, whether civil or criminal, is much more common than a civil action.

Private nuisance

This tort protects against "indirect" interference with the claimant's use and enjoyment of land, such as excessive noise and the emission of smells or noxious fumes. Direct interferences, such as unlawfully walking across a neighbour's land or dumping rubbish in his garden, are dealt with by the tort of trespass to land (which is outside the scope of this text). Private nuisance is commonly defined as an unreasonable interference with the use or enjoyment of land.

The central issue in private nuisance is the issue of reasonableness and what constitutes unreasonable interference. In nuisance the law does not concentrate so much on the reasonableness of the defendant's conduct but rather on the unreasonableness of the interference; it seeks to strike a balance between the rights of occupiers to use their property as they choose and the rights of their neighbours not to have their use of land interfered with. This was traditionally summed up in the Latin phrase *sic utere tuo ut alienum non laedas.* This can be translated as "you must use your own property in such a way as not to harm that of others." In *Sedleigh-Denfield v O'Callagan* (HL, 1940) Lord Wright said a useful test is what is reasonable according to the ordinary usage of mankind living in a particular society. The approach taken by the courts to the protection of such interests is one of compromise, a "rule of give and take, live and let live": *Bamford v Turnley* (1862); *Walter v Selfe* (1851). A modern application of these principles can be seen in *Barr v Biffa* (CA, 2012) where unpleasant smells emanating from a waste tip operated by Biffa constituted an unlawful interference with the claimants' land because on the evidence they constituted a significant detriment and went beyond what was generally acceptable. In *Murdoch v Glacier Metal* (CA, 1998) the claimant was alleging noise nuisance. He was able to demonstrate that the noise was slightly in excess of an official standard. The court held that that was not decisive. The question was whether in all the circumstances the noise nuisance was excessive. In order to determine that factors such as the location, the nature of the activities carried on by the claimant and defendant respectively and all other circumstances had to be taken into account. The official standard was merely one factor, not the be all and end all.

CHECKPOINT

The claimant may bring an action in private nuisance where the defendant unlawfully interferes with his use or enjoyment of his land or of some right (such as an easement) that he may have in relation to it. Such activity is normally in itself perfectly lawful, but it becomes a nuisance when the consequences of pursuing it extend unreasonably to the land of his neighbour.

In *Crown River Cruises Ltd v Kimbolton Fireworks Ltd* (HC, 1996) the claimants claimed in negligence, nuisance and under the principle in *Rylands v Fletcher* for damage caused by the defendant's fireworks display to their floating barge, which was permanently moored to provide a landing stage, and also a passenger vessel moored alongside it on the River Thames. Kimbolton Fireworks argued that that the essence of nuisance was an interference with the use or enjoyment of land, not a floating barge. In rejecting this argument the court held that a permanently moored barge, occupied under a mooring licence, could give rise to the possibility of an action in private nuisance.

There are two distinct kinds of harm which can give rise to a claim in private nuisance.

(a) indirect interference by tangible, physical damage

- To cause an encroachment upon the claimant's land of some tangible thing such as tree roots may be actionable in nuisance (*Davey v Harrow*

Corp (CA, 1958)). The distinction between this form of invasion and a trespass is that, in this case, the interference is seen as indirect. Logically the roots are trespassing.

- Causing physical damage to the land, or to the buildings or vegetation upon it, may constitute a nuisance, as where a drain becomes blocked and floods the claimant's land (*Sedleigh-Denfield v O'Callagan* (HL, 1940)), or a building is allowed to fall into disrepair with the result that parts of it fall on the claimant's land (*Wringe v Cohen* (CA, 1940).

KEY CASE

SEDLEIGH-DENFIELD V O'CALLAGAN (1940)
Without the defendant's permission, and therefore technically trespassing, Middlesex County Council laid a pipe in a ditch on the defendant's land. The workmen involved did not place a grid near the mouth of the pipe to prevent leaves and debris blocking it. The defendants were aware of the pipe and the ditch was regularly checked and cleaned out twice a year by their groundsman on their behalf. Some years later, after a heavy rainstorm the pipe became blocked and caused flooding on the claimant's adjoining land.,

Held: (HL) The overflow of water onto the land of another constitutes physical damage and is actionable in nuisance. The defendants were liable for the nuisance because they ought to have appreciated the risk of flooding and taken reasonable steps to abate it. They had in effect accepted and adopted the pipe, even though it had actually been installed by a trespasser. They were the landowners and therefore ultimately responsible.

Comment
(1) In *Leakey v National Trust* (CA, 1980) a land slip was held to constitute a nuisance. In this case the National Trust occupied a piece of land which was geologically unstable. They were aware that landslips took place. In all the circumstances, Including the resources available to the National Trust, they were responsible for the landslips.
(2) *Hunter v London Docklands Development Corp* (HL, 1997) held that a deposit of dust is capable of giving rise to an action in nuisance.

(b) indirect interference with the right to have quiet and comfortable enjoyment of land

In the cases at (a) above the interference is evidenced by tangible, physical damage, but it may equally be a nuisance merely to interfere with a neighbour's right to quiet and comfortable enjoyment of his land. This may take a variety of forms, such as creating stench, dust, smoke, noise, vibration:

It may also extend into an interference which is moral rather than physical. In *Thompson-Schwab v Costaki* (CA, 1956), the use of a house in a respectable, residential area for prostitution was held to be an actionable nuisance (see also *Laws v Florinplace* (HC, 1981)). In this latter type of case involving so-called "amenity" (i.e. intangible) damage it appears, at least superficially, that the tort is concerned with the protection of the claimant personally, rather than the protection of property. On the other hand, it could be argued that the presence of a brothel is likely to affect property values, and therefore does impact directly on the land itself.

CHECKPOINT

Hunter v Canary Wharf Ltd (HL, 1997) makes it clear that private nuisance is a tort which concerns injury to land, regardless of the nature of the alleged damage. This means that the claimant must show that the land itself has been adversely affected, one consequence of which is that no action should lie in respect of personal injury (see, e.g. Lord Lloyd in *Hunter*). The Court of Appeal reiterated this principle in *Dobson v Thames Water Utilities Ltd* (2009) where a claim for damages arising from the emanation of odours and mosquitoes from the defendants' sewage treatment was rejected because the claimants had no legal interest in the land affected.

In *Hunter* a unanimous House of Lords held that no action lay for interference with television reception caused by the erection of a large building. This was equated to an interference with the view from a property. There has never been a legal right to such a view. Similarly there is no right to receive television signals from a particular location. The law seeks to achieve a balance between two competing interests, namely that of the defendant to use his land as he wishes and that of his neighbour not to be seriously inconvenienced by this. Not every interference is actionable, therefore, because people must be expected to tolerate some degree of inconvenience in the interests of peaceful co-existence. An interference becomes unlawful only where the defendant has put his land to an unreasonable use.

Where, however, the alleged nuisance causes tangible damage the claimant will usually have little difficulty in establishing an unlawful interference with his rights (though see, e.g. *Ellison v Ministry of Defence* (HC, 1997)); this is either because, in the case of such damage, many of the factors involved in the balancing exercise to determine whether the defendant's user of land is reasonable are irrelevant, or because such damage usually tips the balance irreversibly in the claimant's favour. On the other hand, in the case of amenity damage the claimant must prove a substantial interference with the ordinary comfort and convenience of living such as would adversely affect the average person, and it is in this context that the balancing exercise becomes more critical.

Where the action is for interference with a servitude, such as an easement, the claimant need only show a substantial degree of interference. It will then be treated in the same way as a claim for physical damage to property, so that no balancing exercise is necessary and the defendant's conduct is irrelevant, i.e. liability is strict.

Unreasonable interference

"The very essence of a private nuisance . . . is the unreasonable use by a man of his land to the detriment of his neighbour" (Lord Denning M.R. in *Miller v Jackson* (CA, 1977)). The defendant's actual or constructive knowledge of that detriment is a factor in determining whether the interference is unreasonable, but a number of other factors, including the character and duration of the interference, must also be considered.

KEY CASE

MILLER V JACKSON (1977)

In 1972 the claimant bought a house. It was built in such a place that it was inevitable that cricket balls from a cricket ground nearby would be hit into the garden. Cricket had been played on the ground since 1905 but the claimants contended that since the houses were built it had become a substantial interference and claimed in negligence and in nuisance.

Held: (CA) Because of the pleasure derived from cricket and its social utility in keeping village communities together, Lord Denning concluded that cricket balls coming into the property of those living near to the ground could not be a nuisance. However, the majority considered that the social utility of cricket could not justify a substantial interference with the claimants' enjoyment of their land. The playing of cricket was held to constitute an unreasonable interference with the claimant's enjoyment of land and was therefore a nuisance.

Comment

In this case no injunction was granted to restrain the cricket, instead damages were awarded. The court took the view that the utility of the activities of the club outweighed the claimant's interest, at least to the extent that damages were to be regarded as an adequate remedy.

Whether the defendant has unreasonably used his land cannot be gauged solely by reference to the nature of his conduct, because some foreseeable harm may be done which the law does not regard as excessive between neighbours under a principle of "give and take, or live and let live" (*Kennaway v Thompson* (CA, 1980)).

In deciding the issue of reasonable user, the court may have regard to the following matters:

1. Degree of interference
Where physical damage to property has been done, a relatively small interference may amount to a nuisance, but in other cases the interference must be substantial, something more than ordinary everyday inconveniences, such as the claimant will be expected to put up with.

CHECKPOINT

In *Walter v Selfe* (HC, 1851), the test was said to be whether there was: "an inconvenience materially interfering with the ordinary comfort physically of human existence, not merely according to elegant or dainty modes and habits of living, but according to plain and sober and simple notions among the English people".

It is therefore a question of degree as to whether the interference is sufficiently serious, and a good illustration is *Halsey v Esso Petroleum Co Ltd* (HC, 1961) where the defendants were held liable for, inter alia, nuisance caused by a nauseating smell emanating from their factory and by the noise at night both from the plant at their depot and from the arrival and departure of petrol tankers (discussed below under *Rylands v Fletcher*). On the evidence this went beyond what was tolerable even in a mixed commercial and residential district. Each case will of course turn on its precise facts.

2. Nature of the locality
A person living in an industrial town cannot expect the same freedom from noise and pollution as one who lives in the country, but this is not a relevant consideration where there is physical injury to property.

The nature of the locality is irrelevant where the interference causes physical damage. In *St Helen's Smelting Co v Tipping* (HL, 1865), the defendants were held liable for the emission of fumes from their factory in a manufacturing area which proved injurious to the claimant's shrubs.

St Helen's Smelting Co v Tipping (1865)

The claimant purchased a very valuable estate which was within a mile and a half of a large smelting works. Fumes from a copper smelter damaged trees and crops on the claimant's land. The defendant contended that the whole neighbourhood was devoted to similar manufacturing purposes and that the smelting should be allowed to carry on with impunity.

Held: (HL) The defendants were liable. The court drew a distinction between nuisances causing property damage and those causing personal discomfort. Lord Westbury highlighted that the locality rule applies only to cases of personal discomfort and does not apply where there is physical damage to the claimant's property. Property damage must not be inflicted wherever the defendant is carrying on the activity.

Comment

An interference which would not be permissible in one area may be in another. In *Sturges v Bridgman* (1879) Thesiger L.J. said: " ... what would be a nuisance in Belgrave Square would not necessarily be so in Bermondsey." This case involved premises in Harley Street. The claimant was a doctor. Harley Street is well-known as a location for medical practice. The defendant occupied premises in an adjoining street which he used for his business as a manufacturing confectioner. This involved the use of machinery to mix the various products. The claimant built a consulting room in the garden of his property close to the defendant's workshop. Noise and vibration from the defendant's machinery interfered to an acceptable extent with the use of the consulting room. Because this was an area characterised by residential and professional use, this level of interference was held by the court to be unacceptable. The result might well have been different had it been the claimant who was the atypical user of premises.

Conversely, in *Murdoch v Glacier Metal Co Ltd* (CA, 1998) night time factory noise was held not to constitute an actionable nuisance having regard to all the circumstances including, inter alia, the proximity of the claimant to a busy bypass, notwithstanding that the level of noise was marginally greater than the World Health Organisation's recommended level, above which the restorative value of sleep could be affected.

A grant of planning permission is not a licence to commit a nuisance, but where the effect of the change of use in pursuance of planning permission is to alter the character of the neighbourhood, the question of whether a nuisance arises must be decided by reference to that character as altered and not as it was previously (*Gillingham BC v Medway (Chatham) Dock Co Ltd* (HC, 1992)). On the other hand, if the effect of the grant cannot be regarded as changing the character of the neighbourhood, there may be an actionable nuisance even though the interference inevitably results from the authorised use (*Wheeler v J.J. Saunders Ltd* (CA, 1995)). *Watson v Croft Promo-Sport Ltd* (CA, 2009) applied the principle in *Wheeler* where owners of a home located close to a motor racing circuit were awarded damages for the diminution in value of their property and loss of amenity. The Court of Appeal rejected the argument put forward by the motor circuit operator that there was no actionable nuisance because the nature and character of the locality had been changed by the planning permission.

KEY CASE

WHEELER V JJ SAUNDERS LTD (1995)

The defendants had obtained planning permission for two pig-weaning houses to facilitate the intensification of pig farming on a site already used for that purpose. In response to the claimant's claim in nuisance the defendants contended that, since they had obtained planning permission, any smell emanating from the pigs kept in the weaning houses could not amount to a nuisance.

Held: (CA) The defendants were liable. Staughton L.J. said:

"It would in my opinion be a misuse of language to describe what has happened in the present case as a change in the character of the neighbourhood. It is a change of use of a very small piece of land, a little over 350 square metres according to the dimensions on the plan, for the benefit of the applicant and to the detriment of the objectors in the quiet enjoyment of their house. It is not a strategic planning decision affected by considerations of public interest. Unless one is prepared to accept that any planning decision authorises any nuisance which must inevitably come from it, the argument that the nuisance was authorised by planning permission in this case must fail."

3. Social utility

The mere fact that the defendant's act is of benefit to the community will not in itself relieve the defendant of liability. Since nuisance is concerned with a balancing of conflicting interests, however, it may be that the claimant will have to bear minor disturbances. Once again it is a question of degree and if there is physical damage or the interference is substantial, the public interest should not be allowed to prevail over private rights (*Kennaway v Thompson* (CA, 1981); cf. *Miller v Jackson* (CA, 1977)). In *Adams v Ursell* (HC, 1913), the smell from a fried fish shop was held to constitute a nuisance to nearby residents, notwithstanding the defendant's argument that he was providing a valuable service to poor people in the neighbourhood. It should of course be borne in mind that the fried fish shop was actually in a relatively affluent neighbourhood.

KEY CASE

KENNAWAY V THOMPSON (1981)

The claimant had built a house near a man-made lake (a former gravel pit) and was disturbed by water-skiing and speed-boat racing which the defendant club was beginning to organise on the lake. She was aware that some level of activity was taking place. However over a period of time the number of events, size and noise of boats and the overall level of interference increased substantially. The defendants were held liable for the nuisance created by the noise but they argued that an injunction should not be granted on the ground that there was a public interest in permitting the water sports to continue.

Held: (CA) The public interest in having sports facilities available was taken into account. The claimant was therefore granted an injunction. The terms of the injunction reflected the fact that some level of water sport activity on the lake was permissible. The injunction limited activity to the level which was reasonably acceptable in the circumstances.

Comment
(1) The court was not prepared to give unconditional priority to the public interest and the decision in *Miller v Jackson* was criticised. However, the injunction granted to the claimant was formulated in terms which did amount to a compromise that was obviously influenced by public interest. Motor-boat racing was permitted to continue on the lake subject to the injunction restricting the number and extent of racing activities in each year and the noise level of boats using the lake at other times.
(2) In *Dennis v MoD* (HC, 2003) the claimants were the occupiers of a property close to RAF Wittering. This air force base housed a large number of aircraft. Training and operational missions caused very considerable noise nuisance. There was a public interest in ensuring that military training could take place. However, it was held that the level of interference was unacceptable, constituted a nuisance and was actionable.

4. Abnormal sensitivity

A man cannot increase the liabilities of his neighbour by applying his own property to special uses, whether for business or for pleasure (*Eastern and South African Telegraph Co Ltd v Cape Town Tramways Co Ltd* (PC, 1902)).

5. State of affairs

It is often said that the interference must be continuous or recurrent rather than merely temporary or occasional. An injunction will not normally be granted unless there is some degree of permanence in the defendant's activities, except in extreme cases (see, e.g. *De Keyser's Royal Hotel Ltd v Spicer Bros Ltd* (HC, 1914); cf. *Murdoch v Glacier Metal Co Ltd* (CA, 1998)). The duration of the interference, and the times at which it occurs, are important in determining whether the defendant is liable. A man who builds an extension on to the back of his house no doubt causes inconvenience to his neighbour, but he is not liable for nuisance if he takes all reasonable care to see that no undue annoyance is caused (*Harrison v Southwark and Vauxhall Water Co* (HC, 1891)). If, on the other hand, he conducts his operations at unreasonable hours, or takes an inordinately long time, or uses inappropriate methods and thereby increases the level of interference, he may be liable (*Andreae v Selfridge & Co Ltd* (CA, 1938)).

An isolated escape is probably not actionable as a nuisance (*S.C.M. (United Kingdom) Ltd v Whittall & Son Ltd* (HC, 1970)), though it may afford evidence of the existence of a dangerous state of affairs upon the defendant's land. In *Spicer v Smee* (HC, 1946), for example, defective electrical wiring which started a fire and caused damage to adjacent property was held to constitute a nuisance. In *Crown River Cruises Ltd v Kimbolton Fireworks Ltd*

(HC, 1996), the holding of a firework display in circumstances where it was inevitable that for 15–20 minutes burning debris would fall upon nearby property of a potentially flammable nature was held to constitute a nuisance. Furthermore, there may be liability in negligence or under the rule in *Rylands v Fletcher* (see below) in respect of a single escape.

6. Intentional annoyance

Malice: an activity which is not of itself unlawful may become a nuisance when the defendant's activities are motivated by malice. If the defendant carries out his activity with the express purpose of annoying his neighbour, he will be liable, even though the degree of interference would not constitute a nuisance if done in the ordinary and reasonable use of property (*Christie v Davey* (HC, 1893)).

KEY CASE

CHRISTIE V DAVIE (1893)
The claimant, a music teacher, lived in a semi-detached house. The claimant organised various musical activities involving himself, his family, and his pupils. They all represented bona fide musical activity, although the report is silent as to the quality of the performances. The defendant, who lived next door, was annoyed by the music lessons and other performances and in retaliation he banged on the party wall, beat trays, whistled and shrieked.

Held: (HC) Conduct which is motivated by malice may convert what would otherwise have been a reasonable act into an actionable nuisance. An injunction was granted but North J. indicated that he would have taken a different view of the situation if the defendant's acts had been "innocent". However, the truth of the matter was that the defendant was not pursuing a legitimate activity of his own, merely seeking to disrupt the claimant's activities.

Comment
The presence of malice in the defendant's conduct in the use of their own land may tip the balance towards finding the user unreasonable. In *Hollywood Silver Fox Farm Ltd v Emmett* (HC, 1936) the defendant's premises adjoined the claimant's silver fox farm. In attempting to prevent the foxes from breeding the defendant discharged guns on his own land as near as possible to the boundary of the claimant's land in order to scare the foxes. Macnaghten J. considered the intention of the defendant to be relevant in nuisance and an injunction and damages were awarded.

An anomalous case is *Bradford Corp v Pickles* (HL, 1895) where, in order to induce the claimants to buy his land, the defendant abstracted percolating water, which flowed in undefined channels beneath his land and which fed the claimants' reservoir. His motive was held to be irrelevant and he was therefore not liable. This is distinguishable from *Emmett* on the ground that the claimant had no right to receive the water, so that there was no interest to be protected. The right to make noise on one's land, however, is qualified by the right of one's neighbour to the quiet enjoyment of his land. A landowner's right to abstract subterranean water flowing in undefined channels, regardless of the consequences to his neighbour and of his motive, was affirmed in *Stephens v Anglian Water Authority* (CA, 1987).

Damage
Damage must usually be proved, either in the form of tangible injury to land or to property upon it, or in the form of amenity damage as evidenced by substantial personal discomfort, though nuisance to a servitude may be actionable per se (*Nicholls v Ely Beet Sugar Factory Ltd* (HC, 1936)). In the light of *Hunter v Canary Wharf Ltd* (HL, 1997), it seems that no claim will lie in respect of personal injury or for damage to personal property where the land itself is not adversely affected.

Who can sue?
It is now clear that only a person with a proprietary or possessory interest in the land can sue, as originally established in *Malone v Laskey* (CA, 1907). A majority of the House of Lords so held in *Hunter v Canary Wharf Ltd* (HL, 1997), overruling the Court of Appeal on this point in *Khorasandjian v Bush* (CA, 1993) and in *Hunter* itself. Thus, a freeholder, a tenant in possession and a licensee with exclusive possession may sue, as may a landlord out of possession whose reversionary interest is adversely affected.

> **KEY CASE**
>
> **MALONE V LASKEY (1907)**
> Vibrations on the defendant's property caused the collapse of a cistern in the adjoining premises. The claimant, the wife of the occupier of the adjoining premises, suffered injury as a result.
>
> **Held:** (CA) She had no claim in private nuisance because she had no proprietary or possessory interest in the land.

If the claimant does have the requisite interest he can recover in respect of a continuing nuisance even though the damage occurs before he acquires his interest and before he is aware of it (*Masters v Brent London BC* (HC, 1978); *Delaware Mansions Ltd v Westminster City Council* (HL, 2001)).

Who is liable?

1. The creator

The creator of the nuisance is liable whether or not he occupies the land whence the interference emanates (*Hall v Beckenham Corp* (HC, 1949)). He remains liable even if he parts with possession and is no longer able to stop the nuisance without committing trespass.

2. The occupier

The occupier will be liable if he creates the nuisance, but, apart from this, he may incur liability either in respect of the acts of others upon his land (*Sedleigh-Denfield v O'Callaghan* (HL, 1940)) or where the nuisance existed before he became the occupier. He may also be answerable for those whom he allows on to his land as guests (*Att Gen v Stone* (HC, 1895)), at least if he knew or should have known of the interference.

CHECKPOINT

Although the general rule is that an employer is not liable for the defaults of his contractor, he will be liable if he is under a non-delegable duty where:

- there is a withdrawal of support from neighbouring land (*Bower v Peate* (HC, 1876);
- operations are conducted on or adjoining the highway (*Tarry v Ashton* (HC, 1876); see Ch.10).

It seems that he will also be liable whenever the work that a contractor is employed to do creates a foreseeable risk of nuisance. In *Matania v National Provincial Bank Ltd* (CA, 1936), the occupier of premises who employed contractors to carry out alterations was held liable for nuisance by dust and noise caused to other occupants in the building. In *Spicer v Smee* (HC, 1946), it was said that "where danger is likely to arise unless the work is properly done, there is a duty to see that it is properly done", but this proposition is probably too wide (*Salsbury v Woodland* (CA, 1970)). The point is that the property owner is responsible for harm which inevitably results from the instructions that he has given for work to be carried out. If however the work could have been carried out without this harm occurring, but it is carried out incompetently and the harm does occur, liability shall attach to the contractor and not to the employer.

Nuisance created by a trespasser

If a nuisance is created by a trespasser, the occupier is liable not only if he adopts the nuisance for his own purposes (*Page Motors Ltd v Epsom and Ewell BC* (HC, 1982)) but also if, with actual or constructive knowledge of its existence, he fails to take reasonable steps to abate it (in which case he is said to "continue" the nuisance). This principle was laid down in *Sedleigh-Denfield v O'Callaghan* (HL, 1940) and has since been extended to dangerous states of affairs which arise naturally upon the land.

Liability for a dangerous state of affairs arising naturally on the land

In *Goldman v Hargrave* (PC, 1967), a tree on the defendant's land was struck by lightning and caught fire. The defendant had the tree felled and decided to let the fire burn itself out, but it eventually spread to and damaged the claimant's land. The defendant was held liable because, with actual knowledge of the danger, he failed to take reasonable steps to abate it (followed in *Leakey v National Trust* (CA, 1980)). It must be noted that liability in this situation is based on a negligence principle, rather than the normal rules applicable to private nuisance.

KEY CASE

GOLDMAN V HARGRAVE (1967)

A redgum tree, 100 feet high, on the defendant's land was struck by lightning and caught fire. The defendant caused the land around the burning tree to be cleared and the tree was then cut down. He did not extinguish the fire after doing this in the belief that the fire would eventually burn itself out. However, it kept smouldering and subsequently the wind increased and the fire spread to the claimant's land.

Held: (PC) Occupiers who become aware of the existence of a nuisance arising out of a natural condition on their land are bound to take positive action. Therefore the occupier was liable for failing to take adequate precautions to extinguish the fire in the face of foreseeable risk.

Comment

In *Leakey v National Trust* (CA, 1980) the Court of Appeal extended the principle in *Goldman* to include nuisances caused by the natural condition of the land itself and held that ownership of land carries with it a duty to take whatever steps are reasonable in all the circumstances to prevent hazards on the land, however they might arise, from causing damage to a neighbour.

Nuisance created by a natural occurrence

In *Holbeck Hall Hotel v Scarborough BC* (CA, 2000), natural coastal erosion caused a catastrophic land slip. As a result the claimant's hotel was damaged by lack of support from land owned by the borough council and had to be demolished. The Court of Appeal held that a "measured" duty of care to a neighbouring landowner could arise as a result of a danger due to lack of support caused by a land slip in just the same way as it arose out of an escape or encroachment of a noxious thing. The scope of the defendant's duty, however, was to avoid damage to the claimant's land which they ought to have foreseen. They were not liable for a catastrophic collapse which they could only have discovered by further geological investigation. In other words this was again a liability based on negligence. In *Vernon Knight Associates v Cornwall County Council* (CA, 2013) the Court of Appeal considered what was fair, just and reasonable between the neighbouring parties in relation to the measures necessary to prevent flooding. In finding the local authority liable the court took account of the fact that it was a public authority with substantial resources.

Where a nuisance has been created by the defendant's predecessor as occupier of the land in question, the claimant must prove that the defendant knew, or ought to have known, of its existence (*St Anne's Well Brewery Co v Roberts* (CA, 1928)).

3. The landlord

Where the premises are let the normal defendant is the tenant. The landlord will, however, be liable in the following circumstances.

First, if he expressly or impliedly authorises the nuisance, as where the interference arises as a result of using the land for the very purpose for which it was let (*Harris v James* (HC, 1876); *Tetley v Chitty* (HC, 1986)). In *Smith v Scott* (HC, 1973), a local authority was held not to have authorised the commission of a nuisance by a "problem" family which it had housed next to the claimant. The basis of the decision is that the acts complained of were voluntary acts by the tenants. The letting of the property merely provided the tenants with the opportunity to commit these acts. They were not obliged to do so, and while it was undoubtedly convenient for the Council to subject the claimant to the "neighbours from hell", the actual behaviour was that of the tenants.

In *Hussain v Lancaster City Council* (CA, 1999), the council was not liable in respect of a long term campaign of racial harassment against a shopkeeper by the local authority's tenants because the acts complained of did not involve the use of the tenants' land. *Hussain* was distinguished in *Lippiatt v South Gloucestershire Council* (CA, 1999), where the council allowed trespassers to park their caravans on a piece of its land bordering the claimant's farm. The council could have evicted the travellers from its land but had failed to so and was therefore held liable for the travellers' repeated acts of interference.

Secondly, the landlord is liable if he either knew or ought to have known of the nuisance before letting the premises.

Thirdly, if the premises fall into disrepair during the period of the lease, he is liable if he has reserved the right to enter and repair (*Heap v Ind Coope & Allsopp Ltd* (CA, 1940)), and such a right will readily be implied in a short-term tenancy (*Mint v Good* (CA, 1951)); today the Landlord and Tenant Act 1985 provides that, where a dwelling-house is let for less than seven years, there is an implied covenant by the landlord to keep in repair the structure and exterior of the premises, and certain installations for the supply of essential services. The landlord is clearly liable where he is under an express covenant to repair, but it was held in *Brew Bros Ltd v Snax (Ross) Ltd* (CA, 1970) that he does not escape responsibility by extracting that obligation from his tenants, provided that he knows or ought to know of the nuisance.

CHECKPOINT

Liability for premises adjoining a highway
In one particular case, that is where premises adjoining a highway collapse and cause injury to a passer-by or to an adjoining owner, liability is, according to *Wringe v Cohen* (CA, 1940), strict, subject to a defence either that the defect was due to a secret and unobservable process of nature or to the act of a trespasser (but in the latter case see *Sedleigh-Denfield v O'Callaghan* (above)).

KEY CASE

WRINGE V COHEN (1940)
Because of want of repair, a wall to the defendant's premises collapsed and damaged the claimant's shop. The house was let to a weekly tenant but the defendant was liable to keep the premises in repair. He did not know that the wall was in a dangerous condition and that it had, as a consequence of this, become a nuisance.

Held: (CA) The defendant was liable. A landlord who has an obligation to repair or who reserves the right to enter and repair may be liable. The court stated:

- "If, owing to want of repair, premises on a highway become dangerous and, therefore, a nuisance, and a passer-by or an adjoining owner suffers damage by their collapse, the occupier, or owner if he has undertaken the duty of repair, is answerable whether he knew or ought to have known of the danger or not."

Apart from these common law obligations the landlord may also be liable under the Defective Premises Act 1972, s.4. This provides that if the landlord is under an obligation to his tenant to repair, or has an express or implied power to enter and repair, he owes a duty to take reasonable care to see that all who might reasonably be expected to be affected by defects in the state of the premises are reasonably safe from personal injury or damage to their property. A right to repair will be implied where the landlord could, if necessary, obtain an injunction to enter and effect repairs (*McAuley v Bristol City Council* (CA, 1992)).

The Human Rights Act 1998
A common law nuisance may further constitute an interference with a claimant's rights under art.8 of the European Convention on Human Rights (respect for private and family life) and/or Protocol 1, art.1 (protection of property). Since the **Human Rights Act 1998** came into force such rights may be relied on in domestic courts but Human Rights principles require a fair balance between competing interests.

In *Marcic v Thames Water* (HL, 2003), sewers provided by Thames Water had caused flooding which discharged both surface water and foul water on to the claimant's garden. Many thousands of other householders were at a similar risk of flooding as a consequence of the discharge from overburdened sewers in the Thames area. Thames Water claimed that the cost of work required to alleviate the flooding would result in a total expenditure in excess of £1 billion and they sought to rely on lack of resources to justify their decision to take no steps to abate the nuisance. The House of Lords held that there was a statutory scheme which determined the rights and responsibilities of Thames Water. This scheme was intended to be comprehensive and as a result excluded private law remedies.

The decision of the Grand Chamber of the European Court of Human Rights in *Hatton v United Kingdom* (ECtHR, 2003) makes clear that the Convention does not accord absolute protection to environmental considerations. It requires a fair balance to be struck between the competing interests of the parties involved. Parliament achieved this balance in *Marcic* through a statutory regulatory scheme and the involvement of an independent regulator under the Water Industry Act 1991.

Defences

1. Prescription: 20 years' continuance
A right to commit a private nuisance may be acquired by 20 years' continuance thereof, though it may be that this is only so where the right is capable of existing as an easement, such as the right of eavesdrop which

involves water running off onto neighbouring premises. It has been doubted whether the defendant can acquire a prescriptive right to cause unlawful interference by such things as noise, smoke, smell or vibration in which the degree of inconvenience is variable and may at times cease altogether. The claimant must have full knowledge of the nuisance before the period begins to run, and there must have been an actionable nuisance during the 20 years.

In *Sturges v Bridgman* (CA, 1879), as we have seen, the claimant built a consulting room at the end of his garden and complained of noise from the defendant's premises. The defendant's argument that he had been pursuing his trade for more than 20 years failed, because the interference did not become actionable as a nuisance until the claimant extended his premises.

2. Statutory authority

Many nuisance actions arise out of the activities of bodies authorised by statute to conduct those operations. It is generally a defence to prove that the interference is an inevitable result of what they were obliged or empowered to do, so that there will be no liability without negligence (*Manchester Corp v Farnworth* (HL, 1930)). The following principles were laid down in *Department of Transport v North West Water Authority* (HL, 1984). First, in fulfilling a statutory duty there is no liability without negligence, whether or not liability for nuisance is expressly preserved in the Act. Secondly, in exercising a statutory power, liability depends upon whether nuisance is expressly preserved; if it is, negligence need not be proved, but if it is not, there is no liability in the absence of negligence (see also Ch.9).

Precisely what a body is authorised or obliged to do depends upon the provisions of the Act.

A liberal interpretation was given in *Allen v Gulf Oil Refining Ltd* (HL, 1981), where authority to acquire land and build a refinery was held to confer, by necessary implication, the right to operate the refinery. Since there was no express provision for liability in nuisance, the defendants were held not liable for the inevitable consequences of working the refinery, however liability could exist in relation to nuisance arising from choices made by the defendant. E.g. if there was statutory power to make a railway connection to the site, and the defendant chose to locate the railway installations adjacent to neighbouring residential property, there might be liability in relation to the resulting noise nuisance. But this assumes that the railway installations could have been located elsewhere on the site resulting in a lesser degree of interference with the claimant.

3. Coming to nuisance

It is no defence that the claimant moved into the area of the nuisance (*Sturges v Bridgman* (CA, 1879); *Miller v Jackson* (CA, 1977)).

4. Other defences

Consent and contributory negligence are valid defences, although not likely in nuisance actions. Necessity, act of God, and act of a stranger are defences provided that there is no negligence. It is no defence, however, that the nuisance was the product of the combined acts of two or more persons, though the act of any one individual would not be unlawful (*Lambton v Mellish* (HC, 1894)).

Remedies

The claimant may recover damages for any resulting loss which is of a reasonably foreseeable kind (*The Wagon Mound (No.2)* (PC, 1967)).

The remedy of an injunction is an equitable one and will therefore only be granted where damages would be inadequate. If the interference is trivial or temporary it is unlikely to be granted, but it should not be refused simply on the ground that the defendant's activity is in the public interest. For the factors to be considered in determining whether damages should be awarded in lieu of an injunction see *Shelfer v City of London Electric Lighting Co* (CA, 1895). The principles laid down in that case were applied in *Jaggard v Sawyer* (CA, 1995) where the fact that the defendants had acted openly and in good faith, and that the claimant had delayed in seeking interlocutory relief, were considered to be relevant (though not conclusive) factors in deciding that the grant of an injunction would be oppressive.

CHECKPOINT

Injunction an equitable remedy

- The majority decision in *Miller v Jackson* (CA, 1977) not to grant an injunction in respect of the frequent escape of cricket balls from the defendant's land because the cricket club was a valuable local amenity, was held to be wrong in *Kennaway v Thompson* (CA, 1981). However this criticism is somewhat unfair, since the decision in *Miller v Jackson* resulted from the illogical approach of Lord Denning. Geoffrey Lane LJ dealt with the case in an entirely orthodox way, but was not supported by his colleagues.

- An injunction is a flexible remedy and terms may be imposed, for example as to the types of activity permitted and the times at which it may be conducted. This was done in *Kennaway* (above) but the court refused to do so in *Tetley v Chitty* (HC, 1986), distinguishing *Kennaway* on the ground that, in that case, the defendants had been pursuing their activities before the claimant moved into the area.

TETLEY V CHITTY (1986)
Residents in Rochester complained of noise from a go-cart track which could be heard in their houses. Medway Borough Council had granted planning permission for the go-cart track on its land and had granted a lease to a go-cart club. The local authority, having leased the land, was no longer in occupation of it.

Held: (HC) The general rule is that a landlord who has leased premises is not liable for nuisances arising from them except where the landlord granted the lease for the purpose which constitutes the nuisance. Here, the local authority was liable: excessive noise was a very predictable consequence of the use for which the land had been let. Indeed any configuration of the go-kart track would result in an actionable level of interference.

The standard of liability

A question of some considerable difficulty is the extent to which fault (i.e. negligence) is relevant to an action in nuisance. According to the House of Lords in *Cambridge Water Co v Eastern Counties Leather Plc* (HL, 1994), subject to the concept of reasonable user liability is generally regarded as strict; that is to say that if the defendant's user is unreasonable it matters not that he took all reasonable care to avoid the interference. This at least is the position where the defendant actively created the dangerous state of affairs which caused the damage; in other cases, as has been noted, the claimant will generally have to prove fault.

A distinction must be drawn between a claim for damages and an application for an injunction to restrain future harm. In the latter case the defendant will inevitably become aware of the interference at the latest when the claimant institutes proceedings, so the question of fault is then largely irrelevant; the defendant's conduct is deliberate as soon as he has knowledge of the interference, and the court is simply concerned with whether the degree of interference exceeds that which the claimant can reasonably be expected to tolerate.

Where the defendant could not reasonably have foreseen the possibility of interference of the type which in fact occurs he is not liable. If he later acquires actual or constructive knowledge of a potential danger he may be liable in negligence if he fails to take steps to abate it, but it seems he cannot be liable once that danger has passed out of his control. What is not clear from *Cambridge Water* is the position where the defendant knows that his activity creates a possible risk and takes all reasonable care to avoid it. To suggest that the defendant would not be liable in the absence of fault seems to run counter to dicta in Lord Goff's judgment that the defendant would be strictly liable if the risk materialised. On the other hand it is not easy to see how the defendant can be said to have put his land to an unreasonable use for so long as the activity is conducted with reasonable care without causing any interference to his neighbours. It would appear that the question of the extent to which liability is truly strict therefore requires further elucidation.

PUBLIC NUISANCE

A public nuisance may be defined as an unlawful act or omission which interferes with a public right, or which materially affects the comfort and convenience of a class of Her Majesty's subjects who come within the sphere of its operation; whether the number of persons affected is sufficiently large to warrant the epithet "public" is a question of fact (*Att Gen v PYA Quarries Ltd* (CA, 1957)). At common law, public nuisances cover a wide variety of activities such as carrying on an offensive trade, selling food unfit for human consumption and obstructing the highway.

Public and private nuisance
Public nuisance is a crime in respect of which the Attorney-General may, if a criminal prosecution is felt to be inadequate, bring a "relator" action for an injunction to restrain the offending activity.

> **CHECKPOINT**
>
> The same conduct may amount to both a private and a public nuisance. However, an individual may only sue in tort in respect of the latter if he has suffered "particular" damage, which means loss or damage over and above that suffered by the rest of the class affected. This encompasses personal injury, and there is clearly no requirement that the claimant must have an interest in the land.

In *Halsey v Esso Petroleum Co Ltd* (HC, 1961), the claimant's washing was damaged by the emission of acid smuts from the defendants' factory, as was the paintwork of his car which was parked in the road outside his house. The damage to the washing was actionable as a private nuisance, since it occurred on the claimant's land and therefore interfered with his rights as landowner, whilst that to the car amounted to particular damage for the purposes of an action in public nuisance. The term "particular damage" may also include loss of an economic nature consequential upon the interference.

In *Tate & Lyle Industries Ltd v GLC* (HL, 1983), the claimants were held entitled to recover the cost of dredging to facilitate access to their jetty, which had been obstructed by the defendants' building works. This access was a constituent part of their right of navigation on a public waterway. (See also *Lyons, Sons & Co v Gulliver*, CA, 1914).

KEY CASE

TATE & LYLE FOOD AND DISTRIBUTION LTD v GLC (1983)
Ferry terminals constructed by the defendants in the River Thames caused excessive silting. This disrupted the claimant's business by obstructing access to their jetty and they had to spend large sums on dredging operations. Their claim in private nuisance was dismissed because: (1) the jetty itself was unaffected and (2) they had no private rights of property in the river bed.

Held: (HL) In order to succeed in an action for public nuisance a claimant must suffer "particular damage" over and above the damage sustained by the public generally. Here, it was the claimant's public right to use the river which had been damaged and their claim lay in public nuisance alone. The expenditure incurred by the claimants on dredging constituted particular damage over and above the ordinary inconvenience suffered by the public at large, and was therefore recoverable.

Nuisance on the highway

Perhaps the most common instance of public nuisance is an unlawful obstruction or interference with the public's right of passage along the highway. In *Castle v St Augustine's Links* (HC, 1922), for example, the defendant golf club was held liable for so siting one of its fairways that golf balls were frequently sliced on to the highway, with the result that the claimant was injured while driving along the road when a ball crashed through the windscreen of his car. In *Wandsworth London BC v Railtrack Plc* (CA, 2001), droppings from feral pigeons roosting under a railway bridge created a hazard over the footpath and to pedestrians and therefore constituted a public nuisance.

To conduct one's trade in such a manner as to cause a foreseeable obstruction is actionable, and if such obstruction causes loss of custom to other traders, that is special damage (*Lyons, Sons & Co v Gulliver* (CA, 1914)). The claimant must in all cases prove damage.

Where damage is done by a projection over the highway, there may be a distinction between artificial and natural things. In the case of the former, liability is strict (*Tarry v Ashton* (HC, 1876)), whereas in the case of natural projections (e.g. trees) it seems that negligence must be proved and, even though the source of the nuisance is plain to see, the occupier will not be liable until he has actual or constructive knowledge that it is a danger (*British Road Services Ltd v Slater* (HC, 1964)). With regard to premises adjoining the highway, the nature of the liability imposed by *Wringe v Cohen* (CA, 1940) has already been mentioned.

A highway authority is under a duty to maintain the highway and may be liable in negligence, nuisance or, normally, for breach of statutory duty under the **Highways Act 1980**. This right of action for non-repair does not, however, extend to claims for pure economic loss (*Wentworth v Wiltshire CC* (CA, 1993)). The Act provides that it shall be a defence to prove that the authority had taken such care as in all the circumstances was reasonably required to make sure that the part of the highway to which the action relates was not dangerous for traffic. Nor does the authority owe a duty of care to exercise its statutory powers for the benefit of road users (*Stovin v Wise* (HL, 1996)).

THE RULE IN RYLANDS V FLETCHER

INTRODUCTION

Although the law of tort is predominantly fault-based there are instances in which liability may be imposed without negligence on the defendant's part. Thus, there may be strict liability for damage caused by defective products (see Ch.7) and an employer's vicarious liability for the torts of its employees is similarly not dependent on fault on the part of the employer (see Ch.10). It has also been seen that liability in nuisance may be strict where the defendant created the source of the interference, in the sense that, if the defendant's user is unreasonable, it is irrelevant that he took all reasonable care to avoid it. Strict civil liability is also imposed by certain statutes; see, e.g. **Nuclear Installations Act 1965**.

Apart from the above instances a form of strict liability may arise under the rule in *Rylands v Fletcher* (HL, 1868) and in respect of the escape of fire.

Although the rule in *Rylands v Fletcher* has its origins in nuisance it had, until recently, come to be regarded as having evolved into a distinct principle governing liability for the escape of dangerous things. In *Cambridge Water Co Ltd v Eastern Counties Leather Plc* (HL, 1994), it was said that it would lead to a more coherent body of common law principles if the rule were to be regarded as an extension of the law of nuisance to cases of isolated escapes from land (even though the rule is not limited to escapes which are in fact isolated). The point here is that a private nuisance must normally arise out of a state of affairs which implies some degree of continuity or repetition. However, the *Rylands* principle has been restated with certainty in *Transco v Stockport Metropolitan BC* (2003), where the House of Lords held that the strict liability rule, which had stood for nearly 150 years, should not be discarded, but they did confirm that it was a branch of private nuisance. In consequence, it does not cover claims for personal injury. Earlier decisions awarding damages for personal injury under the rule are therefore no longer good law.

CHECKPOINT

The rule in *Rylands v Fletcher* was stated by Blackburn J. as follows

> "We think that the true rule of law is, that the person who for his own purposes brings on his lands and collects and keeps there anything likely to do mischief if it escapes must keep it in at his peril, and, if he does not do so, is prima facie answerable for all the damage which is the natural consequence of its escape."

KEY CASE

RYLANDS V FLETCHER (1868)

The defendant mill owners employed independent contractors, who were apparently competent, to build a reservoir on their land to provide water for their mill. Beneath the site there were some disused mine shafts and passages which, unknown to the defendants, were connected to the claimant's mine. The contractors negligently omitted to block the old shafts and when the reservoir was filled the water burst through them and flooded the claimant's mine.

Held: (HL) The House of Lords affirmed the decision of the Court of Exchequer Chamber holding the defendants liable but Lord Cairns rested his decision on the ground that the defendant had made a "non-natural use" of his land. This was actually a qualification of the rule stated by Blackburn J, although Lord Cairns' language suggested that he was not aware that he was amending or qualifying the decision in the court below.

Comment

(1) There is overlap between *Rylands v Fletcher* and nuisance but the rule in *Rylands v Fletcher* is concerned with escapes from land rather than interference with land. In *Transco v Stockport MBC* (2004) the House of Lords was asked to review the application of the *Rylands* principle in modern conditions. Although the law of negligence has been greatly expanded since *Rylands* was decided and a claimant who is entitled to succeed under the rule would now also have a claim in negligence, their Lordships rejected the abolition of the strict liability rule. Personal injury claims must be pursued in negligence.

(2) The word "dangerous" is not interpreted literally and there is no requirement that the thing which escapes must be dangerous in itself. Water is not dangerous in itself. However massive quantities of water can be dangerous. Obviously dangerous things such as explosives and gas clearly come within the rule in *Rylands v Fletcher* but the rule has also been applied to such items as a "chair-o-plane" in a fairground: *Hale v Jennings Bros* (1938). This is not an inherently dangerous item, but obviously can become so if, as happened in the case, it comes loose from its moorings and is projected at a distance.

(3) The defendant must be in control of the dangerous thing. However, it is not necessary for the defendant to have a proprietary interest in the land from which the dangerous thing escapes. In *Rigby v Chief Constable of Northamptonshire* (HC, 1985) when the police discharged a CS gas canister from the highway, Taylor J. commented that he could:

> "see no difference in principle between allowing a man-eating tiger to escape from your land on to that of another and allowing it to escape from the back of your wagon parked on the highway."

Things brought on to the land

There is no liability under this rule for an escape of things naturally upon the land such as self-sown vegetation (*Giles v Walker* (CA, 1890)), or an outcrop of rock which falls by the process of weathering (*Pontardawe RDC v Moore-Gwyn* (HC, 1929)). The defendant may however be liable in nuisance or negligence in accordance with *Goldman v Hargrave* (above), and will also be liable if he is instrumental in causing the escape of something naturally upon his land, as where the blasting of explosives caused an escape of rock (*Miles v Forest Rock Granite Co Ltd* (CA, 1918)). It must now be taken as clear that forseeability is an element necessary to establish liability under *Rylands v Fletcher* as under nuisance.

Likely to do mischief

The rule has over the years been applied to a wide variety of things including water, gas, electricity, fire, explosions, vibrations, noxious fumes, flag-poles and fairground swings.

In *Cambridge Water* the House of Lords rejected any rationalisation of the rule in *Rylands v Fletcher* into a broad principle of liability for damage caused by extra hazardous activities, inclining to the view that this was a matter best left to Parliament. It was also held that, by analogy with nuisance, the rule did not apply unless damage of the relevant type was foreseeable as the result of an escape, though it was made clear that liability was strict notwithstanding that the defendant had exercised all reasonable care and skill to prevent the escape.

KEY CASE

CAMBRIDGE WATER CO V EASTERN COUNTIES LEATHER PLC (1994)

The defendants, an old established leather manufacturer, used a chemical solvent PCE in their tanning process. PCE evaporates quickly in the air but is not readily soluble in water. In the course of the process, before a change of method in 1976, continual small spillages had gradually built up a pool of PCE under their premises. The solvent seeped into the soil below and contaminated the aquifer from which the claimants drew their water. At first instance the claim in *Rylands v Fletcher* was dismissed because it was held that there was no non-natural user of the land. The nuisance action failed because at the time the contamination was taking place it was not foreseen that the quantities of the chemical would accumulate or that if it did, there would be any significant damage.

> **Held:** (HL) The claims in negligence and nuisance failed for lack of foreseeability. The action in *Rylands v Fletcher* also failed because the defendants had not known, and could not reasonably have foreseen, that the seepage would cause the pollution.

Escape

There must be an "escape from a place where the defendant has occupation or control over land to a place which is outside his occupation or control" (*Read v J. Lyons & Co Ltd* (HL, 1947). In *Transco* (2003) (above), the House of Lords held that there had been no "escape" when the water which leaked from the council's service pipe remained on its land. Provided there has been a non-natural user, the thing which escapes need not be the subject-matter of the accumulation (*Miles v Forest Rock Granite Co Ltd* (CA, 1918)).

WHO CAN SUE UNDER THE RULE?

Whether the claimant needed to be an occupier was unclear but an affirmative answer was given in *Weller v Foot and Mouth Disease Research Institute* (HC, 1966), and dicta in *Read v Lyons* support that view. There are also a number of authorities to the contrary (see, e.g. *Shiffman v Order of St John* (HC, 1936); *Perry v Kendrick's Transport Ltd* (CA, 1956)). However, in *Transco* (2003) (above), the House of Lords has reaffirmed the approach taken in *Cambridge Water*, that only those with rights over land may sue under *Rylands v Fletcher*.

It is doubtful if the rule applies to the intentional projection of things on to the claimant's land. In this case trespass is the more appropriate cause of action (*Rigby v Chief Constable of Northamptonshire*), although the view was expressed obiter in *Crown River Cruises Ltd v Kimbolton Fireworks Ltd* (HC, 1996) that liability could extend to an intentional release which was not deliberately directed towards the claimant.

Non-natural user

It has already been noted that the defendant is not liable under the rule for an escape of something naturally upon the land. In *Cambridge Water* it was said that the concept of non-natural user limits liability under the rule just as the concept of reasonable user does in a nuisance action, though the relationship, if any, between the two was not discussed.

RICKARDS V LOTHIAN (1913)

By a malicious act an unknown third party blocked a domestic water system. The water overflowed and caused damage to the claimant's premises on the floor below.

Held: (PC) There was no liability under *Rylands v Fletcher* because the supply of water via normal domestic installations was a natural use of land. Lord Cairns' requirement of "non-natural use" has been interpreted to construe "natural" as meaning something which is ordinary and usual and "non-natural use'" is equated with extraordinary use or activity.

Comment

In *LMS International Ltd v Styrene Packaging & Insulation* Ltd (2005) a polystyrene product was being cut when a spark accidentally caused large quantities of flammable polystyrene blocks to catch fire. The defendant's means of storing and manufacturing the product "involved a very real risk" that a fire would spread to adjoining premises.The use of the defendant's land was held to be non-natural and they were liable under *Rylands v Fletcher* for a fire caused to adjoining premises.

It is clear from *Cambridge Water* that there is no liability for deliberate accumulations unless there has been a non-natural user by the defendant, which was defined in *Rickards v Lothian* (PC, 1913), in the following terms:

> "It must be some special use bringing with it increased danger to others, and must not merely be the ordinary use of land or such a use as is proper for the general benefit of the community."

A distinction must therefore be drawn between an "ordinary" and an "extraordinary" use of land, though the concept of non-natural user has enabled the courts to adopt a flexible approach and to adapt the application of the rule to changing circumstances of time and place (see *Read v Lyons*, where there are dicta to the effect that a munitions factory in time of war was a normal use of land). In the past, domestic water supplies, household fires, electric wiring in houses and shops, the ordinary working of mines and minerals and the keeping of trees and shrubs (unless, perhaps, poisonous: *Crowhurst v Amersham Burial Board* (Ex., 1878)) have been held to be natural uses. In *Transco* (2003) (above), the piping of a water supply to flats in a tower block constituted an ordinary use of the council's land.

NUISANCE AND RYLANDS V FLETCHER

It should be noted that the bulk storage of water, gas or electricity and the collection of sewage by a local authority have at various times been held non-natural. The approach adopted in *Mason v Levy Auto Parts of England Ltd* (HC, 1967) was to equate the concept of non-natural user with that of abnormal risk, so that the court took account of the quantity of the accumulation of combustible material, the manner in which it was stored, and the character of the neighbourhood, and conceded that those considerations might equally have justified a finding of negligence. This approach was adopted more recently in *LMS International Ltd v Styrene Packaging and Insulation Ltd* (above).

Although, according to the original formulation of the rule, the defendant must have collected the thing "for his own purpose", this did not at one time necessarily mean that he should derive any personal benefit (*Smeaton v Ilford Corp* (HC, 1954)). Where, however, the accumulation is for the public benefit pursuant, for example, to the provision of a public service (*Dunne v North Western Gas Board* (CA, 1964)) or indeed to ordinary manufacturing processes (*British Celanese Ltd v A. H. Hunt (Capacitors) Ltd* (HC, 1969)) the more modern tendency has been to deny the application of the rule.

The status of the above authorities will now have to be reconsidered in the light of *Cambridge Water* and in that case it was said that the storage of large quantities of chemicals on industrial premises was "an almost classic case of non-natural use" even in an industrial area. Furthermore, the fact that the chemical in question was commonly used in the particular industry, and that the defendants' operations served to support a local industrial community, was not sufficient to render the use natural. Unfortunately there was no real discussion of the relationship between public benefit and non-natural user, so the matter awaits further clarification.

Personal injury

It was unclear whether the claimant could succeed in a claim for personal injuries, and there was no discussion of this point in *Cambridge Water*. The view of Lord Macmillan in *Read v Lyons* was that the claimant would have to prove negligence, at least if he is a non-occupier, but there is authority to the contrary (*Shiffman v Order of St John*; *Perry v Kendrick's Transport Ltd* (see earlier in this Chapter)).

Although claims for personal injury had been admitted in the past, in *Transco* (above), Lord Hoffman expressed the view that damages for personal injuries are not recoverable under *Rylands v Fletcher*.

Remoteness of damage

Following *Cambridge Water* the test for remoteness would appear to be reasonable foreseeability, as it is in nuisance, although the case does not speak in terms of remoteness as such.

In referring to the phrase "likely to do mischief if it escapes" taken from the original formulation of the rule, it was said that the general tenor of the statement was that:

> "knowledge, or at least foreseeability of the risk, is a prerequisite of the recovery of damages ...".

It is not entirely clear from this whether both the escape and the consequences thereof must be foreseeable or merely whether, given that an escape has occurred, the consequences alone must be foreseeable, though the actual decision seems to support the former analysis.

Defences

There are a number of defences, the first three of which mentioned below, together with the concept of non-natural user, have gone a long way towards introducing elements of fault into this area of the law.

1. Act of God

An act of God is an operation of natural forces "which no human foresight can provide against, and of which human prudence is not bound to recognise the possibility". But this is not to say that the defendant will escape liability merely because the event is not reasonably foreseeable.

Two cases may be contrasted
- In *Nichols v Marsland* (CA, 1876), the defendant was held not liable when an exceptionally violent rainfall caused his artificial ornamental lakes to flood his neighbour's land.
- This decision was criticised in *Greenock Corp v Caledonian Ry* (HL, 1917) where, on similar facts, the defendant was held liable on the

ground that it is insufficient for him to show that the occurrence was one which could not reasonably be anticipated. He must go further and prove that no human foresight could have recognised the possibility of such an event. For practical purposes the defence is therefore of very limited application.

2. Act of a stranger

The defendant is not liable if the escape is due to the unforeseeable act of a third party over whom he has no control. In *Rickards v Lothian* (PC, 1913), the occupier of a lavatory was not liable when an unknown person deliberately blocked up the overflow pipe and caused flooding on the claimant's premises. The defence is not available, however, if the act is one which the defendant ought reasonably to have foreseen and guarded against. In *Northwestern Utilities Ltd v London Guarantee and Accident Co* (PC, 1936), the defendants' gas main was fractured by a local authority in the course of constructing a sewer. The defendants were held liable in negligence for damage caused by an explosion of the gas because they knew of the work being carried out and, in view of the risks involved, should have checked to make sure that no damage had been done to their mains. In cases such as this a claim based on *Rylands v Fletcher* merges into a claim for negligence, though according to Goddard L.J. in *Hanson v Wearmouth Coal Co* (CA, 1939), the onus is upon the defendant to prove both that the escape was caused by the independent act of a third party and that he could not reasonably have anticipated and guarded against it.

For the purposes of this defence a trespasser is a stranger but employees within the course of their employment and independent contractors are not. The defendant is probably responsible for the acts of his family and guests, although the issue is not entirely free from doubt and may depend upon the degree of control which he can be expected to exercise over them. In *Hale v Jennings Bros* (CA, 1938), the defendant was held liable for the deliberate act of a lawful visitor in tampering with a potentially dangerous machine.

3. Consent of the claimant

Express or implied consent to the presence of the dangerous thing is a defence unless the defendant was negligent (*Att Gen v Cory Bros & Co Ltd* (HL, 1921)). Consent may be implied where a thing is brought on to the land for the common benefit of the claimant and defendant as, for example, where one cistern supplies water to several flats. A further aspect of implied consent is that a person who enters into occupation of property as a tenant takes it as he finds it in so far as she knows of the presence of the dangerous thing (*Peters v Prince of Wales Theatre (Birmingham) Ltd* (CA, 1943)). In

Northwestern Utilities Ltd v London Guarantee & Accident Co Ltd (PC, 1936), the issue of common benefit was held not to be relevant as between the consumer of a product such as gas or electricity, and the supplier and, notwithstanding dicta in *Dunne v North Western Gas Board* (CA, 1964) to the contrary, such a view would seem to accord with *Cambridge Water*.

4. Default of the claimant
If the claimant's own act or default causes the damage, no action will lie. In *Dunn v Birmingham Canal Navigation Co* (EC, 1872), the claimants persisted in working their mine beneath the defendant's canal and failed in their action when water flooded the mine. Where the claimant is partly at fault the defence of contributory negligence will apply.

CHECKPOINT

If damage is caused only by reason of the extra-sensitive nature of the claimant 's property he may not, by analogy with nuisance (see above), be able to recover (*Eastern and South African Telegraph Co Ltd v Cape Town Tramways Co Ltd* (PC, 1902)).

However, in *Hoare & Co v McAlpine* (HC, 1923) it was thought not to be a good defence that a building damaged by vibrations was exceptionally unstable.

5. Statutory authority
This may afford a defence as in nuisance and the same principles of law apply.

REVISION CHECKLIST

You should now understand:

- [ ] **Nuisance covers *indirect* interferences with use or enjoyment of land and it differs from the tort of trespass which protects against *direct* interferences.**

- [ ] **Although public nuisance is a crime as well as a tort, private nuisance is only a tort.**

- [ ] **A claimant in private nuisance must have an interest in land to sue; public nuisance is not linked to the claimant's interest in land and it protects against personal injury which is not recoverable in private nuisance.**

- [ ] **The principle in *Rylands v Fletcher* governing liability for the escape of dangerous things.**

QUESTION

Kofi owns a house and large paddock in a quiet rural village. Kofi's next door neighbour, Soo, manufactures "natural herbal remedies" in a room she has had specially built on to her house. Soo uses plants she grows in her garden for the products she manufactures and she fertilises the plants with manure from the local stables. Kofi has told Soo that the manure stored in her garden attracts flies and the smell coming into his property from her manufacturing has become unbearable, even with the windows closed. Soo was quite unsympathetic towards Kofi's complaint. She explained that she had been granted planning permission for the extension where the manufacturing is taking place. Soo suggested that if Kofi does not like the smell then he should move elsewhere. Angered by Soo's attitude, Kofi decided to hold a rock concert in his paddock in order to "teach her a lesson". He sold five hundred tickets and the loud music and fireworks display from Kofi's land kept all the villagers awake through the night. An exceptionally powerful firework exploded and caused injury to Tom, one of the musicians playing on the stage. The exploding firework also injured Issy, a cyclist passing on the road outside Kofi's house.

Advise Kofi of his rights and liabilities in respect of the above situations.

ANSWER

Kofi would complain that the emission of smells and the flies coming from Soo's garden constitute an unreasonable interference with his use and enjoyment of land giving rise to a claim in private nuisance. Not every interference will amount to a nuisance; it is only when the defendant's activity, measured by the standards of an ordinary person it becomes unlawful. Although there is no set formula for determining what is unreasonable and much depends on the facts in each case, the approach taken by the courts is one of compromise, a "rule of give and take, live and let live": *Bamford v Turnley* (1862); *Sedleigh-Denfield v O'Callagan* (1940). This must be applied in the context of a quiet rural village.

The law would seek to achieve a balance between the right of Soo to use her land as she wishes and the right of Kofi not to be seriously inconvenienced by this. Therefore, not every interference amounts to an actionable nuisance because people must be expected to tolerate some degree of inconvenience in the interests of peaceful co-existence. *Miller v Jackson* (1977), *Kennaway v Thompson* (CA, 1980).

The interference from Soo's land is causing "amenity" (i.e. intangible) damage which would become unlawful only if the court found that she put her land to an unreasonable use. If, however, the alleged nuisance had caused tangible damage then Kofi would have little difficulty in establishing an unlawful interference with his rights: *Halsey v Esso Petroleum Co Ltd* (1961)

In carrying out the balancing exercise the court takes account of the nature of the locality. A person living in an industrial town cannot expect the same freedom from noise and pollution as one who lives in the country. The grant of planning permission is not a licence to commit a nuisance. In *Wheeler v J.J. Saunders Ltd* (1995) it was held that an actionable nuisance was established even though the interference inevitably resulted from the authorised use. This was approved in *Watson v Croft Promo-Sport Ltd* (2009).

However, Kofi may find himself liable in nuisance by holding a rock concert on his land with the express purpose of annoying Soo. Even if the interference would not constitute a nuisance if done in the ordinary and reasonable use of property Kofi may be still be liable because his conduct was motivated by malice (see *Christie v Davey* (1893) and *Hollywood Silver Fox Farm Ltd v Emmett* (1936)).

The same conduct may amount to both a private and a public nuisance. The loud music and fireworks at the pop concert materially affected the comfort and convenience of the villagers (who may qualify as a class of Her Majesty's subjects) so Kofi may be liable in public nuisance for this interference: *Att-Gen v PYA Quarries Ltd* (1957). However, an individual villager would only be able to recover damages in public nuisance if he had suffered "particular" damage, which means loss or damage over and above that suffered by the rest of the villagers (the class affected): *Tate & Lyle Industries Ltd v GLC* (1983).

Tom may seek to base his claim on the tort in *Rylands v Fletcher* (1866) because there would be no need for him to show the existence of a duty of care or a breach of that duty. *Rylands v Fletcher* is concerned with escapes and liability under the rule applies to *"things brought on to the land"* which are *"likely to do mischief"* if they *"escape"*. The requirement of "non-natural use" has been established as part of the rule and the courts have interpreted "natural" to mean something which is ordinary and usual and "non-natural use" is equated with extraordinary use or activity carrying with it additional risk. The question of whether the use of fireworks amounts to a non-natural use of land would need to be determined but, in any event, Tom would not succeed in *Rylands v Fletcher* because for the rule to apply there must be an "escape" from the defendant's premises: *Read v J Lyons & Co Ltd* (1947). Issy's claim under the rule will also fail, as the rule is now seen as an aspect of private nuisance. It covers harm to land but not personal injury: *Transco v Stockport* (2003). Both Tom and Issy might have a claim in negligence, if the explosion was due to careless planning or execution of the display, or under product liability if the firework itself was defective.

Defamation and Privacy

INTRODUCTION

Defamation is an unusual tort. It protects reputation rather than person, property or wallet, and there has recently been considerable controversy over how it operates in practice. This led initially to the development of common law restrictions—such as the rejection of cases where there was not "a real and substantial tort", and more recently to provisions of the Defamation Act 2013 which seek to restrict claims to those of real substance and arising primarily in England and Wales.

There are other peculiarities of defamation. The limitation period is shorter than for other torts, only 12 months. Actions also abate on the death of the claimant. Reputation is strictly personal. Defamation was never covered by legal aid, although this is no longer a distinguishing feature. It was also until recently usually tried by jury. This is no longer the case, although it will take some time for the implications of this to lose significance, in particular the distinction between the role of the judge in deciding whether words were capable of a defamatory meaning and the role of the jury in deciding whether they did bear that meaning. Until now many defamation cases have been resolved in preliminary hearings. If the judge rules that words cannot bear a particular meaning, or cannot be said to refer to the claimant, there is no action to go to trial.

LIBEL AND SLANDER

A defamatory statement or representation in permanent form is a libel, but if conveyed by spoken words or gestures, a slander. Apart from the written word, pictures, statues and waxwork effigies are libels. In addition, radio and television broadcasts are treated as publication in permanent form pursuant to the Broadcasting Act 1990, as are words spoken during a public theatrical performance pursuant to the Theatres Act 1968. Material on the internet is libel. This was assumed in *Godfrey v Demon Internet* (HC, 1999) and has never been doubted.

Reading out a written defamatory document to a third party is, on the balance of authority, a libel: *Forrester v Tyrrell* (CA, 1893). To dictate defamatory material to a typist is clearly a slander, but if it is then put into a letter and sent to a third party the dictator publishes a libel through his agent. As far as defamatory matter on records and recorded tapes and discs is concerned, there is a divergence of opinion among writers as to whether this is libel or slander, but in principle, as the material is in permanent form, it is libel.

KEY CASE

MONSON V TUSSAUDS (1894)

The claimant had been tried for murder in Scotland and had argued that the victim was killed by the accidental discharge of his own gun. The jury returned a verdict of not proven. Shortly after the trial, the defendants placed a model of the claimant and his gun in their exhibition of wax figures in a room which gave access to the Chamber of Horrors. The claimant applied for an interlocutory injunction to restrain the display of the wax figure until the trial of a libel action.

Held: The injunction was not granted but the action was properly framed in libel. Lopes L.J. stated that:

" ... Libels are generally in writing or printing, but this is not necessary; the defamatory matter may be conveyed in some other permanent form. For instance, a statute, a caricature, an effigy, chalk marks on a wall, signs or pictures may constitute a libel."

Comment

Libel, defamatory material in a permanent form, should be distinguished from slander which takes a transient form; for example, spoken words, gestures, or mimicry.

CHECKPOINT

An important distinction between libel and slander is that libel has always been actionable per se, without proof of special damage, whereas slander requires proof of such, except in the following circumstances:

- a direct imputation of a criminal offence punishable in the first instance with imprisonment (words conveying mere suspicion of the offence will not suffice).
- words calculated to disparage the claimant in any office, profession, calling, trade or business held or carried on by him at the time

> of the publication: s.2 of the Defamation Act 1952. If, therefore, the natural tendency of the statement is to injure or prejudice the reputation of the claimant in his calling the words will be actionable per se.

Special damage means loss of some financial or material advantage such as loss of one's job, of business contracts or of the value in money of the hospitality of one's friends (but mere exclusion from their society is not enough). The damage must not be too remote in accordance with general principles (see Ch.4), moral damage, such as injury to feelings or resentment will not qualify and generally illness caused by mental anxiety induced by slander not actionable per se is considered too remote.

Under the **Defamation Act 2013** s.1, a statement is not defamatory unless there is serious harm to the claimant. In the case of libel and the two exceptional types of slander, that harm does not have to be "special" damage. However "actionable per se" now means little, if anything.

Where a third party causes loss to the claimant as a result of the statement, that may or may not break the chain of causation depending upon what the defendant ought reasonably to have anticipated. Unauthorised repetition makes the damage too remote unless there is a legal or moral duty to repeat, or the defendant intends the repetition or if that is the natural and probable consequence of the original publication: *Speight v Gosnay* (CA, 1891); *Slipper v BBC* (CA, 1991); *McManus v Beckham* (HC, 2002).

In essence defamation may be defined as the publication of a statement which tends to lower a person in the estimation of right-thinking people generally: *Sim v Stretch* (HL, 1936) or which tends to make them shun or avoid him. The latter part of the definition makes it clear that the words need not bring the claimant into ridicule or contempt, but may arouse only feelings of pity (*Youssoupoff v M.G.M. Pictures Ltd* (CA, 1934)).

KEY CASE

SIM V STRETCH (1936)
When Edith Saville, a maid who had left the claimant's employment, went to work for the defendant he sent a telegram to the claimant saying:

> "Edith has resumed service with us today. Please send her possessions and the money you borrowed also her wages to Old Barton. Sim."

The claimant alleged that the telegram meant that he was in financial difficulties and had to borrow money from his housemaid.

Held: (HL) The words in question were not reasonably capable of that defamatory meaning.

Comment

The case is not important in itself, but for the dictum of Lord Atkin, referred to above, which has become the general definition of what is defamatory. It is not the only such judicial formulation. See also:

In *Parmiter v Coupland* (1840) Parke B held a defamatory statement to be one "which is calculated to injure the reputation of another, by exposing him to hatred, contempt or ridicule." In *Youssoupoff v MGM* (1934), Slesser LJ expressed the opinion that a defamatory statement could be one which tends to cause people to shun or avoid the claimant.

In *Berkoff v Burchill* (CA, 1996), a majority of the Court of Appeal held that to describe a film actor and director as "hideously ugly" was capable of being defamatory in that it could lower his standing in the public's estimation and make him an object of ridicule. A trading corporation can sue for a defamatory attack upon its commercial reputation: *South Hetton Coal Co Ltd v North Eastern News Association Ltd* (CA, 1894). Under the **Defamation Act 2013** s.1(2) a body trading for profit must prove serious financial harm. Local government, other organs of government and political parties may not sue, because to permit otherwise would be to inhibit freedom of speech and would thus be contrary to the public interest: *Derbyshire CC v Times Newspapers Ltd* (HL, 1993).

The aim of the law is to strike a balance between freedom of speech and the right of a person not to have their good name sullied so that, whilst liability is strict in the sense that the defendant's intention is generally irrelevant, a number of defences are available. However, when considering the role of defamation in protecting reputation, it should be remembered that the competing right to freedom of expression is also increasingly offered protection by the law. It is of course a convention right under article 10 of the European Convention on Human Rights. However this right may be regulated in order to protect the rights of others. The regulation must be in accordance with the law, and a proportionate means of meeting the right of others in a democratic society, namely one which is open and plural, and allows for vigorous debate on matters of public concern: *Lingens v Austria* (ECtHR 1986). So where a conflict between these competing rights arises, the English courts must strike a balance between the protection of reputation and freedom of speech. Traditionally, the common law protected freedom of expression through the defences to defamation (it is for this reason that an understanding of the defences to defamation is as important as understanding the elements of liability) but the law of defamation only extends to untrue statements. Where harm is caused to a claimant by words or images which are true and therefore no remedy in defamation is available, the emerging law of privacy (discussed below) may provide protection.

WHAT THE CLAIMANT MUST PROVE

Whether the action is for libel or slander the claimant must prove on the balance of probabilities that (1) a defamatory statement (2) referring to him was (3) published and (4) he has suffered serious harm. The words are presumed to be untrue. If the claimant establishes these matters, the burden of proof is on the defendant to establish a defence.

Statement must be defamatory

The words must be defamatory in accordance with the definition already given, though it need not be proved that anyone who actually heard or read them believed them to be true. Where the statement tends to discredit the claimant only with a special class of persons, he may not succeed unless people generally would take the same view. In *Byrne v Deane* (CA, 1937), for example, it was held not to be defamatory to say of a club member that he had informed the police of an illicit gambling machine on the club premises, because right-thinking persons would not think less well of such a man, since "right-thinking persons" believe that the law should be enforced, and that there is an obligation to assist the forces of law and order.

KEY CASE

BYRNE V DEANE (1937)
A golf club had some gambling machines unlawfully kept in the club house. These were removed by police after somebody had informed of their illegal presence. Soon after this a verse appeared on the notice board of the club which ended with the lines: "But he who gave the game away, may he byrnne in hell and rue the day." The claimant brought an action for libel alleging that by these words the defendants meant, and were understood to mean, that he was guilty of underhand disloyalty to his fellow members.

Held: (CA) The claimant's claim failed. It could not be defamatory to "allege of a man ... that he has reported certain acts, wrongful in law, to the police ...".

Comment
There is a tongue in cheek element to the decision. If one takes Lord Atkin's approach in *Sim v Stretch*, we are concerned with the impact on "right thinking people". Strictly, the Court of Appeal is correct, right thinking people disapprove of crime, and do not think ill of an informer. However, there was a serious breach of solidarity within the club community.

Problems may arise, however, where the general public is divided in its opinion. Thus, to say of another that she went to work during a strike would certainly lower her in the estimation of a considerable number of people and ought perhaps on that basis to be defamatory. Others would approve her actions. Is this an area in which the law could and should be intervening?

The circumstances in which the statement is made may be important; words spoken at the height of a violent quarrel, for example, are not actionable if those who heard them understood them as mere abuse. The question in all cases is what interpretation the reasonable man would put upon the statement. In *Charleston v News Group Newspapers Ltd* (HL, 1995), the defendants published a potentially defamatory headline and photograph, but the text of the accompanying article plainly negated the defamatory meaning. The claimant was held to have no cause of action because the meaning to be ascribed to the words was the meaning which, taken as a whole, they conveyed to the ordinary, fair-minded reader, not to the limited category of those who only read headlines.

In *Hartt v Newspaper Publishing Plc*, (1989) the Court of Appeal said the right-thinking person is not unduly suspicious but can read between the lines and engage in a certain amount of loose thinking, but is not avid for scandal, and will not select one bad meaning where other non-defamatory meanings are available.

CHECKPOINT

The meaning of words
It is a question of law whether particular words are capable of a given defamatory meaning; if so, the trier of fact must decide whether they do bear that meaning: *Capital & Counties Bank Ltd v Henty & Son* (HL, 1882). Traditionally, the judge ruled on points of law and the jury on points of fact, but now the judge will direct himself as to the meanings the words can bear, before deciding as the judge of fact what meaning they do bear.

If a statement is plainly defamatory in its ordinary sense it is actionable (subject to any defence), unless the defendant can successfully explain away the defamatory meaning. Conversely, the words may be prima facie innocent but, in the light of extrinsic facts known to persons to whom the statement is published, bear some secondary defamatory meaning. This is a true, or legal, innuendo and is illustrated in *Tolley v J. S. Fry & Sons Ltd* (HL, 1931). The claimant, a well-known amateur golfer, was portrayed in an advertisement for the defendants' chocolate. He successfully pleaded an innuendo, namely that the advertisement meant that he had received payment for his services and had thereby breached the rules of the golfing authorities and forfeited his amateur status. The "innuendo facts" were that he was an amateur, and that amateurs could not benefit financially from playing, directly or indirectly. The extrinsic facts upon which the claimant relies in support of the innuendo must be known to the recipients of the statement at the time of publication and the claimant must, as a general rule, specify the persons whom he alleges to have knowledge of those facts: *Grappelli v D. Block (Holdings) Ltd* (CA, 1981).

It is plain from *Cassidy v Daily Mirror Newspapers Ltd* (CA, 1929) that it is immaterial that the defendant is unaware of the extrinsic facts, as long as some of those to whom the words are published are so aware.

KEY CASE

CASSIDY V DAILY MIRROR NEWSPAPERS LTD (1929)
The defendants published a photograph of Mr Cassidy with a woman, below which was carried an announcement of their engagement. The information on which the defendants based their statement came from Mr Cassidy alone and they had made no effort to verify it from any other source. Mr Cassidy was already married although he lived apart from his wife. However, he did occasionally stay with his wife at her flat. She brought an action in libel claiming that readers who knew her as Mr Cassidy's wife would assume that she had been lying about whether she was married to him.

Held: (CA) The defendants were liable. The story would be understood by others to refer to the claimant and the newspaper's complete ignorance of the circumstances could not prevent the statement from having a defamatory meaning.

Comment
In 1929 the natural assumption of Mrs Cassidy's acquaintances might well have been that she was his kept mistress and "living in sin". Today, with divorce much more prevalent, the natural assumption might be that she was now divorced.

Where the claimant does not rely upon extrinsic facts but merely contends that a particular meaning is to be attributed to the words themselves, there is said to be a "false" innuendo which, unlike the legal innuendo, does not give rise to a separate cause of action. In *Lewis v Daily Telegraph Ltd* (HL, 1964), the defendants published a statement that the fraud squad was investigating the claimants' affairs. The claimants alleged that readers would understand this to mean that they were guilty of fraud. It was held that those words could not bear that meaning, but simply meant that there was a suspicion of fraud, which the defendants admitted was prima facie defamatory but which they could prove to be true (see also *Mapp v News Group Newspapers Ltd* (CA, 1998)).

CHECKPOINT

This has more recently been formulated as *Chase* meanings. In *Chase v News Group Newspapers Ltd* (CA, 2002) Brooke L.J., drawing on Lord Devlin's speech in *Lewis,* identified three possible defamatory meanings that might be derived from a publication alleging police investigations into the conduct of a claimant. The *Chase* level one meaning is that the claimant was guilty. The *Chase* level two meaning is that there were reasonable grounds to suspect that the claimant was guilty. The *Chase* level three meaning is that there were grounds for investigating whether the claimant was guilty. It is important to identify which level the words used can and do mean, as this is the meaning which must be shown to be true.

The claimant is entitled to ask the defendant to specify what meanings he claims the words bear, and vice versa. The provision of evidence to show that, for example words are true can only be undertaken if it is clear what meaning or meanings the words can bear. The meanings claimed by the defendant are known as "Lucas-Box meanings" (from *Lucas-Box v News Group* (CA, 1986). The process of clarifying the potential meanings is often a complex one. The objective is to clarify what the "sting" of the defamation is, i.e. how exactly it impacts on the claimant's reputation. The task is often complicated by the fact that the author and editor of the statement are consciously trying to go as near as possible to defaming someone as they safely can, and therefore using language subtly, to insinuate bad things about their victim, rather than making clear assertions.

Reference to the claimant

There must be a sufficient indication that the claimant is the subject of the statement. In most cases, where the claimant is named, this presents no difficulty. The claimant need not be named, however, nor need there be any key or pointer in the statement to indicate them in particular, provided that there is material proven to exist by which people might reasonably draw the inference that it referred to them: *Morgan v Odhams Press Ltd* (HL, 1971).

MORGAN V ODHAMS PRESS LTD (1971)

A newspaper, the *Sun*, alleged that a named girl had been kidnapped by a dog-doping gang because she was threatening to inform the police of their activities. The alleged members of the gang were not named. At the relevant time the girl in question had been staying at the claimant's flat and the claimant produced six witnesses who swore that they understood from the article that he was connected with the gang.

Held: (HL) The story was capable of a defamatory meaning. There was no rule that the article should contain some kind of direct key or pointer to indicate the claimant; the question was whether readers who knew of the circumstances would reasonably have understood the article as referring to the claimant.

The information does not have to be generally available, as long as it is enough for a significant number of people who know of the claimant to make the connection. Where a defamatory statement makes no reference to the claimant, she may rely on a later publication which clearly identifies her with the original statement: *Hayward v Thompson* (CA, 1982).

It has long been the case that there is no requirement that the defendant must have intended to refer to the claimant: *Hulton & Co v Jones* (HL, 1910). The material in this case was an account of events in a French holiday resort which was apparently intended to be fictitious. A character named Artemus Ward was referred to as sexually mis-conducting himself. The claimant persuaded the court that the piece was to be treated as factual reportage, and that persons known to him had linked him to the story because his name was also Artemus Ward, although nothing in his circumstances tallied with the details in the material. Even if the statement is true of one person it may still be defamatory of another. Thus, in *Newstead v London Express News-papers Ltd* (CA, 1940) the defendants were liable for their report that Harold Newstead, a 30-year-old Camberwell man, had been convicted of bigamy, which was true of one such individual but untrue of the claimant, who bore the same name, was about the same age, and who also came from Camberwell. The claimant recovered one farthing in damages, so presumably would fail to show "serious harm" under the Defamation Act 2013.

In respect of a defamatory statement directed at a class of persons (e.g. doctors) no individual member of that class may usually sue unless there is some indication in the words, or the circumstances of their publication, which indicates a particular claimant. But if the reference is to a sufficiently limited class or group (e.g. the directors of a company) they may all be able to sue if it can be said that the words refer to each of them individually. These principles were established in *Knupffer v London Express Newspaper Ltd* (HL, 1944).

Publication

There must be publication to at least one person other than the claimant or the defendant's spouse, but there is no publication by a typist or printer merely by handing the statement back to its author: *Eglantine Inn Ltd v Smith* (HC, 1948). The defendant is liable if he intends further publication, for example by writing a letter to the correspondence editor of a newspaper: *Cutler v McPhail* (HC, 1962). So, too, is he liable if he is negligent, as where he puts a letter in the wrong envelope or speaks too loudly in a crowded room.

A defendant is only liable for foreseeable publication, so he will not be liable if a statement is overheard by one whose presence is not to be expected, or if a letter is read by one who has no authority to do so.

In *Huth v Huth* (CA, 1915), a letter in an unsealed envelope was opened and read by an inquisitive butler in an admitted breach of his duty. There was no publication because it was not part of the butler's duty to open the letter and his conduct was not a foreseeable consequence of the defendant's sending the letter—which was addressed to his wife.

An unauthorised repetition or republication by a third party will break the chain of causation unless the statement is published to one who is under a legal or moral duty to repeat it, or the repetition is foreseeable as a natural and probable consequence of the original publication: *Speight v Gosnay* (CA, 1891); *Slipper v BBC* (CA, 1991).

Every repetition of a defamatory statement is a fresh publication so that, as regards printed matter, the author, editor and publisher are all liable. At common law a mechanical distributor of print, such as a library or newsagent, was presumptively liable for publication but had a defence of innocent dissemination if he could prove that he did not know the work contained a libel, and that that lack of knowledge was not due to negligence in the conduct of his business: *Vizetelly v Mudie's Select Library Ltd* (CA, 1900).

LEGISLATION HIGHLIGHTER

Section 1 of the Defamation Act 1996 now codifies the defence in *Vizetelly* and extends its availability to all those who are not the "author, editor or publisher" as defined in the Act:

- "author" means the originator of the statement, but does not include a person who did not intend that his statement be published at all;
- "editor" means a person having editorial or equivalent responsibility for the content of the statement or the decision to publish it; and
- "publisher" means a commercial publisher, that is, a person whose business is issuing material to the public, or a section of the public, who issues material containing the statement in the course of that business.

The defence now therefore extends to printers, distributors, retailers, broadcasters of live programmes containing the statement where there is no effective control over the person making it, and internet service providers (other than those who actually host material). Under the **Defamation Act 2013**, s.10, no action can be brought against anyone other than the "author, editor or publisher" as defined above unless it is not reasonably practicable to bring an action against the "author, editor or publisher".

The defendant must show that he took reasonable care in relation to the publication of the statement and that he did not know, and had no reason to believe, that what he did caused or contributed to the publication of a defamatory statement.

A person may be liable for failing to remove defamatory matter placed upon premises by a third party: *Byrne v Deane* (CA, 1937). The extent of his duty to do so presumably depends upon whether he has control of the premises where the statement is displayed and the ease with which it can be removed. In this case, the material was placed on a notice board in a golf club. The club secretary clearly had both the legal right to remove it, and the opportunity to do so.

KEY CASE

GODFREY V DEMON INTERNET (1999)

Statements defamatory of the claimant were posted by an unknown person on an internet newsgroup hosted on the defendant's server. The claimant notified the defendant about this material but the defendant did not remove the material from the internet for about two weeks. The defendants claimed that they were not responsible for postings by users on their internet sites.

Held: Although the defendants successfully showed that they were not the author, editor, or publisher of the defamatory statement within the meaning of the Defamation Act 1996, they could not show that they had taken reasonable care in relation to its publication and the defence of innocent dissemination under s.1(b) of the Act was therefore unavailable to them.

Comment
The question in *Metropolitan International Schools v Designtechnica Corporation, Google UK and Google Inc* (HC, 2009) was whether Google should be regarded as a "publisher" of the words complained of (whether before or after Google had been notified of their defamatory comments) or whether it was a mere facilitator. Google was held not to be liable for publication of the statements. A facilitator, such as Google, is not actually operating the site where the material is posted. It is really an indexer, and as such not a publisher. This is not affected by the provisions of the 2013 Act.

The position with regard to publication on the internet is now governed by section 5 of the **Defamation Act 2013**. The operator of a site has a defence if he can show that he did not post the material in question, but the defence is lost if the operator does not respond properly to a notice of complaint. The draft regulations implementing s.5 indicate that a complaint must identify the posting, and the elements complained of. On receipt of a complaint, the operator must contact the originator of the material. The possible outcomes are that the material is taken down, or that the poster objects to this, in which case the operator must notify the complainant. In that case, the policy of the Act is that the complainant takes action against the poster, rather than the operator, but the details are not entirely clear.

Each statement can normally only be published once. The 12-month limitation period runs from the date of first publication: s.8 of the **Defamation Act 2013**. So, for example, a newspaper article which appears in the print edition, but is then archived on the internet, is published on the date of the print edition, and no action can be brought if it is accessed on line several years later. This applies where the statement is substantially the same, so minor differences of editing or formatting will not constitute a new publication. The rule does not apply if the manner of the subsequent publication is substantially different, so if the initial statement has a very limited circulation, and the later publication is in the mass media, the second publication will have its own limitation period.

Harm

LEGISLATION HIGHLIGHTER

In all cases, whether libel or slander, there are new requirements under the Defamation Act 2013. Section 1 of the Act provides:

(1) A statement is not defamatory unless its publication has caused or is likely to cause serious harm to the reputation of the claimant.

(2) For the purposes of this section, harm to the reputation of a body that trades for profit is not "serious harm" unless it has caused or is likely to cause the body serious financial loss.

Effectively, while the principle that a business may sue in defamation is retained, it will have to prove special damage, and this must be "serious". It is not clear if this is an absolute standard, or contextualised to the particular claimant, although in principle it should be.

While an individual does not have to prove "special" damage, he must prove serious harm to his reputation. This harm must be within the jurisdiction. Exactly what this means will be determined through the cases, but decisions on the "real and substantial tort" test developed recently indicate that very limited publication will not usually count: *Jameel v Dow Jones* (CA, 2005), *Davison v Habeeb* (HC, 2011), unless it is to people who know and/or have an interest in the claimant: *Berezovsky v Michaels* (HL, 2000); *Ansari v Knowles* (CA, 2013).

The claimant must have a reputation in this country, although it is accepted that the material complained of may itself be sufficient to bring the claimant to public notice and create a reputation: *Jameel*. The "seriousness" of the alleged defamation is also relevant: *Tesla v BBC* (HC, 2012). The overall impact on reputation must be weighed up—looking at the nature of the allegation, the extent of publication and all other factors: *Cammish v Hughes* (CA, 2012). Where the publication is largely outside the jurisdiction this indicates that there is likely to be no real and substantial tort here: *Karpov v Browder* (HC, 2013). Claims will be struck out if there is no arguable case for serious harm, but this should not be a "mini-trial": *Ansari v Knowles*.

There is a further restriction introduced by the Defamation Act 2013. A defendant who is not based in the UK or elsewhere in the European Economic Area can only be sued here if this is 'clearly the most appropriate place' to bring proceedings, having regard to all publication world-wide: s.9. The overall intention is partly to eliminate claims which are trivial, because publication is limited and harm is not significant, and partly to discourage "libel tourism"—using the English courts to resolve issues which are essentially unconnected to the UK, but where there has been token publication here.

DEFENCES

These play a greater role in defamation, and are generally specific to defamation (and perhaps related torts such as malicious falsehood). The main exception is consent, which is a defence here as elsewhere. The **Defamation Act 2013** has made considerable changes to the defences. Most of the common law defences have been abolished and replaced with statutory defences, usually covering largely the same issues. In theory, the large body of case law on the abolished defences is no longer the law, but past experience of similar exercises suggests that counsel and judges will continue to refer to them as they interpret and apply the new statutory provisions.

Absolute privilege
Statements made in Parliament cannot be called in question anywhere else: Article 9 Bill of Rights 1689. This includes evidence given to a select committee: *Makudi v Triesman* (HC, 2013), and also parliamentary papers: *Lake v King* (1667). Neither can statements made during court proceedings by witnesses, counsel or the judge. In both these cases, the public interest in freedom of speech is deemed to outweigh any issue of reputation.
Absolute privilege is a complete defence.

Absolute privilege also attaches to fair and accurate contemporaneous reports of court proceedings in the UK and elsewhere: s.14(3) Defamation Act 1996. Note that the coverage of this section was extended by s.7 Defamation Act 2013.

Qualified privilege: reports

At common law a number of reports benefit from qualified privilege. This privilege can be lost on proof of malice—that the defendant is including material which he does not believe to be true. These reports include fair and accurate reports of parliamentary proceedings and of public judicial proceedings. The common law privilege in relation to the latter is wider than the statutory absolute privilege in that it applies to any form of publication made at any time.

Under s.15 of the Defamation Act 1996 a wide range of public documents—minutes of, and documents published by, a whole range of public bodies, as well as media reporting of these, benefit from qualified privilege. The reports so protected are to be found in Sch.1 to the Act and are divided into two categories, those in the first being privileged "without explanation or contradiction", and those in the second "subject to explanation or contradiction". The defence is lost as regards those in the second category if the claimant requests the defendant to publish a reasonable statement by way of explanation or contradiction and the defendant refuses or neglects to do so. This statutory privilege does not extend to the publication of any matter which is not of public concern and the publication of which is not for the public benefit (s.15(3)). Whether the report is "fair and accurate" and the question of "public concern" and "public benefit", should be left to the trier of fact: *Kingshott v Associated Kent Newspapers Ltd* (CA, 1991).

Qualified privilege: general

This applies when someone is under a legal, social or moral duty to make a communication, and the recipient has an equivalent interest in receiving it. E.g. an employee reporting the misconduct of a fellow employee to his manager. The nature of the duty and interest is fairly tightly limited, so that, for example, there is no duty to tell an acquaintance that his wife is cheating on him. *Watt v Longsdon* (CA, 1930) clearly illustrates this.

KEY CASE

WATT V LONGSDON (1930)

The defendant, a company director, received a letter from the foreign manager of the organisation. The letter alleged that the claimant, who was managing director of the company abroad, was immoral and dishonest. The defendant informed the company chairman of his suspicion that the claimant was misbehaving with women. He also communicated the statements, which were false, to the claimant's wife.

Held: (CA) The communication to the chairman was privileged because both publisher and receiver had a common interest in the affairs of the company. The publication to the claimant's wife was not privileged because the defendant had no social or moral duty to inform her about unsubstantiated allegations even though she might have an interest in hearing them.

This defence is not directly affected by the new Act. However, it does not count as privilege in relation to the defence of honest opinion.

In *Makudi v Triesman* (HC, 2013) the defendant had made defamatory comments about the claimant to a parliamentary committee. These were covered by absolute privilege. He was then asked to testify to an investigative panel set up by the Football Association. Testimony to the panel was covered by qualified privilege.

Qualified privilege may be lost if the defendant publishes the statement more widely than is necessary for the protection of an interest. However, a publication by the defendant to third persons who have no interest or duty is nevertheless protected if it is reasonable and in the ordinary course of business. If, for example, X sends to Y a letter defamatory of Y which he first dictates to his secretary in the ordinary course of business, Y cannot sue for the publication to the secretary provided that the letter is written to protect or further the aims of the business: *Bryanston Finance Ltd v de Vries* (CA, 1975).

LEGISLATION HIGHLIGHTER

Public Interest: s.4 Defamation Act 2013

(1) It is a defence to an action for defamation for the defendant to show that—

    (a) the statement complained of was, or formed part of, a statement on a matter of public interest; and

    (b) the defendant reasonably believed that publishing the statement complained of was in the public interest.

(2) Subject to subsections (3) and (4), in determining whether the defendant has shown the matters mentioned in subsection (1), the court must have regard to all the circumstances of the case.

(3) If the statement complained of was, or formed part of, an accurate and impartial account of a dispute to which the claimant was a party, the court must in determining whether it was reasonable for the defendant to believe that publishing the statement was in the public interest disregard any omission of the defendant to take steps to verify the truth of the imputation conveyed by it.

(4) In determining whether it was reasonable for the defendant to believe that publishing the statement complained of was in the public interest, the court must make such allowance for editorial judgement as it considers appropriate.

(5) For the avoidance of doubt, the defence under this section may be relied upon irrespective of whether the statement complained of is a statement of fact or a statement of opinion.

(6) The common law defence known as the *Reynolds* defence is abolished.

The *Reynolds* defence, or journalistic qualified privilege, emerged quite recently. The case itself was decided in 1999. There was felt to be a lacuna, in that the print and broadcast media had the public function of investigating and reporting on suspected misconduct, which was an important part of the public debate, but they were not covered by qualified privilege as there was no duty to disclose. A "new" form of privilege, available where the material was published in accordance with proper standards of responsible journalism, did emerge. It was acknowledged as being essentially a public interest defence, rather than privilege: *Flood v Times Newspapers* (SC, 2012)

The statutory defence does not only benefit the media. However, it is journalists who are likely to rely on it. It is likely that the factors to be considered in relation to reasonableness will be similar to those taken into account under *Reynolds*.

Jameel v Wall Street Journal Europe (HL, 2006) concerned an article suggesting that the claimants' bank accounts were involved in funding terrorism, which was found to be defamatory. The Court of Appeal rejected the newspaper's defence of qualified privilege but the House of Lords, focusing on the "public interest" aspect of *Reynolds* privilege, allowed the newspaper's appeal and said that the defence was being applied too cautiously by the lower courts. Journalists are under a professional duty to report on matters of public interest and the public has an interest in receiving such information. Where a publication is in the public interest, the duty and interest are taken to exist and, in the context of editorial judgment, the question then is whether responsible steps had been taken to gather and publish the information.

Flood v Times Newspapers Ltd (CA, 2010) concerned responsible journalism and whether the steps taken by the journalists to verify the information were adequate to meet the test. An article published by the defendant newspaper stated that police were investigating an allegation that an officer had accepted bribes in exchange for confidential police information. This was either a *Chase* level two or level three allegation. The article named Flood as the officer and set out the details of what had been alleged. The Supreme

Court, disagreeing with the Court of Appeal, considered that it was consistent with the principles of responsible journalism to publish this information.

Although the statutory defence replaces *Reynolds*, it seems to cover the same ground, and the analysis in *Flood* is likely to be influential.

LEGISLATION HIGHLIGHTER

Peer-reviewed statement in scientific or academic journal etc.: s.6 Defamation Act 2013

(1) The publication of a statement in a scientific or academic journal (whether published in electronic form or otherwise) is privileged if the following conditions are met.

(2) The first condition is that the statement relates to a scientific or academic matter.

(3) The second condition is that before the statement was published in the journal an independent review of the statement's scientific or academic merit was carried out by—

    (a) the editor of the journal, and

    (b) one or more persons with expertise in the scientific or academic matter concerned.

(4) Where the publication of a statement in a scientific or academic journal is privileged by virtue of subsection (1), the publication in the same journal of any assessment of the statement's scientific or academic merit is also privileged if—

    (a) the assessment was written by one or more of the persons who carried out the independent review of the statement; and

    (b) the assessment was written in the course of that review.

(5) Where the publication of a statement or assessment is privileged by virtue of this section, the publication of a fair and accurate copy of, extract from or summary of the statement or assessment is also privileged.

(6) A publication is not privileged by virtue of this section if it is shown to be made with malice.

(7) Nothing in this section is to be construed—

    (a) as protecting the publication of matter the publication of which is prohibited by law;

    (b) as limiting any privilege subsisting apart from this section.

(8) The reference in subsection (3)(a) to "the editor of the journal" is to be read, in the case of a journal with more than one editor, as a reference to the editor or editors who were responsible for deciding to publish the statement concerned.

This is a new defence. It is apparently intended to give statutory effect to the decision in *British Chiropractic Association v Singh* (CA, 2010) that arguments about the efficacy of treatments were really issues of opinion rather than fact. However, the case related to a statement in a newspaper, rather than a peer-reviewed journal, so it is more a matter of honest opinion. However, a lot of the discussion in the case was of peer-reviewed material, so the new defence does relate to this.

LEGISLATION HIGHLIGHTER

Truth: s.2 Defamation Act 2013

(1) It is a defence to an action for defamation for the defendant to show that the imputation conveyed by the statement complained of is substantially true.

(2) Subsection (3) applies in an action for defamation if the statement complained of conveys two or more distinct imputations.

(3) If one or more of the imputations is not shown to be substantially true, the defence under this section does not fail if, having regard to the imputations which are shown to be substantially true, the imputations which are not shown to be substantially true do not seriously harm the claimant's reputation.

(4) The common law defence of justification is abolished ...

Truth, formerly justification, is generally an absolute defence, though the defendant has the onus of proving the truth of the statement. He need only show that the statement is substantially true and whether the defence is lost through a minor inaccuracy is a matter for the court. In an old case, it was alleged that the claimant had been involved in fraud in three named towns. The defendant proved this in relation to two of the places, and that was held to be sufficient—the "sting" was fraudulent behaviour, rather than where it occurred. However in another old case the claimant sued when he was described as a "libellous journalist". The defendant proved that the claimant had once been held liable for libel. This did not establish the defence, as the "sting" was that the claimant was regularly, or habitually, libellous. The justification must meet the actual sting, at least substantially.

The defendant must have admissible and cogent evidence of truth, and the more serious the allegation, the more cogent the proof must be, as Brooke L.J. observed in Chase:

"Although the standard of proof is the balance of probabilities, the more improbable an allegation the stronger must be the evidence that it did occur before, on the balance of probabilities, its occurrence will be established. I take these principles from such cases as *McPherson v Daniels* (1829); *Berezovsky v Forbes Inc* (HL, 2001); *McPhilemy v Times Newspapers Ltd* (CA, 1999); and *Re H (minors)* (HL, 1996)."

Normally a statement must be taken as a whole, although a lengthy document such as a book can be considered in sections. Where a statement contains a series of allegations, the claimant may seek to "cherry-pick" one which is clearly untrue. In such a case he will argue that the defendant cannot then rely on the publication as a whole and will presumably fail to prove truth. But, if the claimant seeks to adopt this approach, the allegations must be distinct (which is a question of fact and degree) and, if a number of allegations should properly be taken together because they have a common "sting", the defendant is entitled to justify that sting as a whole: *Polly Peck (Holdings) Plc v Trelford* (CA, 1986).

The defendant must, as a general rule, prove that the statement is true and cannot simply rely on the fact that another made it: *Truth (N.Z.) Ltd v Holloway* (PC, 1960); *Stern v Piper* (CA, 1996). However, while hearsay and rumour cannot constitute justification for what amounts to an assertion that the rumour is well founded, there may be circumstances in which the existence of a rumour entitles a person to repeat it and to plead in justification that such a rumour is in fact abroad: *Aspro Travel Ltd v Owners Abroad Group plc* (CA, 1995). This is in effect a *"Chase* level three" meaning—the existence of the rumours constitutes grounds for investigation.

Where the defendant's allegation is that the claimant has been convicted of an offence, s.13 of the Civil Evidence Act 1968 (as amended by s.12 of the Defamation Act 1996) provides that proof that he stands convicted of it is conclusive evidence that he did commit it. The fact that the claimant's conviction is "spent" under the Rehabilitation of Offenders Act 1974 does not prevent the defendant from relying upon justification, but in this case the defence is defeated by proof of malice.

Honest opinion: s. 3 Defamation Act 2013

(1) It is a defence to an action for defamation for the defendant to show that the following conditions are met.

(2) The first condition is that the statement complained of was a statement of opinion.

(3) The second condition is that the statement complained of indicated, whether in general or specific terms, the basis of the opinion.

(4) The third condition is that an honest person could have held the opinion on the basis of—

    (a) any fact which existed at the time the statement complained of was published;

    (b) anything asserted to be a fact in a privileged statement published before the statement complained of.

(5) The defence is defeated if the claimant shows that the defendant did not hold the opinion.

(6) Subsection (5) does not apply in a case where the statement complained of was published by the defendant but made by another person ("the author"); and in such a case the defence is defeated if the claimant shows that the defendant knew or ought to have known that the author did not hold the opinion.

(7) For the purposes of subsection (4)(b) a statement is a "privileged statement" if the person responsible for its publication would have one or more of the following defences if an action for defamation were brought in respect of it—

    (a) a defence under section 4 (publication on matter of public interest);

    (b) a defence under section 6 (peer-reviewed statement in scientific or academic journal);

    (c) a defence under section 14 of the Defamation Act 1996 (reports of court proceedings protected by absolute privilege);

    (d) a defence under section 15 of that Act (other reports protected by qualified privilege).

(8) The common law defence of fair comment is abolished . . .

This defence is quite complex. It is important to distinguish statements of fact from those of opinion, but it is often not easy to do so because fact and opinion are mixed together in the same passage. It is a statement of fact to say that "X is a liar". It is a statement of opinion to say "because X is a liar, he should never hold public office". But the actual statement might be "X cut a ridiculous figure in the press conference. Sometimes defiant, sometimes close to tears, his answers became incoherent and his earlier lies came back to haunt him. This pathetic specimen should never be entrusted with any public responsibility again. Once a liar, always a liar." At common law it was possible to prevent a "rolled up defence" that insofar as the statements were of fact, they were true, and insofar as they were comments or opinions they were honest. It is not clear if this will still apply to the statutory defences.

The ingredients of the defence are that it applies to a statement of opinion which (a) is honestly held by the defendant, (b) is one which could be honestly held on the basis of either actual facts, or facts asserted to be true in a privileged statement and (c) there is sufficient indication of the matters on which the opinion is based.

Whether the opinion is honestly held will involve examining the factors considered in *Horrocks v Lowe* (HL, 1975). Passions can run high in political or other disputes, and often this will result in objectively unsustainable, but honestly held views. Some evidence will be needed that the defendant was "putting on" his opinions, and this will only rarely be available.

KEY CASE

HORROCKS V LOWE (1975)

The claimant, a Conservative Party councillor in Bolton, complained that at a council meeting the defendant, a leading Labour Party opposition member, made defamatory remarks about him. The trial judge held that the occasion was privileged but that the defendant, being in the grip of gross and unreasonable prejudice, was guilty of malice.

Held: (HL) However prejudiced or irrational, the claimant's belief in the truth of what he said on that privileged occasion entitled him to succeed in his defence of qualified privilege.

Comment

In *Spring v Guardian Assurance* (1994) the Court of Appeal decision that imposing a duty of care in negligence would undermine the defence of qualified privilege, which can only be defeated on proof of malice, was overruled by the House of Lords. The majority held that the preservation of the integrity of the law of defamation would not be sufficient to deny the claimant a remedy. It may therefore be possible to frame an action in negligent misstatement if the defamatory statement causes actual loss.

The courts are unlikely to investigate closely how far the facts justify the belief. This provision is there to deal with the opinion which blatantly flies in the face of all the facts, and it will be surprising if the court start to investigate areas of legitimate controversy. *British Chiropractic Association v Singh* (CA, 2010) appears to have provided a logical basis for this approach.

In *Kemsley v Foot* (HL, 1952) a relatively low threshold was set for the indication of the basis of the opinion, and this is likely to remain the case. The statement was mainly an attack on the Beaverbrook newspapers, but these were described as "lower than Kemsley". This was seen as referring to the fact that Lord Kemsley controlled some newspapers, and "lower than" was seen as an expression of opinion.

Offers to make amends

The **Defamation Act 1996** provides, by ss. 2–4, for the defence of an offer to make amends. Although described as a defence, it is more a limitation of liability, since it starts from the assumption that there has been an actionable defamation. The offer, which must be in writing, must be not only to make a suitable correction of the alleged defamatory statement and a sufficient apology to the claimant, but also to pay such compensation and costs as may be agreed or determined to be payable. If such an offer is accepted, no proceedings may be brought or continued in respect of the publication concerned, but if it is not, the defendant has a defence unless he knew or had reason to believe that the statement referred, or was likely to be understood as referring, to the claimant and was both false and defamatory of her. It is presumed that the defendant did not have the requisite knowledge of, or reason to believe, those matters until the claimant proves otherwise. An offer to make amends cannot be made after serving a defence in defamation proceedings and, once made and relied upon by way of defence, no other defence may be raised. The offer may be relied on in mitigation of damages whether or not it was relied on as a defence.

PRIVACY

Since the enactment of the **Human Rights Act 1998**, which incorporates the European Convention on Human Rights (ECHR) into English law, privacy is now an emerging area of law. When considering situations where an individual claims a legal right to the protection of personal or private information from misuse or unauthorised disclosure, the courts are required to have regard to the ECHR. Although art.8 of the ECHR provides an explicit right to respect for a private life for the first time in English law, this must be balanced with art.10 which protects the right to freedom of expression. One of the concerns of the courts is that if respect for a private life is defined too widely it could lead to an undesirable restriction on the freedom of the press to report and comment on matters of public importance.

CHECKPOINT

Privacy is a difficult concept to clearly define

- The distinction between public information and private information is not always clear.
- One definition of privacy was provided by Louis Brandeis, later Justice Brandeis of the US Supreme Court, in the USA, in 1890 as: "the right to be left alone". This appears to echo John Stuart Mill a generation earlier in England.
- The Calcutt Committee, Report on Privacy and Related Matters (1990) reported: "nowhere have we found a wholly acceptable statutory definition of privacy."
- The following working definition of privacy was adopted by the Report: The right of the individual to be protected against intrusion into his personal life or affairs, or those of his family, by direct physical means or by publication of information.

KEY CASE

WAINWRIGHT V HOME OFFICE (2003)
The claimant was visiting her son in prison. As part of a security measure within the prison, she and another son were taken to separate rooms and strip searched by prison officers. She claimed that the strip searches amounted to invasion of privacy and a breach of article 8 of the ECHR

Held: The House of Lords confirmed that there is no tort of invasion of privacy and doubted that the European Court of Human Rights jurisprudence required a principle of privacy to comply with article 8.

Comment
In *Peck v UK* (2003) and *von Hannover v Germany* (2004) the ECtHR subsequently confirmed that a positive obligation in respect of privacy rights is imposed by article 8.

Although there is no tort of invasion of privacy in English common law as confirmed by *Wainwright v Home Office* (HL, 2003), privacy is a value underlying the common law doctrine of breach of confidence, and this has been developed following the incorporation of art.8 of the ECHR into English law into a tort of interference with privacy. Breach of confidence was originally a cause of action arising from the breach of a duty to keep confidence arising from a confidential situation, transaction, or relationship, but it now focusses on the private nature of the information, not on any obligation of confidentiality.

In *Douglas v Hello! Ltd* (HL, 2005), the couple had entered into an exclusive agreement with a magazine (*"OK"*) for publication of their wedding photographs. They claimed against *Hello!* magazine for breach of confidence arising from publication of unauthorised photographs taken at their wedding on the ground that they had asserted the right to control what images should be published. Much of the judgment dealt with the dispute between the publishers, for whom the right to report the wedding was a valuable trade asset. Although there was no existing law of privacy under which the claimants were entitled to relief, the photographic representations of the event were held to have the necessary quality of confidence and deserved protection as the equivalent of a trade secret.

In *Campbell v MGN Ltd* (HL, 2004), the House of Lords held that protection of privacy in England is based on a tort of misuse of private information. This tort has to take account of both art.8 (right to respect to private and family life) and art.10 (right to freedom of expression) of the ECHR. The test is whether there is a reasonable expectation of privacy.

The case concerned revelations that Naomi Campbell was attending Narcotics Anonymous. Given Campbell's previous statements that she strongly disapproved of drugs, the publication of the fact that she had taken drugs and was receiving treatment was held necessary to set the record straight. However, the publication of details of that treatment and a photograph of her leaving the clinic was an unjustified intrusion into her private life.

In balancing the competing interests under the Human Rights Act 1998, significant weight was given to the photograph and its inclusion in the publication added greatly to the intrusion and Campbell's art.8 right to privacy was therefore held to outweigh MGN's competing interest in freedom of expression under art.10.

In *Mosley v News Group Newspapers* (HC, 2008), the material and images published in newspapers and on their website were held to be inherently private in nature and infringed Mosley's rights of privacy under art.8 ECHR. The court found that the degree of intrusion was not proportionate to the public interest supposed to be served in publishing the information.

In *Von Hannover v Germany* (ECtHR, 2004) a positive obligation in respect of privacy rights was found to be created by art.8. In failing to take steps necessary to restrain publication of certain photos of a purely private nature taken in a climate of harassment, the German courts did not strike a fair balance between the competing rights at issue in protecting the private life of Princess Caroline of Monaco. In *McKennitt v Ash* (HC, 2006), the English courts followed this decision and held that a pre-existing obligation of confidence gave rise to a reasonable expectation of privacy. Unless the information holds some important public interest value, the right to private and family life under art.8 will not be outweighed by the art.10 right to freedom of expression. In upholding McKennitt's right to prevent publication of significant parts of a book on the ground that details of her personal and sexual relationships were intrusive and distressing, the court placed great weight on there being a pre-existing obligation of confidence on Ash, her former close friend.

KEY CASE

MCKENNITT V ASH (2006)

McKennitt, a well-known folk musician claimed that a substantial part of the book written by Ash, her former close friend, revealed personal and private details about her that she was entitled to keep private. In the course of their friendship Ash had acquired confidential information about McKennitt's personal and sexual relationships, her personal feelings and in particular in relation to her deceased fiancé and the circumstances of his death. The trial judge made a ruling to prevent the further publication and found that Ash realised that substantial parts of the book would fall within the scope of a reasonable expectation of privacy or a duty of confidence. Ash appealed against this decision on the ground that the matters the judge found to be confidential were not merely McKennitt's experiences, but hers as well, and contended that this gave her a property in the information. She further claimed freedom of speech on the ground that she was entitled to tell her own story and that included her various experiences with McKennitt.

Held: The Court of Appeal considered whether the information in question was private in the sense that it was, in principle, protected by the right to privacy under article 8 and whether the passages containing details of McKennitt's personal and sexual relationships would fall within the scope of a reasonable expectation of privacy. In upholding McKennitt's right to prevent publication of significant parts of the book on the ground that details of her personal and sexual relationships were intrusive and distressing, the court placed great weight on there being a pre-existing obligation of confidence. Ash's claim that her article 10 right to freedom of expression outweighed McKennitt's right to private and family life under article 8 was rejected.

Comment

The weight given by the courts to preserving the public interest in employees respecting obligations of confidence that they have assumed is further illustrated by the decision in *HRH Prince of Wales v Associated Newspapers* (2006). The claimant contended that a private leaked travel journal about his 1997 visit to Hong Kong which set out his private and personal thoughts, constituted confidential information. The defendant argued that the information in the journal was not confidential as it was of a political nature and related to the Prince's public life in office, in which there was powerful public interest. The court considered *McKennitt v Ash* and examined the balance between protecting confidential information and copyright on the one hand and the extent of press freedom on the other, particularly where the information relates to a well-known person. The Prince's right to keep the information in the journal private was upheld: all staff who may have encountered the journal were subject to confidentiality undertakings and therefore the Prince did have an expectation of privacy in respect of the journal.

REVISION CHECKLIST

You should now understand:

- [ ] Defamation requires a claimant to show: (1) a defamatory statement; (2) publication to a third party; (3) that the statement referred to him; and (4) that its publication caused or is likely to cause serious harm;

- [ ] The reforms introduced by the Defamation Act 2013;

- [ ] The function of the defences to defamation in balancing the competing rights of freedom of expression with protection of reputation;

- [ ] In balancing protection of reputation and free speech, art.8 and art.10 of the ECHR are of crucial importance;

- [ ] The history of the protection of privacy in English law and the impact of the Human Rights Act 1998 on this emerging area of law.

QUESTION AND ANSWER

QUESTION

To what extent do the reforms in the Defamation Act 2013 strike a fair balance between freedom of expression and the protection of reputation?

ANSWER

The defences to defamation are one of the most important protections of freedom of speech in English law. In addition to the requirement in the Defamation Act 2013 for claimants to show that they have suffered serious harm before suing for defamation, a single publication rule has been introduced and the presumption in favour of a jury trial has been removed. The Act has also placed the main common law defences on a new statutory footing (although it is likely that cases under the old law will continue to be influential). It has introduced a number of new defences and modernised the rules protecting website operators from libel claims arising from defamatory user comments.

On certain occasions the public interest requires that freedom of speech must outweigh the protection of individual reputation and this is achieved through the defence of privilege. The defence of absolute privilege (which is not directly affected by the Act) gives protection to statements made on occasions where freedom of speech is essential, such as statements made in Parliament or in a court of law. It is an absolute defence, and provides a complete defence, regardless of how careless the defendant has been in publishing the statement or whether he has been motivated by malice.

The defence of qualified privilege affords less protection than absolute privilege but it is much wider in scope than absolute privilege. The situations covered by qualified privilege are many and varied, but generally require a mutuality of interest—the defendant must have a duty to pass the information to the third party, who must in turn have a legitimate interest in receiving the information. Reporting allegations of sexual misconduct by a fellow employee which could bring the company into disrepute would count. However it was held that there was no duty to pass this information to the employee's wife, even though she clearly had an interest: *Watt v Longsdon* (1930). However, qualified privilege is defeated by malice; the crucial issue is the honesty of the defendant's belief in the truth of the statement. If the defendant honestly believed the statement to be true, qualified privilege will not be lost even if the belief is arrived at from unreasonable prejudice or was irrational (see *Horrocks v Lowe* (1975)).

The attempts by large corporations to stifle scientific and academic debate with the threat of libel proceedings were highlighted in the case of *British Chiropractic Association v Dr Singh* (2010). These concerns were addressed in the Defamation Act 2013. The Act creates in s.6 a new defence of qualified privilege relating to material in scientific or academic journals, whether published in electronic form or otherwise, which has undergone a responsible peer-review process.

Section 4 of the Defamation Act 2013 creates a new defence of publication on a matter of public interest. This new defence is intended to reflect the principles established in *Reynolds v Times Newspapers* (2001) and in subsequent case law. The *Reynolds* 'privilege' has been abolished and replaced by s.4 of the Act. The defence may be relied on irrespective of whether the statement complained of is one of fact or opinion.

The new s.4 defence encapsulates the "reportage" defence developed by the common law where the statement complained of was an accurate and impartial account of a dispute to which the claimant was a party, the defendant does not need to have verified the information before publication: *Roberts v Gable* (2008).

Where the statement complained of is substantially true the Defamation Act 2013 section 2 (1) provides a statutory defence of truth (to replace the common law justification defence). Truth is a complete defence to an action in defamation, although since the law presumes a defamatory statement to be untrue, the onus is not on the claimant to prove the statement was false; the burden of showing the truth of the statement is on the defendant. Where a statement is shown to be true, even if it was made with malice, there is no liability in defamation (apart from exceptions in the Rehabilitation of Offenders Act 1974).

However, the burden of proving truth is reduced because the defendant does not have to prove the literal truth of every word in the facts of the defamatory statement if he can justify the sting in the libel. This was established in *Alexander v North Eastern Railway Co* (1865) and this approach is confirmed in the Act which provides that if a defendant can establish the "essential" or "substantial" truth of the sting of the libel there is no need to prove that every word of the statement was true.

A new defence of honest opinion which replaces the common law defence of fair comment has been introduced by section 3 of the 2013 Act. Honest opinion, like justification, is a complete defence to an action in defamation. Although the statutory defence of honest opinion is largely a restatement of the current law, the cases interpreting what amounts to a statement of fact and what is a statement of opinion continue to be relevant. The requirement for the opinion to be on a matter of public interest is not contained in the 2013 Act, which gives protection to all opinion. Prior to the Act, honest comment failed if the claimant could show malice on the part of the defendant. However, what the defendant now needs to show is an honest belief in the truth of the opinion.

Honest opinion, which protects honest expressions of opinion based on true fact, is viewed as the essential protection of the fundamental right of free speech. It is important to note that honest opinion does not mean that the opinions protected must be fair-minded or reasonable. Honest opinion protects opinions honestly held, however obstinate, prejudiced, or exaggerated.

The assessment of the statement is made on the basis of how the ordinary person would understand it. This reflects the test approved by the Supreme Court in *Joseph v Spiller* that "the comment must explicitly or implicitly indicate, at least in general terms, the facts on which it is based".

The defence of honest opinion must be based on true, or privileged, facts. The 2013 Act additionally gives protection in situations where defendant is not the author of the statement, but is publishing statements made by others. In these circumstances honest opinion will succeed unless the claimant can show that the defendant ought to have known that the opinion stated was not held by the author.

Concern about the chilling effect on freedom of speech in respect of internet publication has resulted in greater protection for website operators and online intermediaries from liability for online content for which they are not responsible: *Tamiz v Google Inc* (2013). Section 5 of the Defamation Act 2013 aims to protect the website operator by shifting more responsibility for defamatory content to the author of web posts. Section 5 does not replace the existing law; it is a new defence aimed at forums and blog sites who print, distribute and host user-generated content. The defence is available where an action for defamation is brought against a website operator in respect of a statement which it did not post. The defence is defeated where the operator acted with malice in respect of posting the statement. However, the defence is not defeated just because the website operator moderates the statements posted by others.

Handy Hints and Useful Websites

Dealing with problem questions in tort

Problem-based questions in law are intended to test your ability to identify and apply the relevant legal principles to a given hypothetical factual scenario. The key to achieving a good grade in answering a tort problem question is to: (a) demonstrate your knowledge of the law by identifying the actual legal issues behind the facts of the problem being posed and (b) demonstrate your understanding of the law by applying the relevant law to the facts in question.

A tort problem question sets you a task. This is usually to "Advise X" or "Advise the parties on their rights and liabilities (if any) in respect of the issues raised" by the question. It is therefore important when answering problem questions to ensure that you address the question and always *complete this task*. For example, "In conclusion", you should always "advise X" or "advise the parties" in question on their rights and liabilities in respect of the specific issues raised by the problem.

Planning your answer is particularly important in tort because problem questions frequently contain a number of different issues and they can sometimes involve a number of potential claimants and defendants. It is also important to remember that there is not necessarily a "right" answer to a tort problem but there is a correct approach. One approach that students find helpful is to use the IRAC mnemonic by following the steps listed below.

Identify the legal issue/s
Rule define and explain the legal rule and/or principle
Apply the rule/principle to the facts in question
Conclusion which sums up the advice to the party/parties

Identify the legal issue/s

Identify clearly the factual issues on which advice is sought. This important stage in your answer involves identifying *what the question is about from a legal point of view*. As you are reading through the question you must take care to spot and make a note of these issues and any defences which may be available. At this point you might discover a party who has no recognisable legal claim or a claimant who does have a claim but who will have no legal remedy or reduced damages because the facts show that the defendant will be able to establish one of the defences. Each of the separate issues identified as you read through your examination paper should be isolated and dealt with separately in your answer.

Once you have decided on the questions that you intend to attempt, *before* you start writing out your answer, for *each* of these questions you should: (a) outline the issue/s and the loss/damage suffered in each case (b) identify the potential claimants and defendants and (c) list any defences that might be applicable. Not only will this approach give your answer a clear structure, it will also provide you with a helpful reference point as you work through your answer. This can be particularly helpful in an exam situation where time management is important to ensure that you don't spend a disproportionate amount of your time on any one question.

Rule: define and explain the legal rule and/or principle

Identify the principles of law which are relevant to the issue(s) and explain the legal principles, giving authority (case law or statute, as appropriate). Identifying the relevant law is a filtering process and this process should include discussion of any areas where the state of the law is in doubt. On the basis of this process any irrelevant law should be filtered out at this stage and only the law which is pertinent to your answer should be retained.

Apply the rule/principle to the facts in question

The law must be applied to support your discussion. It is at this stage that you must focus on constructing a logical argument and make a sensible attempt to apply the law to the factual issues. At this stage you should also identify any additional factual information about the problem which a court would need to come to a firm conclusion.

Conclusion

You should conclude your answer with a short paragraph containing your advice. If you have worked through your answer in a logical order there will be no need for a lengthy conclusion. You should note that in summarising the advice it will not usually be possible to come to a firm conclusion about the outcome of a dispute since there is likely to be additional factual information required. In some cases, the uncertain state of the law would make the outcome impossible to predict with certainty, even if all the factual information was available. You should distinguish clearly between areas of factual uncertainty and areas of legal uncertainty. Lengthy discussion of possible alternative factual scenarios will only be appropriate if necessary to explain different possible outcomes of the application of the relevant legal principles to the facts, otherwise such discussion will not earn marks but will instead be a waste of precious time.

Common errors in answering problem questions

- Failing to read the question properly
  During examinations many students underperform because, in their haste, they either fail to read the question correctly or to follow instructions.

- Telling "the story" of the case
  In using case law authority, it is not usually necessary to tell 'the story' of the case. Discussion of the facts of the cited case will only be relevant if the student wishes to point out that the facts are so similar to the case in question that it would seem impossible to distinguish them or, alternatively, if you wish to point to some difference between the two fact situations which makes it possible that the two could be distinguished.

- Failing to consider the position of all the parties in a dispute
  Issues should be explored from all sides and advising a particular party will involve considering the arguments which the opposing party or parties will employ.

- Restating the question
  Students sometimes lose precious time rewriting the facts in the question and if you find yourself doing this remember that you are not earning marks.

Like learning to ride a bicycle, to become really competent at answering problem questions you will need to practise: the more you do, the sooner it will become second nature to you. One of the most valuable ways of getting this practice is to prepare written answers to your tutorial/seminar questions

Tips on writing an essay question in tort
Essay questions require students to:
- Identify the central issues raised by the question.
- Explain the key legal principles and policy considerations with clarity and precision.
- Demonstrate an understanding of the relevant principles by applying them to the discussion/argument supported by relevant authority.
- Set out a coherent and well-structured argument with conclusions drawn from analysis of the central discussion.

One of the mistakes students most frequently make when answering an essay question in tort is failing to ensure that they understand what the question is about. The law of tort applies to a wide variety of different situations and the aim of an essay question will usually be to assess your knowledge and understanding of the way in which a specific aspect of the law has developed and evaluate its current position. Your understanding of any particular aspect of tort will be demonstrated by:

(1) outlining the history of the topic under discussion;

(2) using relevant case law or statute to illustrate the key legal principles;

(3) providing examples of how these principles have been interpreted in subsequent cases;

(4) illustrating any exceptions to the key legal principles;

(5) making an evaluation of the present state of the law, highlighting and areas of ambiguity in the current law;

(6) considering arguments for alternative actions or possibilities using cases or journal articles to support these arguments.

It is important to note that whether answering an essay or a problem question in law there is rarely a "right answer" there is simply a right approach. The right approach is to present sufficient and relevant information in a clearly structured and well expressed manner with proper referencing of sources. With a tort essay, it is not always a lack of knowledge that lets a student down—quite often, it is a lack of structure in the arguments and a failure to support the discussion with relevant authority that is the main problem. Therefore, in order to obtain maximum benefit from your study of tort, it is very important to develop good essay writing skills to enable you demonstrate your knowledge and understanding

Chapter 1: Trespass to the person

- Trespass to person covers intentional and direct interference.
- Claims for *indirect* interference with the person must be brought in negligence
- A battery can take place without an assault and even the slightest force may amount to a battery: an unwanted kiss may constitute a battery.

Chapter 2: Duty of Care

As a tort, negligence consists of three elements: a legal duty to take care; breach of that duty; and damage suffered as a consequence of the breach. This chapter is concerned with the duty of care element and it is important to remember that the concept of duty is used as a means of limiting negligence liability. This function of a duty of care was summarised in *Smith v Littlewoods Organisation Ltd* (1987) by Lord Goff:

" ... the broad general principle of liability for foreseeable damage is so widely applicable that the function of the duty of care is not so much to identify cases where liability is imposed as to identify those where it is not ...".

The role of duty of care in limiting negligence liability is particularly relevant in respect of certain defendants such as the police and local authorities.

However, it might be useful at this point to note that the concepts of duty, breach and damage sometimes overlap and the separate elements frequently fail to provide a clear answer as to whether a claim should be allowed. In *Lamb v Camden LBC* (1981) Lord Denning said: "it is not every consequence of a wrongful act which is the subject of compensation". Lines have to be drawn somewhere:

"Sometimes it is done by limiting the range of persons to whom a duty is owed. Sometimes it is done by saying that there is a break in the chain of causation. At other times it is done by saying that the consequence is too remote to be a head of damage. All these devices are useful in their way. Ultimately, it is a question of policy for judges to decide".

Chapter 3: Breach of duty

- Having established the existence of a duty of care the next step for the claimant is to show that the defendant breached that duty. A breach of duty is only established if defendant's conduct fell below the standard required in the particular circumstances.
- It is for the judge to decide what is reasonable or what could have been foreseen and in evaluating the defendant's conduct many factors are taken into account.
- The question of whether breach of duty has occurred arises in vastly more cases than the question of whether a duty of care should be imposed.

Chapter 4: Causation and Remoteness

- Where a breach of duty is established the claimant must first show that the harm suffered was as a matter of fact caused by the defendant's breach of duty. This element is known as causation in fact; if "but for" the defendant's negligent conduct the damage would not have happened then that negligence is the cause of the damage.
- Where causation is in fact established the question of remoteness of damage then arises. This is known as causation in law and provided that

the defendant can show that the damage suffered was too remote a consequence of the breach of duty, liability may still be avoided.
- The principles of causation and remoteness of damage are common to all torts.

Chapter 5: Defences
- Not all possible defences in tort actions are discussed in this chapter: it is concerned with defences which have a particular relevance to claims in negligence. Some defences are specific to particular torts, for example, justification in defamation, and are considered with those torts.
- Contributory negligence operates where the claimant's own fault has contributed to the damage suffered and the damages payable are reduced in proportion to the degree of fault.
- The defence of volenti non fit injuria, i.e. no wrong is done to one who consents. This means that a claimant who voluntarily agrees to undertake the risk of harm is not permitted to sue for the consequent damage. It is a complete defence and if it succeeds the claimant gets nothing.
- The defence of ex turpi causa non oritur action, no right of action arises from a bad cause, means that a defendant is not liable for damage in circumstances where the claimant was participating in an unlawful act.

Chapter 6: Occupiers' Liability
- The liability of occupiers towards persons injured on their premises is governed by two statutes. The Occupiers' Liability Act 1957 is concerned with liability to lawful visitors and provides that all lawful entrants are owed the same "common duty of care".
- The 1957 Act did not deal with trespassers, therefore a subsequent statute, the Occupiers' Liability Act 1984, was enacted to govern the duty of an occupier to persons other than visitors (e.g. trespassers).
- The standard of care imposed by the statutes is very similar to Lord Atkin's neighbour principle in *Donoghue v Stevenson* (1932) in common law negligence.

Chapter 7: Product liability
- In addition to rights under the common law there is an additional form of liability for defective products: the Consumer Protection Act 1987.
- The Act imposes strict liability for defective products which cause personal injury and damage to private property.
- The most notable feature of the Act is that it removes the need for those injured by a defective product to establish fault on the part of the producer.

- Central to liability under the Act is the requirement that the harm is caused by a "defect" in the product but the question of what makes a product defective takes account of what "persons generally are entitled to expect" in relation to a product. All the circumstances in the case are considered in determining what constitutes a "defect" and many of the factors taken into account in common law negligence are relevant to the question *Tesco Stores v Pollard* (2006).

Chapter 8: Employer's Liability

- The liability of an employer to an employee has two aspects. The first, liability for harm caused by employees in the course of their employment, vicarious liability, is dealt with in chapter 10 but it should be noted here that vicarious liability concerns an employer's liability for harm caused *by* his employees.
- The second form of liability which is the subject of this chapter is an employer's personal liability *to* employees in respect of harm suffered at work.
- The employer's duty is a general duty to take reasonable care for the *physical* safety of the employee and advances in medical and scientific knowledge about the effects of asbestos and repetitive strain injury have led to an expansion of an employer's liability to safeguard employees against these types of harm.
- An employer's liability for *psychiatric* harm as the result of occupational stress is also a developing area of liability.

Chapter 9: Breach of Statutory Duty

- Not all statutes give rise give rise to a civil action for breach of statutory duty.
- When the statute is silent as to whether a breach of duty gives rise to a civil action the courts determine the issue by considering a range of factors including the intention of Parliament when enacting the statute.
- Once an action for breach of statutory duty is established, the courts must then determine if the damage suffered is recognised by the statute in question.

Chapter 10: Vicarious Liability and Non-Delegable Duties

Before vicarious liability is imposed on a defendant there are three conditions which must be met:

- There must be a specific employer-employee relationship. This is distinguished from an employer's relationship with a self-employed independent contractor: employers are not usually liable for the torts of independent contractors.

- A tort (an actionable wrong) must be committed by the employee.
- The employee must be acting in the "course of employment" when the tort is committed. If the employee acted outside the scope of employment the employer is not liable. The question of whether an act is within or outside the course of employment is crucial but there is no exhaustive definition of what falls within the scope of employment. In cases involving an employee's intentional criminal conduct, the decision in *Lister v Hesley Hall Ltd* (2001) reflects the role of policy in this area.

Chapter 11: Nuisance and Rylands v Fletcher

- The tort of nuisance protects against "indirect" interference with the claimant's use and enjoyment of land.
- Direct interferences, such as unlawfully walking across a neighbour's land or dumping rubbish in his garden, are dealt with by the law of trespass to land.
- Private nuisance, which is not the same tort as public nuisance, is commonly defined as an unreasonable interference with the use or enjoyment of land.
- Although the same state of affairs may constitute both private and public nuisance, it must be noted that the rules relating to them are not identical.
- The tort in *Rylands v Fletcher* is closely related to nuisance but it differs from nuisance in that it does not depend on the defendant being involved in a continuous activity or an ongoing state of affairs.
- Unlike the tort of trespass to land, *Rylands v Fletcher* does not require a direct and intentional interference.

Chapter 12: Defamation and Privacy

- Defamation aims to balance the competing rights of freedom of expression with protection of reputation.
- Wide ranging procedural and substantive changes to defamation law have been introduced by the Defamation Act 2013.
- New protections for website operators introduced by the 2013 Act are very important.
- Although English Law does not recognise of breach of privacy as an independent tort, the Human Rights Act 1998 requires the article 8 right to respect for privacy to be balanced with the article 10 right to freedom of expression.

USEFUL WEBSITES

www.hmso.gov.uk – Acts of Parliament
www.parliament.uk – House of Lords judgments within two hours of delivery
www.lawcom.gov.uk – The Law Commission

Index

LEGAL TAXONOMY
FROM SWEET & MAXWELL

This index has been prepared using Sweet and Maxwell's Legal Taxonomy. Main index entries conform to keywords provided by the Legal Taxonomy except where references to specific documents or non-standard terms (denoted by quotation marks) have been included. These keywords provide a means of identifying similar concepts in other Sweet & Maxwell publications and online services to which keywords from the Legal Taxonomy have been applied. Readers may find some minor differences between terms used in the text and those which appear in the index.